This Nation/This Church

One People Under God ... with Liberty & Justice ... For All

by

Donald P. Goss

Bloomington, IN  Milton Keynes, UK

authorHOUSE®

AuthorHouse™
1663 Liberty Drive, Suite 200
Bloomington, IN 47403
www.authorhouse.com
Phone: 1-800-839-8640

AuthorHouse™ UK Ltd.
500 Avebury Boulevard
Central Milton Keynes, MK9 2BE
www.authorhouse.co.uk
Phone: 08001974150

First published by AuthorHouse 11/15/2006

ISBN: 978-1-4259-5834-3 (e)
ISBN: 978-1-4259-5833-6 (sc)
ISBN: 978-1-4259-6985-1 (hc)

Printed in the United States of America
Bloomington, Indiana

This book is printed on acid-free paper.

The purpose of this "message" to the leaders and to the citizens of this specifically created Nation/Church is to weld into one "truth" in their hearts and minds, its historical and spiritual journey from conception, through birth, into maturity, pointing out some of the major impediments to eventual achievement of its appointed task; i.e. "To advance the Kingdom of Jesus Christ." These *impediments* cause many unnecessary and dangerous potholes in the path of its travel.

The vehicle of its travel is in very real and imminent danger of being hijacked from the owner/driver, and placed into what many of its passengers are being "assured" is a more comfortable and safer and smoother highway. The would-be hijackers are what we term secularists, and are aided and abetted by two "political" organizations (one, the most unskilled, at the moment not able to place both hands on the steering mechanism) who constantly vie for "position" to steer us around the pot-holes and through the inevitable detours which bring danger to the likelihood of a successful journey. The party not now having steerage responsibility, proving itself to be a very dangerous, active "backseat driver" who is causing steerage and debilitating damage to the vehicle and its roadway; the other only slightly more adept at negotiating the passage.

This message attempts to identify those impediments. They are, some of them, herein described only enough to maintain continuity of the presentation, they will become much more visible to the traveler's eye as they are more in-depth discussed in Appendix B following the body of this report.

Table of Contents

With Appreciation

To my wife, Donna, who lovingly sacrificed too many hours of the early retirement hours which we had looked forward to "doing things" together while trying to wait out my urge to produce a cogent message that accurately portrays a sense of "incompletion" felt by many of our "Lay" acquaintances in the wider church, over a forty plus year experience serving in area, regional, national and "special task" Christian Organizations.

To D. James Kennedy, PhD (and much more), Senior Pastor of the Coral Ridge (Florida) Ministries, whose inspiring televised sermons (many of which are referenced within this dissertation) as well as the Bible Study Series he wrote, opened a vista of theology from which this message to the Christian, Protestant, Institutional Churches has emerged, as has the recorded sum of all the ministries that he founded and in which he participates. I am honored to accept Dr. Kennedy's recognition (unmerited) as a Faith Partner of his ministry and mission.

To Coral Ridge Ministries, from which came as a gift to me, *The New Open Bible* (King James Version), complete with Read-along references, Read-along translations and Topical Index to the Bible, The Christian's Guide to New Life, Book (of the Bible) introductions, Visual Survey of the Bible and Study Aids. This version of the Bible was my understanding of the "flow" of the accurate history of God's people from creation to the present day; and from which comes all-out support for Dr. Kennedy's inspired, courageous, innovative and multifaceted mission. The Coral Ridge Ministry is a ray of hope (to the writer of this message) that the state of God's Nation/Church is certainly strong enough to build the likelihood of success in completing the ministry entrusted to it by its true founder, Jesus the Christ.

To the Reverend Robert H. Schuller, whose 30+ years of televised worship services have long been a must on the list of Donna's and my worship experiences, who like The Reverend Kennedy has added to evangelistic outreach, higher education, Pastor support, food for the hungry and myriad of other "ministries" and whose inspirational story

My Journey (along with several others of his 30 or so books) was also a major source of input to the shaping of this critique.

To Lee Strobel, whose books *The Case for Christ* and *The Case for Faith* both helped me to an understanding of the faith granted to me by God's grace, and served as a resource which illuminated some explanations of the history of God's people, which were highly significant to meaningful description of the time line and cause/effect of certain events stemming from the call of Abraham to be the Patriarch of God's people, through Christ's on-earth ministry, till now.

To Pastor Jim Cymbala, who as Pastor of the Brooklyn Tabernacle wrote *Fresh Wind, Fresh Fire* which describes in graphic and dramatic style the necessity and the benefits of prayer in relation to efficacy of any ministry; and to the personal witness he, his wife and daughter (within the book) provide to the effects of prayer.

To James Davis, a fellow Commissioned Lay Pastor (CLP) who was a constant source of encouragement and who dutifully reviewed the work for "sense" as well as to the other CLPs of my acquaintance, who (some of them unknowingly) contributed to its development through discussions (and arguments) over the more than 15 years of my participation in that ministry.

To the Holy Spirit of God who prompted this "new" message to the churches and to His people; the Spirit who makes all things new.

Introduction

Paul, an Apostle of the Lord Jesus Christ, in his first letter to the Corinthians, found it necessary to correct their "stewardship" of the church he had organized in their midst. The letter was in response to some major differences between them as to whom and what understanding of the Word they would follow. He very strongly reminded them that they were there to follow *no man,* but Jesus Christ who had been crucified and resurrected, and that they, as fellowship of believers, were *called to live* within the "freedom" of His revelation of God's infinite mercy and grace which was also the message they had received from him, who was an Apostle of Jesus Christ. Paul reminded them in very certain language that they were there to *activate* the final and great command of Jesus, which was to complete His *ministry of salvation* to all people, revealed it to them through His ministry and teaching, as it was proclaimed to them by His Apostles.

Paul settled the dispute raging within the church by assigning to two of *his* students, named Aquila and Priscilla, the task of bringing up to date, theologically speaking, the message being preached to them by the person (Appolos) whom a faction of their membership were attempting to elevate above the Gospel he preached. Paul's remedy was successful, and the Corinthian Church began to once more move forward, *for a time.*

In his second letter, Paul warns the Corinthians once more, to examine themselves as the Church to which they aspired to be a part:

- *This will be the third time I am coming to you. "By the mouth of two or three witnesses every word will be established." I have told you before, and foretell as if I were present the second time, and now being absent. I write to those who have sinned before, and to all the rest, that if I come I will not spare – since you seek a proof of Christ speaking in me, who is not weak toward you, but mighty in you. For though He was crucified in weakness, yet He lives by the power of God. For we also are weak in Him, but we shall live with Him by the power of God toward you. Examine yourselves as to whether you are in the faith. Prove yourselves. Do you not know yourselves that Jesus Christ is in you – unless indeed you are disqualified. But I trust that you will know that we are not disqualified. Now I pray to God that you will do no evil, not that we should appear approved, but that you should do what is honorable, though we may seem disqualified. For we can do nothing against the truth, but for the truth. For we are glad when we are weak but you are strong. And this also we pray that you may be made complete. Therefore I write these being absent, lest being present I should use sharpness, according to the authority which the Lord has given me for edification and not for destruction.* (2 Corinthians 13: 1-10)

We, the church, examine ourselves.

In the spirit of Paul's injunction for "the church" to periodically undergo self-examination, this treatise is developed and presented. That, by any other name is a critique.

Webster's New Collegiate Dictionary defines the word *critique* almost as if it were another word for criticize. i.e. "to consider the merits and demerits (of the institutional church) and then judge accordingly." That is certainly appropriate to the intent of our use of the word *critique*. An added dimension to *critique* is that in order for it to be of positive value, the exercise would be less than complete without far ranging fact finding and in-depth discussion of those findings, including input from recognized experts of the fields under study, and from "lay" laborers from within the church, while gleaning ideas from all parties; and finally, presenting as a product from that critique, any ideas for growth and/or improvement of the institutional church's ministry which might be forthcoming.

It should be forthrightly stated at this early juncture in preparation for this examination, that in any of the ideas for growth and/or improvement presented, *there is no delusion on the part of this writer* that such ideas will be a result of the inspiration from the Holy Spirit *exclusively to the writer.* Most of those which will be presented have been around for what seems like eons of time as inspiration *to others* considerably more educated and practiced than this "layman." in Word of God mandates as to creating contemporary ministries, goals and strategies, in successful *calls* for disciple involvement, in eliciting "lay" participation and/or in planning and activating contributory components to the overall mission of the church.

What they *will* represent is an attempt to seek out the myriad of existing *very potentially promising, very innovative* ideas which have been heretofore left aimlessly adrift in a giant sea of creative strategies, in individual lifeboats of *People of God* rescue attempts, some of them actively rowing toward a haven for their own passengers, leaving other afloat in that same sea to sink-or-swim because this boat might sink if we allow you to latch onto us – forgetting that He who walks on water created the church for the very purpose of throwing His safety net to *all* who are in danger of drowning before *they* reach His haven of safety.

The ideas for growth and improvement which are presented will be an attempt an all-encompassing, saving "raft" out of all of the deadwood to which in-danger-of-drowning survivors desperately cling. The deadwood being ideas that were activated for a while, then abandoned for a variety of *"it is no longer worth the cost"* reasons; or that were never enlarged into a wider appeal by "professional" raft builders looking beyond the local eddy.

It is suspected that one of the major handicaps of the present-day institutional church is that it is too "closed door" because it is almost exclusively led by "professional" Christians. The tradition of the church has devolved into the mortal influence (the Adam/ Eve syndrome) of believing that if it even hopes to perpetuate or improve its *denominational* capability to function as the proclaiming body of Christ, *that will best be accomplished* through identifying those *college age* disciples (and the occasional secular professional who hears his/her own "call" and "signs up" for Seminary. They must then have their "new " call, validated by the rigors of Seminary training and go through a rather lengthy process of indoctrination as a "candidate" to the ministry. The candidate disciple is then "ordained" (or certified) into the Professional Christian career field of a particular denomination and "recommended" to one of the "available" ministries. There is a 2000 year long line of recognized and revered, and approved, used by God, leaders who have expended their entire lives in the Institutional Church – most of them "professional" but many of them not.

Most, if not all, professional Christians are quick to credit *non-professional* (Lay) members of the (i.e. Denomination of the) church to which they have committed their *secularly* professional talents, with success or failure of "professional" efforts to establish and/or maintain a "fruit-bearing" Christian Fellowship.

Unfortunately, it has been charged by many professional and non-professional members of the church that too many of those who are ordained seem to fail to adequately recognize that graduates of higher education *other than Seminary*, who, even though they have life-long been followers of Christ but had first chosen to apply their talents, skills and abilities to entities which are tied to something called *secular* pursuits, are mistakenly labeled as "Lay" Christians, and therefore may be routinely considered less than capable of understanding and/or effectively applying themselves to the *Great Commission of Jesus Christ*, through application of their non-denominational talents to Church Ministry. E.g. to exercise "good order" or moderating (chairing, leading) a group from a congregation which is charged with the planning and conducting of worship services, or of "shepherding" congregational ministry as Christ calls for it to be expressed in daily life; or to Baptize those who repent of their "unbelief" and come to accept Christ's gift of redemption, or to "induct" them into their denominational fellowship, or to apply to the "polity" of their denomination to their congregation's ministry, as a "requirement" for their acceptance of the "new birth" into the family of God.

It the above is true, among the consequences of reluctance of "professional" Christians to make use of "Lay" congregation members and leaders could very well be:

1) The "could be" contribution of many old, faithful and productive "fruit-bearing" congregations supporting denominational efforts to minister to the communities that have long hosted the congregation, would simply fade away as the congregation struggles to serve on its own, without leadership. Or they could be expected to follow appointed, part time, guest profess- ional leaders who are either unfamiliar with local issues or who are preoccupied with concerns of their "full-time" congregational "problems." and are written off as "not worth the trouble" of their minor in-put into denominational ministry.

2) Many active and financially contributing members of congregations will elect to transfer their involvement in ministry from their "life-long" and chosen ministry to another "local" church, either of their chosen denomination or evangelical. This they "reluctantly" do rather than to "buy-in" to "yoking"

to another (or two or more) of the same denomination but in a community some distance away, where they ultimately become "uncomfortable" with the addition of new or unfamiliar circumstances of daily life, which they are expected to add to those they have long suffered with and of which they were not relieved, and by operating under *guest leadership* – which is "their" problem to both (or all three or more), and/or yield to the human temptation to leave active participation in ministry altogether. The capacity for and continuity of the denominational ministry they have long been fulfilled with being a part of, in carrying out a serving ministry as needed by their host community *as well as to wider ministry,* is thereby and unnecessarily reduced to the quantity and quality of involvement in any new, revised or "dead" commitment.

3) Citizens of the secular (host) community who have been helpful to ministry programs of the local church out of their respect for "Christian" interest in local needs, lose any belief which they might have been building up, that *this church* really does represent the steadfast, meaningful, merciful, loving, care taking involvement of God in the lives of all people.

4) Any attempt of congregation members to elevate their interest in sustaining or enhancing denominational capability to carry out their ministry, outreach, especially to the community in which they live, by assuming *any* congregational leadership is effectively suppressed by the professionals in the interest of "good order."

5) By filling empty pulpits with a rotation of guest preachers, : hearing" Gospel lessons becomes disjointed and spotty, and opportunities for "serial" presentations are forfeited.

6) The *Church* created by Jesus Christ is thereby camouflaged by a *strategy* for professional protection of a human disciple definition of *"the only means for success"* in completing the mission to which it was called, which destroys the probability of success by the very disciples to whom completion was entrusted.

The foundation of the Church:

It would hardly be fair to critique the Church as it is presently applying itself to the mission for which it was brought into existence without the frame of reference for its creation, the theology of its appointed tasks and the history of man's application of the ministries which have brought it to this point in its history. Parts One, Two and Three of this dissertation describe the understanding of origin, purpose and authorities of and for the church as the base-point from which this critique comes.

First and foremost, we must accept that the Christian Church is much more than "the world's greatest religion." The Biblical book of Colossians (1:24) identifies the Church's existence thusly: "......*for the sake of His Body, which is the Church.*" We therefore enter into this task viewing the Christian Church as *the very, living, body of Christ;* and results of our examination of it within its present time and place would not be meaningful without comparing the Church's present efficacy to society quotient in relation to that which its creator, *Jesus Christ,* had at the time and place of *His earthly ministry.* Perhaps a more contemporaneous way of saying the same thing is: While the Gospel message itself is *always* relevant, is the theology and strategy and methods of proclamation currently being used as relevant to its hearers as it was in Jesus' (and the Apostles) time.

If it is true that "the past is prologue" we are therefore called to view the Church's history as the measuring board for its current evaluation. Even "confessing" the many and mighty and tragic errors contained in Church history, the history of great successes achieved against which we measure its current life are as formidable (almost) as is the ministry of the Christ by whom we are charged to do "better than He:" "...*most assuredly, I say to you, he who believes in Me, the works that I do he will do also; and greater works than these he will do ...*" (John 14:12) Without any attempt whatsoever to *"elevate the servant above the master"* (Matthew 10:24), the Body of Christ *has* done for more people than were alive during Christ's (physical) *on-the-scene* presence. In that sense at least, the Church has indeed done greater works. Christians who make up, by definition, individually and collectively, the Church, by way of example can be credited with:

Making Disciples of All Nations:

In compliance with the final command of Jesus Christ to His Church William Carey, more than 200 years ago launched the world missionary movement. Today, Jesus Christ *is* known in every nation on earth. The *Roman Catholic Church* now conducts, perhaps, the institutional church's major world-wide disciple making ministry, the *Salvation Army* runs a close second. What is popularly known in the United States as *Main Line Denominational Churches*, all have as primary components of their ministry, outreach to the world community through participant missionary programming and/ or funding of "outside the Denomination" ministries. The *Orange County* (California) *Community Church* sponsors a worldwide ministry of proclaiming salvation via TV, and radio, with listeners numbering in the tens, if not hundreds of millions of viewers and/or listeners, as does *Coral Ridge* (Florida) *Ministries* (A more detailed discussion of these ministries is included in Section IV of this critique) A recent study reported on Fox News reveals that Christianity is, today, the fastest growing "religion" in the world; the most explosive figures being reported for Africa and Asia, attributable in most part, to TV and radio broadcasts.

Teaching them to obey all things that I have commanded you:

The total effort of the Christian Church to obey this half of the *Great Commission,* is almost impossible to describe in one sentence or paragraph. Denominations of the Christian Church have, just within the borders of this Christian Nation, been responsible for the founding of many great universities which are recognized throughout the world as Christian institutions. Many local congregations sponsor parochial schools and/or teaching day-care centers; most local churches conduct elementary and/or adult Sunday School classes, some of them conduct advanced "inquirers: classes. Many churches support extra curricular" programs for children and youth. Most denominations support, in one way or another, programming that reaches out to "lost souls" via education programs. *It is universally accepted, that the Institutional Church is the recognized pioneer of "man-in-the-street" education.*

Feeding the hungry, healing the sick, visiting the lonely or imprisoned:

Any exhaustive written description of the achievements of the Institutional Churches as they engage in these ministries would fill libraries of records. But to cite *some* of the major in-country and world-wide efforts will be informative:

The *Salvation Army* is universally renowned for ministering to the poor, hungry, destitute and "unloved." Almost every city in the United States provides Christian sponsored shelter and food for the hungry services to those who have the need.

The *Red Cross* was founded by a Christian. The very symbol of the Red Cross (a white cross on a red field) is a miniaturized "picture" of the cross upon which Christ died.

Most "secular" charities are based upon Christian taught principles, albeit they each claim their principles to be unique to, or best delivered by, *their* organization. (The several denominations of the Christian Church do the same)

Christian Churches *pioneered* and continue to maintain the lead in establishing, equipping and operating state-of-the-art hospitals and medical facilities.

The volumes of records and stories of the Institutional Church's "successes" in carrying out the *Great Commission* of its founder would indeed make the Library of Congress seem to be a minor repository of historical information. There are enough of, and huge enough successes in Church history that there *could be* a major risk of conjuring up a "Lets rest on our laurels and relax a bit" syndrome, especially in congregations where participation in evangelistic outreach extending beyond worship service prayers, local events and/ or "offerings" requires sacrifice of local ministry.

It should also be noted at the outset of this "examination" that in the interest of clarity of communication and to enhance the opening of minds, flowery language will not be used to either obfuscates meanings or to minimize any effect of findings. This follows the pattern set by John (the Baptizer) and of Jesus himself when speaking of or to the Scribes, Pharisees or Sadducees with whom they were dealing.

This dissertation will call what is seen as a spade, a spade.

But there is, herein, no pretense that the *"examiners"* are equal to or above the master (i.e. the Institutional Church), it is simply that in order to "persevere" as contributing disciples within the church, such a presentation is necessary, in order to satisfy one's self, as Paul counseled, to effectively evaluate current strategy and degree of success,

And it should be noted this early in the project, that the cause of the uncertainty and doubt in the hearts and minds of those members

of the Main-line Denominations of the Institutional Christian Church who are leaving the church or who have declined to subscribe to its practices, is the developing conclusion that, at least within the churches espousing the "Reformed, continuing to reform" theology, the leadership of the church, beginning with its seminaries and institutions of learning, is beginning to camouflage a burgeoning tendencies to Political Correctness, by assuring themselves and their laity that it is actually reformed theology.

The successes and strengths of Institutional and Denominational Churches are immeasurably, almost indescribably great in their mission to bring honor and glory to Almighty God, by proclaiming the Gospel of Salvation through Jesus Christ – and through Him alone; in making disciples of those who come to believe; in teaching what Christ taught. In a mission spirit of "it is not possible to do enough," what this critique will speak to is if and how this Nation/Church can build on those strengths as it "examines" whether the Institutional, especially the "main-line" Protestant Churches are assiduously and effectively "keeping their corporate noses to the grindstone" or their "shoulder to the wheel" of mission.

We undertake this self-examination by submitting ourselves to Him who "elected" us to be His body on earth (His Church), called to "proclaim" and to complete His ministry of redemption of the "lost," while He goes and prepares our ETERNAL home

Our Father, who art in Heaven, Hallowed be Thy Name: Thy Kingdom come, Thy will be done, on earth as it is in Heaven.

We, who by your Grace have become members of your earthly body, seek now your counsel. By the gift of your word and through the example of your ministry while among us, you have taught us what You expect from us as your people. You commissioned us to proclaim your ministry of salvation for all people – even to the far corners of your world. You commanded us to Baptize in your name, those who come to believe by your grace as they hear our proclamation and to teach them all that You commanded us. Through your Apostles, you organized us to accomplish your will through your people.

As was true when Paul "examined" the church in Corinth, there is evidence that as your body, we have fallen short of the glory You brought to your people. It is seen in the failure of your people to live, act and be as You described for us to exist as your people; in our failure to make your name known and chosen by those whom we would "save."

We pray now, open our hearts to the Counselor You bring us, help us to accept that which we find will enable us to refurbish the Church we have allowed to become corrupted, help us to succeed in completing your earthly mission to your joy, in Jesus" Name.

PART I
OVERVIEW

CHAPTER 1
The Church:
Its One Foundation

Jesus said to Peter: *".........and on this rock I will build my church, and the gates of Hades will not overcome it. And I will give you the keys to the Kingdom of Heaven and whatever you bind on earth will be bound in Heaven, and whatever you loose on earth will be loosed in Heaven."* (Matthew 16: 18, 19)

Jesus gave to the Church absolute authority, through the Spirit, over the life and well-being of believers who live on earth.

Jesus himself laid the foundation of the church. He did so as He closed out His *"earthly presence"* ministry. He obviously had a purpose for His church. New Testament Scriptures record that reason: *"...that now the manifold wisdom of God might be made known **by the church** to the principalities in the heavenly places, according to the eternal purposes which He (God) accomplished in Christ Jesus our Lord"* (Ephesians 3:10, 11)

Since physical rock has neither natural voice nor other means of communicating, it becomes evident that the Creator of the Church, reserving for himself the role of cornerstone, in appointing Peter (more accurately – Peter's faith) to be the rock upon which the Church would be built, was *symbolizing* the inviolable quality of the Church's foundation. Jesus, in his confrontation with some Pharisees, intertwined with rock, His Apostolic heralds, as He told them in Luke 19:40: *"I tell you that if these should keep silent, the stones would immediately cry out."*

And thus, Jesus is popularly believed *and taught* to have created His church. But those who rely only upon this action of Jesus to be the origin of the Church fail to adequately take into account the total foundation upon which Jesus was actually *reconfiguring* His church.

In the Old Testament, the *rock* foundation is first referenced in Genesis (49:24) as: *"......because of the Shepherd, the rock of Israel ...."* Deuteronomy (32:3, 4) identifies the true rock: *"I will proclaim the name of the Lord, He is the rock, His name is perfect ......"*; 2 Samuel (22, 23) assures us: *The Lord is my rock, my fortress ...."* The Book of

Psalms refers five times to the Lord as the rock of His people. Isaiah (26:4) asserts: *"......the Lord is the rock eternal......"* and in 51:1, Isaiah is, perhaps, the best known Prophet of God to instruct God's people to look to the Lord for counsel and guidance in their daily lives, and to identify His people (who are righteous) as being sons of the "rock" which is God: *"...look ...to the rock from which you were cut";* and Daniel (2:34) speaks of the rock (God) which, in Nebuchadnezzar's dreams, destroyed the great king's golden statue *"......and filled the whole earth ......"*

We can therefore safely accept that the Biblical rock – is God the Father, one with His Son, Jesus, and has been since the Creation itself. In that same frame of reference, Genesis (1:27) tells us: *"So God created man in His own image, in the image of God He created him, male and female He created them ......";* Verse 28 tells us why: *Then God blessed them and said to them, "Be fruitful and multiply, fill the earth and subdue it, have dominion over the birds of the air and over every living thing that moves on the earth"*

If we believe that God, having appointed man (Adam) to be the "steward" of His creation, can it be so terribly wrong to accept that God created man and endowed him alone among all living creatures, with rational thought capabilities and with responsibility to oversee the rest of creation? All this with absolute freedom to choose for himself whether or not he would live *forever* under God's one (restraining) rule of life, for such a purpose, i.e. that man would, in love and gratitude, become an eternal source of fellowship with his creator.

In the very beginning, God established the role He had in mind for mankind to play in His creation.

God, in His infinite wisdom, determined that man's loyalty to his "employer" (his freedom) would be validated and matured, and that the objections of one of His angels (Satan), "that man loved his creator only through the medium of "bribery" in the form of his cushy appointment as God's steward of all creation, would be overcome by allowing Satan (in the form of the Biblical serpent) to tempt man, through his helpmate, into designating himself as arbiter of what would be right and wrong in life.

But man, in a corruption of his absolute freedom to *choose* to obey *or not to obey* his Creator and Mentor, chose instead, to attempt to elevate himself to equality with God. (Genesis 3:5). Adam, in effect, said: "You did a great work of creation, God, but you don't have to bother any more, I can improve it from here.

Thus did man first "establish" sin, which became known in the framework of Old Testament Scripture as *The Fall,* and is mentioned as such in New Testament writings.

God annulled His contract with Adam and Eve, and in His mercy, choosing not to destroy them, exiled them from Eden. Within His decision to exile, God appointed unto them the consequences of their decision to "fend for themselves." Bur God, in His mercy, determined to give them ample opportunity to "work off" their sin-laden attempts at self-aggrandizement; that opportunity taking the form of allowing the trials, tribulations and hardships of mortal life and for the first time, *mortal death,* which, until their "fall" God had reserved unto himself, *in protection of them*, as they, God hoped, repented of their sinful decision and come back to His utopian Providence.

The single attribute which God steadfastly insists upon from the very beginning of creation to this very day, is the maintenance of freedom of man to *choose* for himself whether to "love, honor and obey" God, as he (man) endures the mortal life consequences which man deliberately brought upon himself, of his determined pursuit of his own glory in place of the "true love" of yielding all glory to the Giver of his Life. I.e. Authority to establish right/wrong relationships between man and man and/or man and God and to trust God *completely* to provide man's his *abundant life.*

The proof-test established by God to enable man to have his exile judgment commuted, is that man would be required to totally repent of his acquiescence to the temptation to raise himself to God's (personal) exalted status; to rebuff his Satan inspired ego altogether; to henceforth trust God *only* to carry him through the maze of human life conditions brought about by his disobedience, and to once more become totally obedient to God's will, His way.

Unfortunately, the history of man, as recorded in God's Word, reveals that every time that God leans toward redeeming His promise of restoring to man the abundant life He started him out with, and lightens the effects of the consequences He allowed to come into being within earthly life, man seems to renew his determination to transfer his allegiances back to *self-glorification*, by reverting to his attitude of, as Frank Sinatra became famous for singing, "I'll do it my way" – who needs God?

The Biblical record of the first 2000 years of man's steadfast determination to establish himself as equal (better yet, *more* equal) to God, reports in fateful detail that God's need to discipline those who stubbornly cling to their rebellious, disobedient attitude is so much greater than is His award of loving, merciful protection for of those who come to faithfully trust His will, His way. This period of man's history includes the "Great Flood" of Noah's time, the action of judgment against family lines, culminating in God's disbursement of (flood) surviving human inhabitants of earth – The Tower of Babel event.

CHAPTER 2
Selecting The Builder

Apparently, God, after 2000 years, grew frustrated with individual man's determination to "do it my way" and decided to choose someone from man's own number whom He could identify as "righteous" enough to appoint to Adam's "dominion" role. This righteous man would become the "new-creation" of God's People, and would: "......*be fruitful and multiply, fill the earth and subdue it ......*" including the proselytizing of those who were outside his designated "family." (Slaves, servants, aliens, etc.)

Enter the covenant of God with Abram. This is considered by many theologians to be the second, Noah being the first, of God's plan to use righteous men to carry out His hope for the redemption of "fallen" mankind, those who chose to emulate Adam, from the self-destructive consequences of their own sin. – His begotten Son, Jesus, being the ultimate effort. Abram, who became the renamed Abraham, was appointed to begin the very first "Church" (People of God). By virtue of *qualifications* eventually required by God, (circumcision and daily living in His prescribed will) for Abraham's full issue to become know as *The People of God*, this first church became an institutional church.

Abraham's difficulties first in accepting the promises of God's "call" and then when once his faith was in place, in putting God's instructions into practice, demonstrate the hardness of man's resistance to *complete* trust in the promises of God. Abraham's "righteousness" was finally accepted by God, through his (Abram's) believing response to God's testing of the totality of his faith – the giving of his only *legitimate* son, through whom God had announced He would keep His promise of creation of a great nation, as a burnt offering to God. Abraham's "nation" grew for 175+ years, when God initiated the next step in the building of His Church.

A "tempering" of this new "People of God" was then achieved by making it necessary, by bringing a famine to the land in which they were living, for Abraham's progeny, Joseph, Isaac and family, to migrate to Egypt; the process of which was one of first establishing the family, through Joseph, in great favor with Pharaoh and then their falling into absolute *dis*favor and ending up as slaves with succeeding Pharaohs. It was a 400 year process.

The tempering having been satisfied, God, responded to His People's all-out and heartfelt prayers, by appointing Moses to lead His people from slavery in Egypt back to the homeland He had promised Abraham would become his nation.

Moses began his mission as a very reluctant leader, filled with great doubt that he was truly the person God needed for such a task. Moses, before the flaming bush, offered all kinds of personal "reasons" to refuse the call. But God refused to take "no" for a response; God demonstrated a power that He has applied to His personal calls from Moses time unto this day:

GOD DOES NOT NECISSARILY CALL THE QUALIFIED TO A CERTAIN TASK – HE QUALIFIES THOSE WHOM HE CALLS

Even as they were being rescued from Egypt, God's People exhibited intransigence in their "willingness" to *faithfully* follow Him. They rebelled against the rules of order demanded by God through Moses, namely, to trust God to care for His people in all situations, by living an obedient to God and service to each other lifestyle. They finally reached a condition of resistance with which God found it necessary to issue ten laws (commandments) of "belief" behavior, by which, *if they were obeyed,* His people would become known among themselves and to all of the world, as a unique people – God's *chosen* people.

God was describing and establishing the only lifestyle for humans which would enable man to complete the mission He gave them; to bring all man-kind back to "Eden." The (Ten) commandments issued by God proclaimed to His People that "law" was God's province and that it (and how they) would apply to every walk of daily life. *There is no separation, according to God, from Church to" secular" life,* for His people.

The crux of the still existing difficulty between God's creation (free thinking man) and his Creator remains, i.e. man's steadfast and determined *mis*application of the freedom granted to him in his creation. The evidence of God's Word is that in man's creation, God desired that mankind would reflect His love and His glory as he "enjoyed" the benefits of all else that God created, enjoying it, preserving it and sharing in it in full fellowship *with* his Creator. *But His people consistently disobeyed His law.*

Once more, *for emphasis:* In order to prove the pureness of their love, that attribute that gives meaning to all other traits which are required of a successful steward of creation and which God hoped man would exercise as His steward, God allowed the angel *Satan* (the "serpent" of Garden of Eden fame) to challenge God's asserted "right" to reign forever as Sovereign of Creation by attempting to *disprove* this hoped for quality of man's love for God or for each other. Satan's challenge took the form of tempting man (Eve) to claim full *in place of dependent* status with their Creator. In great corruption of God's loving trust by endowing him with freedom, Adam chose to ally himself with Satan's attempted destruction of truth by *dis*trusting God's promise to for- ever provide abundant life for man, *if man merely accepts God's Lordship.*

In *continued* perversion of the freedom that God created in him, man *to this day constantly* demonstrates preference for Satan's version of what *really* constitutes freedom. Man continues to test God's mercy and love through constantly making choices which attempts to impose *his* self-seeking (albeit illusionary) dominion over God's direction of his life, even to the point of refusing to believe the revelations brought to him by his Savior, of his *only* hope for salvation, which is the "lifestyle" which God had *since the very beginning of Adam's exile,* decreed would provide man with Heavenly Treasure, eternal health and well-being. That lifestyle to be applied by living in evidence of absolute trust in God through obedience of His Word, His Will, His Ways.

The ultimate paradox is that man "tests" his God-given freedom from slavery to sin, not by achievement for himself, contentment, or personal fulfillment as God promises by man's "discovering" the infinite variety of ways he can please God in "feeding My sheep," but by substitution *aberrant* behavior for God's "call" to become steward of His creation, thereby putting at risk of loss, the very freedom he seeks to prove. Simply put: Man seems determined to prove his freedom by doing what he can *be forgiven for,* rather than in living and doing what God has repeatedly demonstrated will to provide *peace and abundant fulfillment.* Man does this in (false) belief that materiel comfort *now* is better than what he must *wait for, in faith.*

Abraham's appointment as patriarch of God's Chosen People was God's remedial first step in creation of a *Church* that would over-whelm man's historical estrangement from His Will, His Way of a life lived with true and universal love. He created His Church in the midst of Satan driven, rebellious mankind for the purpose of using His people to not merely proclaim, but to fully demonstrate by living it, a fullness of life *which only the creator of ALL life could assure.* Thus God defined the "law" of life for man in his community.

But man continued to stubbornly abuse the freedom which God faithfully and steadfastly afforded him. His people's history is repeated corruption of the worship rites and of life (social) practices which God ordained through Moses, reinstated through Solomon and then Ezekiel after the return of the remnant of His people to His favor from their "disciplinary" exile, brought about by anti-God living and idol worship, which triggered a great *fury in man's Creator.*

The fury of God was against those "official" leaders of His Church (Priests, Pharisees, Sadducees and Scribes) who prescribed and initiated offensive practices by "piling on" their own laws and then rigidly enforcing them. These were leaders who were elevated to Church "officialdom" by human edict rather than by a call from God. And, perhaps most infuriating to God was that these "leaders" of God's Church deliberately misinterpreted the daily life application of the Word of God, which had been entrusted to Church keeping, in order to elevate their own status in the eyes of their oppressors (the Romans) and of their own people. This was their attempt to keep themselves from "worldly" destruction as well as to provide for themselves the "abundance" of life they thought "their" people owed them because of their *assumed* religious stature. The result was anarchy within the life of the People of God and effective suppression of the people's belief (trust) in the providence of the God who was their true hope for eternal life. These leaders were leading the "inferior" People of God by the code: Do as I say, not as I do.

Enter the *incarnation* of God, the Messiah for which they had long prayed and hoped. Jesus Christ was brought to humanity for the purpose of *freeing* His people from the shackles of man-made "holy" law; for their restoration to eternal fellowship with their Creator, for relief from the burdens placed upon them by "legalistically" and falsely led attempts to obey the laws of their God. Jesus Christ finished the task set before Him by God the Father, and then He *restructured* God's Church so that His revelation of the true nature and character of God would be perpetuated until He would return to His People in final achievement of His redemption of "righteous" man.

In accordance with God's divine plan, those who led the People of God (i.e. the Scribes, Pharisees, Sadducees, *the renowned teachers*) refused to accept that Jesus was the Messiah of prophesy and prevented many orthodox "man-on-the-street" followers from becoming converts to what eventually became known as Christianity. But there came a great benevolence for misleading their followers: "*I say then, have they stumbled that they should fall? Certainly not! But through their fall, to provoke them to jealousy salvation has come to the Gentiles ......if by any means I may provoke to jealousy those who are my flesh and save some of them ......*" (Romans 11:11-14) So in the restructuring of the Church, membership in the People of God was opened to "*those who were not My people.*" You and I, Gentiles, became thus qualified for adoption into the People of God.

The Church of God, founded through Abraham, is God's conduit for revealing to today's people – His power, love, glory and grace, and of proclaiming the *only* means for God to "stay" His judgment of death for sinful man (by accepting Jesus' promise contained in John 3:16: "*...for God so loved the world that He gave His only begotten Son, that whoever believes in Him should not perish but have everlasting life.*" and for the building of a community of man which will encourage Him to bring forth His "New Jerusalem.")

Now let us look to our dictionary and learn what is meant in the minds of mere mortals as the "Church." – That was renewed and reestablished by Christ through Peter and the other Apostles, including Paul.

Webster contains at least five definitions: The first one listed does suggest a building, perhaps made of rock, but Webster's application of *rock* fails to God's use of the word. Only one (the 3ʳᵈ) of definitions listed comes even close to indicating the purpose of the Church *as is given in God's Word (the Bible)*, e.g. in Ephesians 3: 10 – 11 mentioned earlier. Webster says: "a body or organization of religious believers: as

(a) "the whole body of Christians." But even that definition falls short of the long-standing foundation upon which Christ (re)established His "New" Church.

What we can thereby confidently deduce is that the "rock" spoken of in connection with Christ's Church is that He himself is the rock, actually the cornerstone – the only *permanent* foundation; that men *in His image* are the building blocks He chooses to complete His creation, cemented together by the blood of His crucifixion, sealed by His resurrection.

Any *meaningful* or instructional substance of a Lay critique of the Institutional Church must begin with an in-depth understanding of its Architect and Builder; must assess the efficacy of its building blocks and should offer, if found to be necessary, possible remedies for any "structural" deterioration which might have developed over its history, and identify and propose those determined to most likely to advance its future hope for successful completion of its mission. This premise is drawn from New Testament teachings by the Lord of the Church – some from His own teachings, some through the Apostles which His Word credits for the explosive growth of the Church which "brought down" the Roman Empire. Perhaps the most succinct of the Apostles' teachings are the epistles to the newly organized churches, from Peter and from James.

1 Peter (2:9) points out to us latter day disciples: *"But you are a chosen generation, a royal priesthood, a holy nation. His own special people, that you may proclaim the praises of Him who called you out of darkness into His* marvelous *light."* And verse 13 tells us: *"Therefore submit your selves to every ordinance of man for the Lord's sake ...... or to governors."*

The gist of Peter's first letter to believers reminds us to *relinquish* the false values, standards and trappings of this world in favor of those revealed and promised to "believers" by Christ. Many lessons in Scripture tell us how. Peter reminds us (1 Peter 1:13-16) *"Therefore, gird up the loins of your minds, be sober, and rest your hope fully upon the grace that is to be brought to you at the revelation of Jesus Chris; as obedient children, not conforming yourselves to the former lusts, as in your ignorance; but as He who called you is holy, you must also be holy in **all** your conduct, because it is written, be holy, for I am holy."*

Before giving this passage the "O yeah, all that will get me is persecuted, pilloried or physically harmed in rejection" we are reminded throughout New Testament Scripture that those who teach this obedience, even the cornerstone of the Church, suffered persecution, pillaring and physical harm like we are not, or very few of us, usually called to endure. Yet they persevered in absolute faith that God in Jesus Christ could and would prevail. And those who gave the Church the "firm foundation" is had to have in order to overwhelm violent, even life threatening resistance to its "rock" as *the only way to eternal life* (those who took their lives into the lion's arena) wielded this weapon of choice, i.e. *trust n His promises*, and did so as His people who *without violence* outlasted, some say brought down their persecutors who applied "of the law" weaponry.

Chapter 2 (1 Peter), verses 13 -17, calls for us to: *Therefore submit yourselves to the ordnance of man for the Lord's sake, whether to the king as supreme or to governors ......Honor all people, Love the Brotherhood, Fear God, honor the King ......"*

We cannot claim obedience to God's Word if we fail to do as the Cornerstone and all the building blocks of this New Church teach us to do.

Perhaps now is the time to remind ourselves that since Jesus brought us (our ancestors) to this "New Promised Land" (these United States) and counseled us (through His Holy Spirit) to form a "Democratic" government, the "kings and governors" we are to submit ourselves to, are those we have also been given a *process by which we can choose for ourselves.* Every church member of voting age has the ***freedom*** to apply his/ser beliefs, *without regard to political affiliation* to their choice of who will govern us – or to become one of the "governors" him/her self.

James, in his epistle (2:14-26) utters a very eloquent statement which says to us: *"Faith proves itself by works."* We would be seriously remiss if we limit that lesson to *individual"* works." Recall, if you will, the Scriptural references to Sodom and Gomorrah and to Capernaum and to Nineveh. Perhaps the key "works" we can take as voting individuals, is to evaluate candidates for any office of "governing" (whatever the level, whatever the role) by his/her application of God's Word to their every day life and decision making, (Not to what he/she can do to increase our material worth) and to vote in accordance with that evaluation, even if:

11

"...but if you should suffer (scorn, "friendly" oppression, loss of material worth) *for righteousness sake, you are blessed. And do not be afraid of their threats, nor be troubled ......for it is the will of God, to suffer for being good than for doing evil."*

Let us begin our critique by establishing in our own minds His authority, authority which only God can claim as "head" of the Church. Lets frame it in the sequence of its history of establishment, including obstacles thereto. Let us discuss and define consequences of problems identified and see if we can *suggest* solutions.

There is one caveat to this critique. Many institutional church congregations and/or individuals do make an honest, sincere and lovingly dedicated attempt to carry out the ministry entrusted to them by Jesus Christ. For those congregations and individuals, Christ's ministry is, rightly, their life purpose and they strive to bring glory to God. *This critique is not addressed to them.* In the manner of a *self-evaluation* each congregation is urged to identify which, if any, part of this dissertation applies to them, a not unholy exercise. Many congregations however, do not make such attempts, they work for personal (ized) recognition or praise. It is to these congregations that John was instructed to write during his sojourn on Patmos.

This dissertation *is* written to address the fact that some present-day congregations or individuals, some regional groups of congregations, sometimes even accruing to the national level, some-times with private, sometimes with open agenda, in a deliberate and/or less than Biblical theology, often disguised as "reformed," in a "human" and errant attempt to sustain the life of "their" church by attracting more members, are falling into the category of ministry such as Paul warned Timothy against as he pastured the church to which he (Timothy) had been called in Ephesus: *"As I urged you when I went into Macedonia – remain in Ephesus that you may charge some, that they may teach no other doctrine, nor give heed to fables and endless genealogies which cause disputes rather than Godly edification, which is faith."*

Now the purpose of this commandment is love from a pure heart, from a good conscience and from sincere faith, from which some, having strayed, have turned aside to idle talk, desiring to be teachers of the law, understanding neither what they say nor the things which they affirm. But we know that the law was not made for righteous persons, but for the unholy, the profane, for murderers of fathers and murderers of mothers, for manslayers' for fornicators, for sodomites, for kidnappers, for liars, for perjurers, and if there is any other thing that is contrary to sound doctrine, according to the glorious gospel of the blessed God which was entrusted to my trust." (1 Timothy 1: 3-11)

Peter (1 Peter 5: 1-9) counsels the elders of the Church to "shepherd" the flock. James (5:14) calls upon the elders of the Church to pray for members of the fellowship who are suffering; verse 19 calls for the Church faithful in Christ to *confront* erring believers. The Apostles, mainly Paul, in other Scriptural writings, also speak to the need to keep the people of the Church righteous and pure, in the hopes of successfully completing their mission of making it possible for all people "to the corners of the world" to spend eternity in the "New Jerusalem."

It is felt by many "Lay" Christians that too many "with-it" seminaries today teach and practice what Paul was warning Timothy against. All in a misguided attempt to equip contemporary and/or *politically correct* – or "non-controversial" leaders (Pastors) to have "successful" churches. And all such teaching, of course, becomes a confusing and errant attempt to "bring theology more accurately into the real world."

The first theology to be corrupted is the assurance that God throughout inspired Scripture that acquired knowledge, in and of itself *is not* power; that knowledge, standing alone, is meaningless and illusionary until God molds it into understanding. It *then* becomes wisdom. " *... for I (Christ) will give you a mouth and wisdom which all your adversaries will not be able to contradict or resist"* (Luke 21:15) and in Ephesians (1:17) Paul prays for us: "......*that the God of our Lord Jesus Christ, the Father of Glory, may give to you the spirit of wisdom and revelation in the know- ledge of Him."* Also, in a note of caution that *ministers are accountable,* Paul teaches in 1 Corinthians (3:18): *"Let no one deceive himself. If anyone among you seems to be wise in this age, let him become a fool that he may become wise, for the wisdom of this world is foolishness with God. For it is written; He catches the wise in their own craftiness, and again: the Lord knows the thoughts of the wise, that they are futile."* Isn't this one of the lessons to be learned in the account of God's intervention in the building of the Tower of Babel? **And isn't this what Christ chastised the scribes, Pharisees and Sadducees for claiming and practicing?**

Wouldn't it be a fascinating statistic to know how many classes on theology in "with-it" seminaries begin and end each session with a prayer for understanding and wisdom?

There can be little or no doubt what role Jesus who created, and the Apostles who "began" the Church had in mind for the congregations of the Church in regard to the *"ungodly"* society into which they formed. Jesus, in Matthew (28:18-20) commanded: *"Go therefore and make disciples of all nations, baptizing them in the name of the Father and of Son and of the Holy Spirit, teaching them to observe all things that I have commanded you' and I will be with you, even to the end of the age."*

The command of the Creator of the Church is unequivocal; the Church is charged to change society by baptizing each individual, from what sinful man has made of it into a society of believers and followers (disciples). The Apostles teach us as Jesus taught them, some of the pitfalls and dangers and hardships and troubles and rewards inherent in the execution of that command. These are taught as *opportunities* for those doing the teaching to acquire absolute faith, as in *"I can do all things through Christ, which strengtheneth me."* (Philippians 4:13) The Apostles assure us of their faith that the hardships they warn us about are more than worthy of their bearing if we look to the "rewards" preserved for us in *"the mansion He goes to prepare for us.* Paul states his faith thusly: *But indeed I count all things lost for the excellence of the knowledge of Christ Jesus as Lord, for whom I have suffered the loss of all things, and count them as rubbish, that I may gain Christ."* All of the Apostles except one lost their mortal lives in giving themselves totally to this faith.

The elements of the broadly stated caveat are covered to a more substantive depth in various issues spoken to in the critique, which follow.

Now we will return to the critique itself, beginning with the authority which can be rightly claimed *only* by the Lord of the Church.

PART II
THE DESIGN OF GOD'S CHURCH

CHAPTER 3
Its Building Materials

"In the beginning God created the heavens and the earth. The earth was without form, and void; and darkness was on the face of the deep. And the Spirit of God was hovering over the face of the waters. ...." (Genesis 1:1 --)

The need for the Church to become a from within voice of God to even His own people stems from man's steadfast and concerted reluctance to understand or to accept the *fact* of God's sovereignty over all creation, even His own creation. Man's reluctance was aided and abetted, even initiated by him who is known as *Satan*. Satan's challenge began with a face-to-face tempting of Eve, Adam's helpmate; and has evolved to this day into a continued lie: *"Scripture is a folk tale."* – In this present day, based upon *pseudo scientific* "knowledge." – As to whether or not there even is a God. The most current such argument and a science based counter-argument going somewhat like this:

With Evolution, Who needs God?

The most successful and by far the most damaging "scientific" argument against the existence of, or need for, a creating God, was *Charles Darwin's theory of evolution*. Damaging in that as a diabolical element of so-called state-of-the-art efforts to indoctrinate school students with "truth," Darwin's theory was popularly and prematurely (prematurely because it was introduced as the only "logical" conclusion to draw from Darwin's study) adopted by main-stream public educators in the 1920s – by "disciples of the master" more than 120 years after it was introduced without verification (proof) which to this day is still failing to appear; and *forced* upon those who rejected it, by the legal system, up to and including the Supreme Court, when some local public education teachers did not, *for obedience to the Word of God* reasons refused to teach the theory as *only* possibility for the beginning of all life.

Darwin's thesis, again as proposed to the legal system by his followers and their lawyers some 120 years later, was: This theory of evolution belies all previous claims of the Bible that a *Supernatural Creator* established the human race and *appointed* "man" to be His steward (manager) of the world and its inhabitants –*and that there can be no life after death.*

Charles Darwin, scientist, whose theory of evolution was the meat and potatoes of the Scopes Monkey trial in the 1920s, made the case so convincingly that the Public Education Community, in their contrived eagerness to replace God theology with man-made dogma, were duped into accepting evolution as the only possible "truth" with which to educate their students. And when parents and other defenders of the Judeo-Christian faith objected to their attempts to eliminate any other theory, such as Big-Bang, Random Chance, Chemical Affinity, et al, from any course of public instruction, the "educators" who were apparently unable to persuade with scientific argument the decision to eliminate, turned to the "legal system" to affirm the righteousness of their decision. The legal system, in the form of a local court jury, susceptible to, or unable to counter erroneously validated scientific "facts," affirmed the educator curricula plans and forbade even *mention* of creation theories in the public school arena. All appeals to the lower court's decision were denied. That decision of delusion *stands* to this day, even in the face of many and massive reports which put forth studies, with evidence, which convinces many if not most scientists to publicly announce that science itself *now* contradicts evolution theory and strongly *supports* the hypothesis that the universe and the earth was brought about by supernatural design and action.

Even Christian schools continue to be obligated to teach the theory of evolution, or their students would forfeit their ability to qualify for "higher" education.

In terms of damage to Christian teachings, prominent evolutionists, many of them holding down tenured chairs in famous universities, candidly put forth the opinion that *if Darwin's theory is true,* these are some of the implications which are most inescapable:

1) there is no inviolable evidence for God;
2) there is no life after death;
3) there is no foundation (except social convention) upon which to base right and wrong;
4) there is no "higher" meaning for life.

5) People just do not have free will.

But is Darwin's theory true?

Time magazine (December 31, 1999) said: Charles Darwin didn't want to murder God, as he put it, but he did!

Evidence within the scientific community over the last thirty or so years, in numerous published and provable analytical papers concludes that the originator of the theory, in their rush to prove their privately devised hypotheses, had glossed over significant nuances in regards to components used in their studies –which transforms the many arguments *against* the theory, from theological to *scientific.* It is fact, that more and more biologists, biochemists and other researchers, not merely Christians, have reached and announced that Darwin's theory's inferences are based on incomplete, flawed, even false information. *An accelerating number of scientific studies now contradict Darwin, by concluding that an "intelligent designer" was behind the origin* and development of life.

In order to test this contention of errant court judgment, please look at some of the reasons why this change in scientific conclusion has occurred. Most succinctly, in his book *The Case for Faith,* author *Lee Strobel* lists dozens of study conclusions in reference to this scientific dilemma, including a study from Darwin himself. In his book *Origin of the Species,* Darwin admitted that if it could be demonstrated that any complex organ exists that could not possibly have been formed by numerous, successive slight modifications, then his theory would break down. Many of the studies listed in *The Case for Faith* identify numerous examples of unchangeable organs of life. *The Case for Faith* is a book well worth the reading.

The clincher in the argument against the theory of evolution could well *be* the report of the recently organized field of microbiology that there is no such thing as a simple organism; all organisms are so complex as to have their components labeled as *machines.*

The whole point of contention (re. evolution) is: Biological evolution can only take place *after* there is some form of living matter that could replicate itself and then grow in complexity through self-induced change. Darwin's theory presupposes that non-living chemicals which are given the right amount of time and circumstances could develop themselves into living matter.

Darwin's presupposition has never been proven correct. In fact, there are many studies listed in *A Case for Faith* which strongly refute it.

The most heralded "scientific" study which does, or claims to prove it is an experiment conducted by Professor Stanly Miller of the University of Chicago, sometime in 1928-29. Miller duplicated, in his laboratory, the atmosphere that *he had decided* was in place those necessary billions (with a B) years ago, as well as the chemicals which he *thought* were present then. He shot huge voltages electricity, simulating lightening, through that contrived atmosphere. After some period of time, he found that amino acids (the building blocks of all life) had been created. Professor Miller never explained to the "powers that were" that of the more than one hundred amino acids that exist, only a few affect life, and even then only if they are combined in a specific manner. The Miller experiment was widely hailed as *proof* that life *could have begun through natural processes.* That experiment was also the primary academic (and legal) support for Darwin's "genius."

It was later discovered that the artificial atmosphere generated for Miller's experiment was not identified by Miller and his associate because there was *evidence* that the elements chosen for the experimental atmosphere were *in fact* present those billions of years ago, they were chosen because *only those elements could ever support* the generation of amino acids.

NASA scientists have lately, in the last thirty years, *proven* that the elements selected for Miller's experiment were in fact *not* present then.

Time Magazine was in error! The point is that evolution is a hypothesis that cannot be proven.

And in reference to the current uproar over separation of Church and State, the United State Supreme Court, by sustaining the lower court decision about teaching Darwin's theory solely in the Public Schools, is in fact, using false science to *dictate* a Government refutation of religious belief.

What is the reason for the inclusion of this issue in a critique of the Church? *The institutional Christian Church, by its failure to apply for legal redress, very effectively supports this governmental establishment of religious dogma and thereby falls short of carrying out its responsibilities re: the "and teach them to observe all that I have commanded you"* – to wit: Creation as announced in Genesis 1.

The issue of evolution is addressed very briefly here; it will be addressed more thoroughly as to its effect on the carrying out of the great commission in chapter 10.

CHAPTER 4
Its Laborers

"Then the Lord God said: "Behold the man has become like one of Us, to know good and evil. And now, lest he put out his hand and also of the tree of life, and eat, and live forever" ...... Therefore the Lord God sent him out of the Garden of Eden to the ground from which he was taken. So He drove out the man; and; and He placed Cherubim at the east of the Garden of Eden and a flaming sword which turned every way to guard the tree of life." (Genesis 3: 22-24)

Man (and woman) was the crowning glory of God's six days of creative work. As free mortal beings that stood in the image of God, they were assigned dominion over the "natural" world cited previously. They alone, of all the creatures of the world are equipped for fellowship with their creator.

Having created man in His own image, God loved His creation so much that He set him up in an ideal environment and set of circumstances which were designed to produce in him a will for intimated fellowship with God through all eternity. Then He gave man a "help-mate" through whom he could be the agent by which God would always continue His creation. To demonstrate His love, God also gave man the freedom to choose whether or not he would obey the one restriction He gave him: *"not to eat the fruit of the tree of life."* And He gave man the opportunity to demonstrate his love for his Creator, by allowing a rebellious angel (Satan) to try to tempt man from his love induced loyalty to God.

Satan (the serpent of the garden) succeeded in his effort to cajole man into believing that he could be equal to his Creator, if he simply ignored "God's injunction to refrain from eating the "forbidden" fruit. *Adam ate fruit of the tree of life!*

In His disappointment with man's decision, God exiled man from utopia. God *exiled* Adam and Eve, but He did not abandon them. God maintained His presence with Adam, and with his progeny, always with awesome love and mercy, always sustaining their freedom to repent their determination that they could "make it on their own" and then in their penance, to turn back to "life" and complete God's intention of eternal life with Him.

Adam's sin may not *seem* like much in man's perspective (all he really did was to take a bite of fruit). But it was a *very* serious sin because the fruit he ate was of the tree of knowledge of good and evil and God had told him *not* to eat it, under penalty of death. Up to this time, Adam had been free of sin – he was morally innocent. When he sinned he lost all innocence and became, "by nature" a sinner. As a sinner, he died. He died immediately, spiritually and *began* to die, physically.

Adam was the first man to ever live upon the earth. Every other human being who has ever lived came from Adam and Eve. Sinners beget sinners. Adam became a sinner before Eve ever conceived and therefore every human being descended from Adam, *except Christ,* is a sinner just as he was. The consequence of Adam's sin is that physical death entered the human race. Remember? Adam was created to have *eternal* fellowship with God; God, however, with a mercy never really understood by mortal minds, devised a way for man to be reinstated to his original station in life. The *first step* of God's way to new life was Adam and Eve's exile from Eden; exile from God's preservation of his human life

But man, in his ultimate conceit, did not trust other men any more than he trusted God. So men learned to compete among themselves for symbols of superiority regarding material things and for personal safety. Life for man became a constant aura of jealousy, enmity, all sorts of tribulation.

The next 2000 years of God's merciful discipline for man because he sins are recorded in Scripture and His efforts to persuade man to *without limit* or *condition* respond to His pure love by freely extending His own absolute and total allegiance to Him, was frustrated by man's constant and continuing determination to "do-it-myself." God allowed man about 1000 years (man time) to come to his senses, but man grew so much more and more crafty in developing new ways of rebellion that God, in His frustrated anger, found one righteous man, *Noah* and his family, worth of saving and then sent a flood over all the earth, destroying all other living creatures.

The sin of man which had brought on the decision of God that unrighteous man should be destroyed was the steadfast corruption

of God's plan for man, through marrying daughters of *ungodly men.*
Siring children to them and adopting their spouse's belief systems – thus
sponsoring a "new" and *"tolerant and evil"* society of man. The society
they established reveled in continuous sin. Genesis (6: 5-7) records:
*"Then the Lord saw that the wickedness of man was great in the earth, and
that every intent of the thoughts of his heart was only evil, continually. And
the Lord was sorry that He had made man on the earth, and was grieved
in His heart. So the Lord said, I will destroy man whom I have created,
from the face of the earth, man and beast, creeping things and birds of the
air, for I am sorry that I made them."*

Noah, whom God identified as an exception to His view of man'
depravity, and his three sons and their wives, who were all shielded from
the consequences of God's anger by the ark which God had commanded
to be built, were, after the flood receded, appointed to repopulate
the earth. They were also "officially" appointed to be stewards of the
restored animal kingdom. Man was also permitted, *for the first time,* to
eat meat – but not blood. Blood is the sustenance of mortal life.

God (re)established the sacredness of human life. He decreed that
"whoever sheds man's blood, by man his blood shall be shed.

For in the image of God He made man. And as for you (Noah) *be
fruitful and multiply ......"* (Genesis 9:7)

The Establishment of (Family) Nations

The sons of Noah, in initial obedience to the covenant between
God and their father, began families, which over the next 500 years,
or so, grew and migrated until they came to a place called *Shinar.*
They decided to dwell there. At that time, they all spoke the same
language.

In Shinar, in the nature they inherited from Adam, i.e. *thinking
of themselves more highly that God"* (Romans 12:1) they said: *"Come,
let us build ourselves a city and a tower whose top is in the heavens, let us
make a name for ourselves, let we be scattered abroad over the face of
the whole earth."* (Genesis 11:4). They began to build what came to be
known as the Tower of Babel. God saw that they were attempting to
raise *their* identity up to His, or higher, and "confused: their language
and scattered them abroad from there, over the face of the earth. They
ceased their building. The families, over the succeeding 500 years, grew
in membership, they became separate nations.

God "calls" a New Righteous man

God, as the next step in His plan to reclaim man from his isolation from His God, identified Abram, from the lineage of Noah's son *Shem,* as a righteous person and made with him, a covenant.

Abram, eventually renamed Abraham, was instructed by God to separate himself from his father and all the other families that descended from Noah, and move to a new land with all of his chattel and his nephew *Lot.* God promised Abraham that he would become the patriarch of a new lineage: God's chosen people. Abraham thus became the first man chosen by God to be the mortal link (agent) by which God began then to do, and had done throughout the history of man and will continue to do until the end of "mortal time." i.e. bring about a "stay," through man's rebirth, of His exile judgment. *Abraham was the first "action" of God's new plan for Him to "restore" man to His original status.* The new People of God became His "Church."

CHAPTER 5
Its Superstructure

"Get out of your country, from your kindred and from your father's house to a land I will show you. I will make you a great nation; I will bless you and make your name great; and you shall be a blessing. I will bless those who bless you, and I will curse him who curses you; and in you, all families of the earth shall be blessed." (Genesis 12:1)

In separating Abram from previous history and from his kindred, God established from the very beginning of their covenant relationship, that he (God) would always be the sole source and arbiter of the promised blessings. God covenanted himself to bring the blessings to pass – by His promise of "I will." What was incumbent upon Abram was to fully trust and to faithfully obey all God's instructions to him.

Abram validated his trust in God when he obeyed God's call to sacrifice the life, by offering him as a burnt offering, of his only son, Isaac, through whom God had already would come the peoples of the promised great nation. Abram believed that this beyond *measure* great God, the almighty, could would *resurrect* his son Isaac in order to keep His promise to Abram. It was after this act of faith that God renamed Abram, *Abraham,* and proceeded to put into action His plan for the "molding" of His people. God gave His people a sign of their identification as His people. He required of Abraham that he and his descendents as well as his servants and slaves be identified by accepting the rite of circumcision.

God's opening covenant in creating His Church, made with Abraham, was continually updated as God brought His people to maturity; or when God determined it to be appropriate for any other reason. The covenant was finally and fully ratified when God sacrificed the very life of *His* only begotten Son; and has never, to this day, been annulled by God. His covenant provides opportunities for blessing in three personal (to Abraham) areas:

1) National: *"I will make of you a great nation"* i.e. a great **nation.**

2) Personal: *"I will bless you and make your name great and you shall **be** a blessing.*

3) Universal: *"......in you all families on earth shall be blessed."*

The covenant with Abraham created an important link in all that God began to do, has, in fact, done all through the history of His Church, *and will do until the end of human history*. It established the one purpose of God for humans into which all of God's programs and works fit; the *universal* promises of the covenant, even to us today, are:

1) Blessings for those people and nations which bless Abraham and all who came from him.

2) "Cursing" upon those people and nations which curse Abraham and Israel.

3) Blessing upon all families on earth, through the Messiah, who according to the flesh is Abraham's son, and provides salvation for the entire world.

Just as there can be no rational doubt that God created the universe and all in it, including man, there can also be little doubt that God *intends* to complete the building of His Kingdom on earth, by using man-power.

And the purpose of the covenant for God was: *"Now therefore, if You will indeed obey My voice and keep My covenant, then you shall be a special treasure to Me above all peoples, for the earth is mine and you shall be to Me, a kingdom of priests and a Holy Nation. ......"* The kingdom (nation) of priests was established more than 500 years before the "Church" – which followed His people's failure to hear His voice.

God was giving man an opportunity to repent his way back - to "Eden."

After Abraham sired Isaac and his life of 175 years ended, God saw to it that Abraham's great-grandson Joseph, led his father, Jacob, along with all the family begotten through his wife Sarah, into Egypt, first in evidence that He (God) could and would deliver on His promises of caring for His people, e.g. first saving them from the famine which came upon Israel and then, over a 400 year "trial" period, molding them into and tempering His People into an identifiable, homogeneous nation, consisting of twelve branches (tribes, each headed by one of Jacob's twelve sons.)

The molding and tempering consisted of bonding them together through their endurance of common tribulation (slavery to Pharaoh) and, when God determined that the tempering was complete, God fulfilled His promise to Abraham to "give" His people the land which He had shown him. God called Moses to "superintend" His people's journey to that land. This journey, called *The Exodus,* was the ultimate sign from God that these were His People and that they would always be under His protection.

In bringing His people, finally, to the land He had promised, God was also establishing His People, *His Church*, for the definitive purpose of their setting and maintaining (for all peoples to learn) by their living of them, the values, standards and mores' He was establishing for *any* person or people who would seek His ever-lasting fellowship. It would be well to remember here that God *did* include in His people, those "outsiders" who for servitude or for any other reason, adopted His People's faith, underwent the rite of circumcision that His People had undergone, and melded into their fellowship. In this way (re: the aliens in their midst) God, from the very beginning of His "Church" – His separate People, provided the way for His People to bring into *their* designated status "outsiders" who "*seek Him with all their heart.*" (Psalm 119:2). God's plan was (is) for His "separate" People to bring into His eternal fellowship, "aliens" who (and if they) subscribed to God's Holy Way, rather than His Peoples becoming corrupted in their earthly sojourn by *assimilating the ways of unbelievers.*

God required of His believers that they live, act and be as He commanded. I.e. This "new" People of God serves a Holy God who requires of them to be holy as well. To be holy as used here means to be set apart – or "separated" from non-believers. They are to be separated from other nations, other cultures, unto God. In Leviticus 18-27, God reiterates to His People what He requires of them to be sanctified as holy. These sanctification "instructions", known to theologians today as *The Holiness Code*, extended to the people (chapters 18-20), to the Priesthood (chapters 21-22) their worship (23,24), their "social" life (25,26) and included "special" vows (27). God saw, *and continues to see* it as necessary, in order to *thus remove* the difference that separates people from God, so that they may walk in eternal fellowship with their Creator.

This *Holiness Code* (Leviticus 18-27) is described for us in Scripture to emphasize God's *intent* that His People would by practicing a God-defined way of life, come to understand that to achieve redemption from their physical state, their *total* life – both worship and social - must be lived in the way and manner prescribed. Man was required to live thus *as a demonstration of total repentance* in order for God to repeal His exile of them from Eden, and to accept man into eternal fellowship with Him.

How the Holiness Code is to be applied to "daily life."

God, in His detailed thoroughness in leading His people, did not leave to chance His people's ability to reap the benefits of establishing themselves as His people. God gave to Moses a pattern of Government which, if His people set up and followed, would reduce the effects of their human, *self-driven corruption* of life under the *Ten Commandments* and the holiness code to levels which they, as "agents" of their God would be able to help each other to overcome. God taught Moses who, as also called for by God, taught the people of God *before they established the nation which God was founding through them:*

"You shall appoint judges and officers in all your gates which the Lord your God gives you according to your tribes, and they shall judge the people with just judgment. You shall not pervert judgment. You shall not pervert justice, you shall not show partiality nor take a bribe for a bribe blinds the eyes of the wise and twists the words of the righteous. You shall follow what is altogether just, that you may inherit the land which the Lord God is giving you" (Deuteronomy 16: 18-20). And God goes even further in His teaching of His people to govern themselves. *"If a matter arises which is too hard for you* (at the tribal level) *to judge between degrees of bloodguiltiness, between one judgment or another or between one punishment or another, matters of controversy within your gates, then you shall arise and go up to the place which the Lord your God chooses, and you shall come to the priests, the Levites, and to the judge there in those days, and inquire of them; they shall pronounce upon you the sentence of judgment ......according to the sentence of the law in which they instruct you, according to the judgment which they tell you, you shall do ......which they pronounce upon you."* And God, through these instructions though Moses, included consequences for any person's failure to comply.

These instructions to His people from God through His agent Moses became the model used by the *Founding Fathers* of the United States for the design of the Constitution (i.e. Covenant) for governance of the people, which became the frame of reference for future continuity of the government. The Constitution will be addressed more appropriately in chapter 7, following.

But as the "Church" (the new nation, Judah) aged, its *mortal* leaders, elevated to leadership by accepting the call of Church members who concentrated their own energies on "secular" interests or who *appointed themselves* by falsely claiming a call from God became corrupted y the power that *thought* they had to "manage" the Church. These false leaders became more and more oppressive to the people; denying their wishes to serve widows and children in the name of God and thereby eroding common trust in the promises of God. In effect, they were driving followers out of the fellowship of believers. This they did through "supplementing" the Holiness Code by legislating new rules and rendering it ineffective for the guidance of true believers. As mentioned elsewhere in this critique, this was the *final straw*, which made the incarnation of Christ, one with God, and His sacrificial death necessary in order to achieve God's desired restoration of His people – to their Creator.

One of the fallacies in the thinking of today's Christian is that because of the death and resurrection off Jesus Christ, God's intent for the Holiness Code no longer applies to His people. Nothing could be farther from the truth! It is true that where the detailed practices of animal sacrifice and worship ritual are concerned, other "offerings" now apply. Peter (2:5) in his first letter to "the Church" instructs us: "……… *you also, as living stones, are being built up a spiritual house, a holy priesthood to offer up **spiritual** sacrifices acceptable to God through Jesus Christ.*" And God "allowed" His temple in Jerusalem to be destroyed *a second time*, and to be no longer available to His People.

But the purpose of His plan – to define a separation of God's People from all others *by how they live, act and are in their hearts,* is still in force. The laws of God as spelled out in the Ten Commandments and as set up in the "code," in order for man to receive redemption were in fact successfully accomplished for all believers by the sacrificial death of Jesus Christ. But Christians are called to continue to be a separate and distinct people, identifiable to all whom they encounter in their worldly journey. Peter, again in his first letter (2:12) defines separation as: *"...... having your conduct honorable among Gentiles, that when they speak of you as evil doers, they may, by your good works which they observe, glorify God in the day of visitation,"*

As Christ said to Nichodemus, to be Christian is to be born again. To be born again is to become a new person, separated from those who have not accepted the sacrifice; separated in spiritual *and life practices,* (even) if never relocated to a new land. The laws of God (pre-Christ) described the way man had to live, act and be in order to "earn" redemption. Baptism into Christ's death, *accepting* Christ's death as their death to sin (Romans 6:3, 4) made the instructions of the code moot to true believers. Acceptance set men free from "worldly" demands on their lives and free from prescribed rituals in place of substance of religious life; this acceptance allows man to, in a spirit of complete love, to live in a fashion that would be a constant demonstration of God's love and mercy for all His people, which (a new holiness code?) Christ spelled out in what we refer as the Beatitudes (Matthew 5:3-12 and Luke 6:20-26)

Christ himself commanded His disciples: *"A new commandment I give to you, that you love one another; as I have loved you that you love one another. By this all will know that you are My disciples."* (John 14:12); and again He topped off that particular teaching with: *"If you love* (accept my teachings) *me, feed my sheep."* (v 15). God decided and made possible through the revelation of His Will, His Way via the life, ministry, sacrificial death of His only begotten Son Jesus Christ, that His People would be separate and distinct from all other, and identifiable to all by the values, standards and mores' they employ as they experience their "exile" (mortal life) from His spiritual being.

And God provided a way for any who became disenchanted with "worldly" life, even to the point of reaching out to them *whether or not* they knew of their need for His mercy (that's called Grace). God established His People, the Church, for the purpose spelled out in Ephesians (3:10) *"...... to the intent that now the manifold wisdom of God might be made known by the Church to the principalities and powers in heavenly places, according to the eternal purposes which He accomplished in Christ Jesus our Lord."* God entrusted to His separated people, responsibility for accomplishing His announced purpose.

Once more, God did not do this by creating an idealistic vacuum. With the resurrection of Jesus from the dead' the issuing of the final and "Great Commandment" and the "enrollment" of the Apostle Paul into His ministry of salvation to all peoples, the separation His People from the world is no longer physical, as when He called Abraham to lead His People to a new and promised land. With the advent of Christ, the separation of God's People is now in their spiritual re-birth. His People were deliberately left, for a resting time, in their worldly state, so that they would have an opportunity to be involved in completing Christ's redemptive ministry, by carrying our His final command to His followers, *"To go therefore, and make disciples of all nations, baptizing them in the name of the Father and of the Son and of the Holy Spirit,* **teaching them to observe all things that I have commanded you......"** (Matthew 28: 19, 20)

The point of *emphasis* here is for the new, refurbished by Christ – one with God – institutional Church to hear and obey the command "Go." Go even into the *local* population, and not to limit themselves to the building of a physical house in which a "called" preacher will deliver sermons to whoever might wander in the door, or to responding to local catastrophic events in the name of "their" Church. *The command to GO is not a command for passivity.*

And He did not leave them without precise and detailed guidance as to what they would encounter as they applied themselves to His command: *"...... If anyone would come after Me, he must deny himself and take up his cross and follow Me"* (Matthew 16:24). John (15:1 – 17:26) sums up in detail Christ's instruction, as well as warnings of worldly, even life threatening animosity to the ministry He was entrusting to them. His final, *face-to-face* teaching as they were on the way to the garden of His arrest dealt with:

1) The relationship of Believers to Christ (John 15:1-11).
2) The relationship of Believers to Each Other (Jn 15:12-17).
3) The relationship of Believers to the world. (Jn 15: 18-25).
4) The promise of The Holy Spirit (Jn 15:26-16:25)
5) The prediction of His death and resurrection (Jn 16:16-33).

......And chapter 17 of John describes Christ's intercession with God the Father on behalf of himself as *man* in travail, His Disciples and all who come to believe through their (and our, their spiritual descendents) ministry and proclamation.

Thus was God's institution, the Church, refurbished, re-staffed and set into motion more than 2000 years ago. The Church re-created by Jesus Christ, with His assurance that the gates of Hades will not prevail against it, stands today, unchanged as to His Final Command to it (its people); but with its outreach to Gentile lands not yet created at the time of Christ's on-earth presence. With "latter-day" dispersion of centers of evangelical opportunity required for response to lands now (since the 1600s) in existence, comes a renewal of the need of which Paul speaks, for the Church to from time to time, with the counsel of the Holy Spirit, examine itself to be assured that these new centers (congregations) continue to be "in Jesus the Christ."

With the expansion of believer populations to new and fertile fields of "harvest" – the "new" world opened to them in the 1600s – a need came to organize, as did Paul, new congregations of the existing People of God, located to more adequately address this unforeseen need and capable of generating new strategies for obeying Christ's final command.

The outreach arm of the Church was relocated; its building plans were restructured. But in the absence of an appointed human leader, the planning and the "leadership" was assumed by The Holy Spirit of God.

CHAPTER 6
A Strategic Relocation

Preparing the Church for relocation:
Note: Since this critique is intended to address the institutional church as it has evolved into the present day, let us not dwell in detail on the convolutions undergone by "The Church" as it matured by enduring hard, albeit many of them self-inflicted, pruning of its branches (John 15:2) if they are unable to bear, or if they corrupt the fruit for which the "vine" was planted, *except to note some of them as they impacted the "smoothness" of the Church's continuing ministry.*

History, Scriptural and secular, records how the early church erred by aligning itself with man-led governments (the original sin?) and became as oppressive to its followers as was the church of the Pharisees, Sadducees and Scribes "governed" by the Sanhedrin, which ultimately became the culmination of its trials, tribulations and troubles; *the final straw* for its adherents, which, in turn, formed the arena into which Christ was "given" to salvage and to reform God's People with a new covenant – paid for with His broken body and shed blood.

This seems to be an appropriate place in this critique to assert that many believers, and many un-wise believers, tend to shrug off the telling of Biblical lessons about God's intervention in the affairs of man, as being allegorical – especially where God's Inspired Word describes a particular intervention as catastrophic to (mortal) life and limb of those targeted by that intervention. But those who do shrug them off fail to take into their "wisdom" that "symbolic representation" (Webster 2a) in no way eliminates the fact of the event described allegorically. The reference here is to such events described in Scripture as the destruction of Sodom and Gomorrah and the killing of "every man, woman and child" in the conquest of the Promised Land, etc. **The incarnation of God in the form of man (Jesus Christ) was not an allegory;** it was an event that did happen, in God's own time, in accordance with ancient (BC) prophecies which were more accurate than most eye-witness descriptions.

*And what we identify as eternal damnation (Hell) is **not** an allegory. Hell is a product of God's love. Hell is the final great complement to the reality of human freedom and to the dignity of human choice.* C. K. Chesterman (Christian) has said: "*Consignment to eternal separation from God is the final gift of God to those who have, by the way they lived their mortal lives, consciously rejected the **hard** virtues of God (holiness, righteousness and justice) even if they were not in opposition to the "soft" virtues of love and tenderness.*

The practices of the early church, recreated by Christ as He returned to His spiritual self, as its founders died off and were replaced by a percentage of self-seeking successors, eventually evolved into what its followers accepted as the "Universal" Church. But its leadership soon corrupted the teachings of Christ and so misinformed its followers, and made them the source of their own wealth and status, through *non-scriptural* material assessments for penitence, that God found it necessary (in the "dark ages") to raise up new "elders" whom He selected (Luther, Calvin, Knox, Zwingly, et. al.) who wrested from the established hierarchy, the "truth" i.e. what became known as a "Reformed" theology of God's Grace.

This "wresting" was so vigorously challenged by the Universal Church hierarchy that it often took the form off, sometimes fatal, violence, but always camouflaged by the Universal Church with a misinterpreted theology which they called truth. This was also the period of Church development wherein differing understandings of scripture by men called by God to *re-form* the Church, fell into the trap of emphasizing "minor" theological, but more often than not disagreements over procedural practices of worship, and caused protestant *denominations* of Christ's new Church to be established and organized. Unlike the twelve tribes that entered the Promised Land, denominations have been unable to unify this Church of Jesus Christ; *they have not yet formed "one body" of Christ on earth.*

Some leaders of these denominations, in order to validate their own theology, fell into the same "pit" as did those who led the original "Universal" Church. They reverted to secular government sponsorship for "lawful" protection of "their" denomination. Unfortunately, with their practice of seeking secular support and member discipline, *denominations* soon retrograded into parochialism, defined as

35

unreasonable and unmerited but adamant loyalty to human pride-of-authorship in reference to individual *theological insight* of Scripture. They quickly formed "traditional" and ritualistic practices *some of which continue to this day*. Any hope of a truly catholic Church vanished, and denominational leaders continue to struggle valiantly though errantly to restore the original Church unity.

We merely mention for continuity purposes, the horrific miscalculations of the Crusades and other self-defeating attempts by successions of Church leaders to deny "Lay" believers promised renewed freedoms, by responding to "timely" opportunities to obey Christ's *Great Commission* to proclaim and to Baptize and to teach, within their local fellowship, within their host community, even within their own family. Government sponsored church became so oppressive of believers that God decided once more, *to intervene.*

The traumatic hardship of worldly life being experienced by His *"ministers"* within as well as between sponsored denominations, became so difficult for them that God decided to intervene, one more time

This is "belief:" God identified, *through their prayers and practiced obedience to* His Will, His Ways; This is recorded history: a small group of believers living in South-east England, (separatists from the "national" Church) who were being routinely persecuted by the governmental authorities at the instigation of the Church of England, for non-conformance to ritualistic and oppressive to "common" believers, rules of worship and the living of daily life. These rules were, ostensibly, promulgated for the purpose of uniting "all believers" in Christ's ministry. In reality, all they accomplished was to abdicate Church "authority" to England's governmental supervision over citizen daily life and practices. These "separatists" whom God identified, found these restraining rules to be contrary to the freedom bought for them by the death and resurrection of the Savior they trusted and gratefully worshiped and followed.

The tactics of the relocation:

When these "rebels" finally decided that they had had enough they determined to leave their homeland and relocate to a place where they could worship *by the way they lived their lives,* in peace and safety, in accordance with their understanding of the Bible, and their conscience. They moved to Holland, which had a more liberal outlook on worshipping. They stayed there for a little more than ten years and then discovered that the "free" culture they were enjoying was in reality adversely affecting their children. They decided to move to the "new" world. They had relocated their church to Holland in the first place because "the world" was restraining their peaceful attempts to worship according to their own theological understanding. They prayed together and meditated and now (led they felt, by the Holy Spirit) they decided to move their church, the keystone of their mortal lives, to America. They set sail on a ship called *The Mayflower*. They landed at a place they were not aiming for, at Plymouth Rock, and established a new home for their Church. *America's founding was the result of a spirit led effort by followers of Jesus Christ, to relocate their Church to a place where they could live and obey the final Great Commission of the Lord of their Church.*

Like Abraham so many centuries before, they followed the Spirit of God to a place that He would show them.

God led His Church to relocate to a land not populated by a corrupt people. As appointed agents of God, God's people founded America. It was an action of God to once more separate His People from the world, until His Church, in difficulty with a "world-full" of skeptics could regroup and renew their spiritual strength so they could "go back" to their spiritual separation identity, and would once more *freely* pursue the ministry entrusted to His People by God through Jesus Christ.

The Apostle Paul, speaking to Greek philosophers in Athens:

"And He made from one blood every nation of men to dwell on all the face of the earth, and has determined their pre-appointed times and the boundaries of their habitation, so that they should seek the Lord." (Acts 17: 26, 27)

The very selection of what became known as *America* to be the location of a new "Promised Land" was God driven. His "scout," Christopher Columbus, declared *in his diary* that it was the Holy Spirit moving in his heart according to the prophesies of the Old Testament that to take the Gospel of Jesus Christ to the new world, that took him through the exploration adventure. His very name, *Christopher*, means Christ Bearer and, as recorded in his diary, he "heard and responded to the call" to bear Christ to the new world.

In *The Mayflower Compact which was signed by all those who were migrating to the new land,* these righteous Pilgrims stated that they came to America *"for the glory of God and the advancement of the Christian faith."* That is why they came and established the first *enduring* settlement in this "new" land. And when *all* the original thirteen colonies got together years later, they ratified a *New England Confederation* agreement, stating: *"We all came into these parts of America with one and the same end and aim: To advance the Kingdom of our Lord Jesus Christ.*

God continues to hope that thus delivered and inspired man (ALL men and women) will zealously undertake to: *Go therefore and make disciples of all nations, baptizing them in the name of the Father, and of the Son and of the Holy Spirit – teaching them to observe all things that I have commanded you, and lo* (if you do that) *I am with you always, even to the end of the age."* (Matthew 28: 19, 20)

PART III
THE CHURCH WE CRITIQUE

CHAPTER 7
The "New" Church In The "New" World

God started America off on the right foot:

The Declaration of Independence of the United States of America declares in part: *"......that all men are created equal, that they are endowed **by their Creator** with certain inalienable rights, that among these are life, liberty and the pursuit of happiness. ......"*

It took a war of rebellion against English tyranny (shades of the conquest of the Promised Land) to affirm that *God's People* would be the inheritors of this new land. After the successful conclusion of this war of rebellion, after the new country, the United States of America came to be, those who fought and sacrificed fame, fortune and their own well-being, and for many, their own blood, for freedom, in unison, *all of them* by vote of the existing thirteen legislative bodies which constituted this new nation, designated, ratified and established rules by which this new nation would *always* function. They first validated their core belief by making permanent their previous joint *Declaration of Independence* which was the framework of their revolutionary struggle. They did so without further public discourse. They made it their "founding" document. They saw no need to expand their statement of faith that God had led them to this point in history, that they would construct their "free" society based upon the Christian beliefs; on their God-given wisdom to "live" their theology. *God conceived a new nation from this relocated church.*

Their "ratification" of their faith took the form of writing and then enacting a constitution, in effect *a covenant between the individual citizens, the states and the Federal Government,* which spelled out the relationships by which the people would who populated the thirteen newly designated states would live in freedom in their pursuit of happiness, and how those states would jointly and severally survive within the framework of their Declaration of Independence. Shortly afterward, while this new nation was still in its infancy, they updated the constitution; they identified four freedoms which would thereafter pillar the foundation guidelines.

One of the four freedoms brought to life, was freedom OF (not from) religion. Together, these four freedoms guaranteed that any of this nation's citizens could freely, without *government* edict or oppression, practice any religion (including Christianity) of their free choice. *The right not to have to endure personal offense by any public display of any religious axiom was NOT specified as one of the freedoms made into law by that first amendment.*

The Constitution ultimately accepted by all states, followed the pattern set up *by* God in His instructions to His original People before the disposed the "native" of the land to which He had brought them. I.e. The thirteen (now 50) states became the *tribal* level, the states' legal system provided the *appointed judges and officers in all your gates,* The Federal Executive Branch became the (Joshua's) national army which drove out the enemy and eventually became their (Israel's) kingdom level of government, the Federal Court System became the *appeal tribunal* for those matters which became "too hard" for the *appointed judges* to decide, and the Supreme Court became the *Priests and Levites* – pronouncing the sentence in those special times or circumstances or issues which could not be satisfactorily adjudicated at the lower level.

The town and city mayors, their council members and their county commissioners, the State governors and legislators and members of Congress were all equated to the *elders* who received definition of their responsibilities to "make it all work" from God through Moses, as recorded in Deuteronomy, *and reaffirmed by Peter, the "Rock" of this new Church: "The elders who are among you I exhort, I am a fellow elder and a witness to the sufferings of Christ, and also a partaker of the glory that will be revealed. Shepherd the flock of God which is among you, serving as overseers, not by constraint but willingly, not for dishonest gain, but eagerly; nor a being lords over those entrusted to you, but being examples in the flock; and when the Chief Shepherd appears, you will receive the crown of glory that does not fade away.* (1 Peter 5: 1-4)

And in terms of Paul's and Peter's admonition to "subject yourselves to those who govern" – this God centered, God inspired charter for His new people opened up a totally new freedom. *The Constitution adopted by this Nation/Church established a unique relationship between governed* and governor; it provided a means for its Christian constituents to select other Christians to govern them.

The fact that the United States was founded as and to be a Christian nation was *certified* in the late 1800s by the only body authorized to make an official certification. The Supreme Court of the United States invested ten years of Court time as they examined *every single document* having to do with the founding of this nation. At the completion of their investigation, the Supreme Court, *in a unanimous decision,* stated: *All these documents attest to the fact that this is a religious people; this is a Christian Nation.* That statement was used by the justices as a foundation to their unanimous decision – The Trinity Decision of 1892.

History, from shortly after that 1892 decision until now, reveals that successors to those (then) current administrators of this Christian Covenant, those who undertook to "supervise" all life within their jurisdiction, have battled disgruntled challengers who have been at least as adept at: *"......to circulate false reports ...... your hand with the wicked to be an unrighteous witness ..."* (Exodus 23: 1-9) as were those whom God saw it necessary to "discipline" as to how to live their lives; and those whom Peter had in mind as he delivered his second letter to the churches: *"But there were false prophets among the people even as there will be false teachers among you, who will secretly bring on destructive heresies, even denying the Lord who brought them, and thereby bring upon themselves swift destruction. ...."* (2 Peter 2: 1-3)

The Constitution of the United States was written and put into practice by Christian men inspired by their acceptance of the teachings of Jesus Christ to define a form of government which would accommodate His teachings. (Actually, in response to those who would obfuscate that statement by exaggerating the truth, there were two Deists among the writers, amounting to less than 6% of those present.) Christian purpose does not appear to be the mainstay of their successors, our latter day "interpreters" of that covenant.

Before we take this thought any farther, perhaps we who are currently responsible for carrying on the original end and aim, should affirm to ourselves the basis of the beliefs which fueled the their Statement of Faith. It resides in the totality of God's Holy Word, and could begin like this:

Donald P. Goss

(Psalm 119:45) *"I will walk about in freedom for I have sought out your precepts* and (Isaiah 61:1) *the spirit off the sovereign Lord is upon me, because the Lord has anointed me to preach the good news to the poor. He has sent me to bind up the broken- hearted to proclaim freedom for the captives and release from the darkness for the prisoners.* Luke, Romans, 1st & 2nd Corinthians, Galatians (twice) and James all speak to freedom to worship the *Lord Holy God, and Him only.* (1 Peter 2:16) counsels us to *"Live as free men but do not use your freedom as a cover-up for evil - - live as servants of God.*

July 4th each year is a day set aside in the United States to celebrate the freedom brought to us by *committed Christians* (and those, few in number, who became their cohorts) who succeeded in their sacrificial and mortal efforts to "guarantee" every one of us, the opportunity to worship the Savior *which they proclaimed* to be the sole author and preserver of the freedom by which we are to, with impunity against governmental oppression, carry out the mission given to us by the Creator of all life. To make known to all men the power and the glory and the love and the mercy and the grace – the holiness of our God; seen through the birth and ministry and sacrificial death and resurrection of His only begotten Son, one *with* our God. *It is for this reason that all who come to our fellowship are welcomed.* **We are not called to welcome them so that we can "pick-up" their culture,** (witness Ezra's cleansing of God's people) *we are called to reveal to them, the Gospel of Salvation for all people.*

We, individually and corporately, descendents of or sworn immigrant to the "chosen" peoples whom the Christian leaders fought and defined freedom for, are the Church of Christ, United States chapter. We are the present people of God, spiritually descended from the first patriarch (Abraham). We are chosen by God through the incarnation of Jesus, His Son, our Christ, and accepted by Him as such by virtue of the faith He has given us as we believe that Jesus prayed *for us* as *"those who will believe in Me through their message ......"* (John 17:20).

The total ministry entrusted by Christ to His Church, specifically the re-development of His People living in the "new world" has been passed to us (current resident, recipients of His grace in America). *We have inherited the "end and aim" of the New England Confederation, to wit – To advance the Kingdom of Jesus Christ, and as we live under the*

Constitution of our "Promised Land" we recognize that advancement takes the form of proclaiming the Gospel of Salvation to ALL who come to us for inclusion to our "freedoms."

We are called to welcome and to "live with" in Peace, those who refuse the faith we proclaim; *we are NOT called to tolerate by excusing without recourse, life and life-styles which are in conflict with Christian doctrine.* History will record, but *God alone* will be the judge of our faithfulness to the "call" of our inheritance.

- Moses warned his people as they were about to enter the land which God had promised them: *"...... and this people will rise up and play the harlot with the gods of the foreigners of the land where they go to be among them and they will break the covenant which I have made with them. Then My anger shall be aroused against them in that day and I will forsake them and I will hide My face from them and they shall be devoured. And many evils and troubles shall befall them so that they shall say in that day, have not these evils come upon us because our God is not among us? And I shall surely hide My face in that day because of all the evil which they have done, in that they have turned to other gods."* (Deuteronomy 32: 16-18)

- The writer of the letter to the Hebrews warns: *" ......For if we sin willfully after we have received the knowledge of truth, there no longer remains a sacrifice for sin, but a certain fearful expectation of judgment and fiery indignation which will devour the adversaries. Any one who has rejected Moses' law dies without mercy ......of how much more punishment do you suppose will be thought worthy who has tramped the Son of God underfoot ...... for we know Him who said: Vengeance is mine, I will repay, says the Lord."* and again: *"The Lord will judge His People."*

The letter to the Hebrews speaks to individual believers. Individuals, collectively, are the People of God *and they are This Nation/Church.*

CHAPTER 8
Continuity Of Architect Soveriegnty

"In the beginning was the Word and the Word was with God and the Word was God. He was in the beginning with God. And all things were made through Him and without Him nothing was made. In Him was life and the life was the light on men. And the light shines in the darkness and the darkness did not comprehend it." (John 1: 1-5)

The Apostle Paul, commissioned directly by Christ himself to proclaim the Gospel of Salvation to the Gentiles (to you and me) tells us in his letter to the Corinthians (1:24): *"...... for the sake of His Body, which is the Church.:* and then continues in verse 28: *"Him we preach, warning every man and teaching every man in all wisdom, the we may present every man perfect in Christ Jesus."* And in verse 29: *"...... to this end I labor, striving according to His workings which work in me mightily."*

The scriptural letter to the Ephesians from the Apostle Paul is popularly labeled by theologians of latter-day vintage as portraying *the Church of Christ.* Colossians, also authored by Paul, can similarly labeled as portraying *the Christ of the Church.* Ephesians brings reader attention to the Body (the Church), Colossians, to the head. Both of them are divided between the doctrinal and the practical. Paul's purpose in these two epistles is to demonstrate that *Christ* is preeminent – i.e. Christ must be first and foremost in everything – in all of life – and the Christian's and the church's life must reflect that priority. Because believers are rooted in Him and collectively *they are His Body on earth,* the Church. Paul pleads that it is absolutely *inconsistent* for them to become "life-blood" to His People, without Him.

Paul and all the other Apostles carried forward the Gospel that Jesus Christ *is* the fulfillment of God's promise of merciful restoration of rebellious man to eternal fellowship with his Creator, as well as the "grace" of bringing the wisdom to them Paul testified unceasingly to Christ's sovereign authority over the total lives of believers *and unbelievers* alike. The Apostles all thus testified by defining Christ's part in the creation and His presence in the "maturing" of His people from the very beginning of His fellowship with man. (re: Genesis 1:26 – 2:16) until the "end of the age." Christ himself informs John in his vision on the island of Patmos: *"I am the alpha and the omega, the beginning and the end"* (Revelations 22:13)

The sources of this Apostolic belief and the evidence which they brought forward in proclaiming that Jesus Christ was who and what He said he was, was the Holy Scriptures upon which the People of God have, from their inception, rested their authority that they truly were and spoke authentically as the People of God. *Be it known, remembered and understood* that the only scriptures available to the Apostles was what existed *before* the advent of Christ. Their proclamation stemmed from their first-hand witness of the events and happenings which they experienced as "under- studies" in the ministry of Christ (and reinforced by the promised Holy Spirit within them) was *exactly* as prophesied in those (what we know as) Old Testament Scriptures.

Though there is ample evidence of the presence of Christ in Old Testament Scriptures from Genesis through Malachi, the most often referenced testimonies used by the Apostles were:

1) The initiation of God's covenant with Abraham and the actions and events leading up to the affirmation of His "new" people. It began with the appointment of Abraham as "first-person" of all succeeding generations, *until* God (when time was fulfilled) *in the form of man* – which was Jesus the Messiah – would finalize their redemption; and

2) The announcements of the life, death and resurrection of the Messiah, told in full detail by the Prophets, each of whom was God's "proclaimer-in-place" all during the struggles of God's people to follow the law (the Ten Commandments and the "daily life" and worship instructions of Exodus 20). The necessity for prophesy in the ministry of salvation conducted by the Messiah was also two-fold:

a. Prophesies were used by God to inform His people of happenings which had not yet occurred, and

b. Prophets were God's appointed counselors, necessary to lead and to reassure His people through the pit-falls of life which kept springing up as some of His church leaders who achieved their status of King or Religious Elder by elevating themselves *through false claims, by (satanic) acclamation of the people or by corruption of the tenets of their succession to their "proper" roles.* (At the time of Jesus' ministry these church leaders were identified as Pharisees, Priests, Scribes and Sadducees.)

At the disposal of the Apostles for "proof" of their proclamation of Jesus Christ as Creator and as Lord of the Church, were more than 330 prophetic texts of the Old Testament, which describe in minute detail the first and second coming of the Messiah into this world. There are 456 "before the fact" accounts of what would happen during His advent – *all of which happened to Christ.*

Fulfilled prophesies are unique to the revelation of God to His People. They were recorded in Scripture. They were available for the building of His Church. *Prophesies are not found in any other religion, or in history or anywhere else in the archives of the world.*

There are, in addition to those mentioned in the preceding paragraph, 1700 other fulfilled prophesies in the Old Testament having to do with various cities, events and nations contiguous to or within 1000 miles of Israel. They do not necessarily have to do with Christ, but do have to do with the efficacy of Scriptural history.

Not only is prophesy vitally important to apostolic efforts in their obedience of Christ's commands, to give form to His Church (Matthew 16:18 & 28:19), but they were vitally important to God himself. He used prophesy to establish himself, *by foretelling to them* as the one true authority in their lives. He told the Israelites (in Isaiah 46: 9-10): *"I am God and there is no other, and there is none like Me ...... declaring the end from the beginning and from ancient times – the things that are not yet done."* He also says to false gods: *"Shew us what will happen. Or declare to us the things to come hereafter, which we may know that you are gods."* (Isaiah 41: 22, 23) And *never* has there been any response to this challenge from God.

Who was this man Jesus? A prophesy of the birth of Christ 500 years before He was born, says to us: *"But thou Bethlehem Ephrathah, though thou be little among the thousands of Judah, yet out of thee shall come forth to Me the one to be ruler in Israel; whose goings forth have been from of old, from everlasting."* (Micah 5:2)

There were two Bethlehems in the land of Israel n 500 B.C. One became the site of a great city; the other was a very small town in the southern part of Judah, just six miles south of Jerusalem – Bethlehem Ephrathah. How could the prophet Micah know that would be "the place" except that he learned it from the mouth of God?

The most often cited prophesy of the coming of the Messiah, His "day" and His judgment and blessing of His People, is from Isaiah. First, His authority to rule: *"For unto us a child is born, Unto us a Son is given, and the government shall be upon His shoulders."*

What did Jesus come among us to do? (Extracted from Isaiah 53): *"...... He is* (to be) *despised and rejected of men ...... He hath borne our griefs and carried our sorrows ...yet we did not esteem Him smitten of God ...(in our place) ... was wounded for our transgressions ...He was bruised for our iniquities; the chastisement of our peace was upon Him ...... and with His stripes we are healed."* And He is the ruler of Israel, God's chosen People.

The first and second coming of the Messiah is also found in Zechariah, as well as is His rejection, horrific death and ultimate triumph.

Daniel (9: 24-27) prophecies the time frame for the Messianic Mission from then time of Daniel to the establishment of God's Kingdom on earth. The sixty-nine weeks (of years) of seventy in *Daniel's vision were fulfilled at Christ's first coming in the midst* of a "troubling" time. Some scripture scholars affirm that the seventieth year has not yet been fulfilled because Christ relates it to His second coming ...... Others believe that the seventieth week pertains to the destruction of the Temple by the Romans.

In summary, the prophesies, collectively, foretell the coming of the one (Christ) who is the seed of a woman, born of a virgin, of the race of the Hebrews, the seed of Abraham, in the line of Isaac and Jacob, of the house of David, whose very date of the beginning of His ministry is predicted by Daniel. Also in the Old Testament can be found the details of His passion and suffering; His death on the cross, His entombment, His resurrection on the third day, His ascension into Heavenly Glory and the promise of His second appearance at the end of time, as we know time. The actual existence of Christ as the creation took place and within the struggles of men as they experienced their "fall" from God's

Grace, is duly recorded. His incarnation as man, so that He could fully reveal the *power, glory, love and mercy* of the God who brought them into being, *an would not abandon them,* was promised in detail through the prophecies – as inspiration for men to repent their determination to become "equal" with their Creator.

About the reliability of the Scriptural Prophesies of the coming Messiah: The latest foretelling of the advent was through the prophet Micah, proclaimed more than 500 years *before* Christ was born. The entire Old Testament was written from about 1400 to 400B.C. There was, after Micah's prophesy, a 400 year hiatus in Scripture writing. God planned it that way so that no one could *ever* say, as skeptics always try to say about these prophecies: "They were written *after* the event; they are history being pawned off as prophesy." Not only was there the hiatus, but God built an impenetrable wall in the midst of those 400 years by having the Old Testament Scriptures translated into Greek (150B.C.) and spread all over the world. *There is no way that any verse of the Old Testament could have been written **after** the birth of Christ.*

As key as the Messianic Prophecies are to attesting to the truth of God's plans and His capacity to bring them into fruition, to use men (and of course, women) to bring about the restoration of fallen man to His eternal glory, the Old Testament Scriptures are also filled with records and events wherein God worked *through* men already in place, to bring salvation to man whenever they rejected His freely given opportunities for them to repent *by coming to obedience to His laws.* This was their rejection of His authorship of an "abundant" life for them. It was man's intransigence in reference to God's offerings that made it necessary for God to make and to fulfill the Messianic Prophesies.

Adam and Eve set the pattern for man's resistance to God's having reserved for him self the ultimate definition of "abundant life." Their exile from Eden was for the "mercy" purpose of disciplining them into repenting their decision to attempt to equalize themselves with Him by acquiring the knowledge and capabilities which He had withheld from them for Himself as their Creator, so that they would learn to trust only Him to deliver the "needs" of their lives.

The 2000 years of God-to-individual relationship mentioned earlier, the "fall," the flood, the Tower of Babel, etc., along with other struggles also recorded in Old Testament Scripture describe a series of cycles of man getting himself into serious trouble from which he could not extricate himself, and then calling of God to rescue him. The cycles consisted of "good times" provided through God's grace, then man's reversion to *"thanks God; I'll take it from here:* egoism, a drift – sometimes a dash- toward self-destruction and then a plea to God to save him. All of which shows how God, with a mercy and love which man cannot to this day comprehend, let alone emulate, always brought him back from the "pit of corruption" (Isaiah 38:17). Throughout all this, God used mortal beings as instruments of His intervention. *But it has always been God acting through His chosen agent, which "rescued" man from the consequences of his folly.*

These cycles have continued throughout the history of His People. They were begun through a very human Abraham, (Abraham's *righteousness* was accepted by God, not on Abraham's obedience to God's instructions to sacrifice his son's life, but solely on his trusting belief {faith} that God was who and what He revealed himself to be) whose "works" left much to be desired. And his descendents steadfastly developed a history of repeatedly living out those same kinds of cycles, and ultimately caused the advent of Jesus Christ so necessary.

The Scriptural record to which references are made identifies many specific humans who were called by God to carry out "saving" tasks. Ant the record reveals, sometimes in intimate detail, that those who were called were not necessarily called because they were "good" people. The common denominator between them was that God ascertained that each had the requisite *human* attribute for the task, and/or each was the person He would make available at the time or place He decided to intervene. Sometimes His intervention was in the form of a warning by Prophesy, of calamitous consequences for His people if they did not repent the lifestyle they were then living. *These warnings from God through the prophets proved not to be hollow threats.* The end of the "monarchy" of Israel came when God carried through on His promises of retribution, delivered by His Prophet Jeremiah, for the rejection of His call for repentance:

"But this is what I commanded them, saying: Obey My voice and I will be your God and you shall be My people. And walk in all the ways that I have commanded you that it may be well with you. Yet they did not obey or incline their ear, but walked in the counsels and the imagination

of their evil heart, and went backward, and not forward." (Jeremiah 7: 23-24) And *"For they have healed the hurt of the daughter of My people slightly, saying* peace, peace when there is no peace. Were they ashamed when *they had committed abomination? No! They were not ashamed nor did they know how to blush. Therefore they will fall among those who will fall, in the time of their punishment they shall be cast down, says the Lord."* (Jeremiah 8: 11-12)

True to His word, God caused Israel to be destroyed, the Temple ransacked and torn apart and the people, except for a few "unimportant" citizens who were sent into a new exile, in Babylon. God, through Jeremiah, in a forecast of mercy, at the same time promised His people that if they endure this durance vile and persevered in faith that He would and could keep His promises, the exile would end in seventy years. The "remnant" of His people who survived would be returned to their homeland; the Temple would be rebuilt and Jerusalem would be restored. As their exile drew to a close, Daniel, an Israelite who had found favor with the king of their captivity, prophesied not only their return, which did happen as God had promised, but Daniel also prophesied *to the day*, the coming of the Messiah. History records that it all did happen as God (through the prophets) had foretold.

And the historical record also teaches us that the person *we would choose* is not the person God chooses. As in all things, God applies His own selection criteria to His "call" decision. *We are again reminded that God, usually, does not call the qualified – He qualifies the person He calls.*

The most well-known such person, being the youthful slayer of *Goliath* who intended to exterminate the people of God, who after being chosen by God and inaugurated to rule over His people as their king, reverted to "human" sin and became a murderer/ adulterer. But when confronted by his religious advisor, Nathan, also called by God for *that* purpose, *repented* his sinful lusts, accepted his "punishment" and devoted the rest of his life - - - to full obedience to God's wise counsel. Because of David's devotion to his "found-again" God, God appointed him to the example for all future kings of Israel to follow, in obeying God's precepts. And David thus became the human ancestor to God's begotten Son, Jesus.

Another stand-out such person was *Moses,* who was called to lead his people out of 400 years of back-breaking slavery in Egypt, to the land that He had promised Abraham would be the homeland of His chosen people. In Moses' appointment, we learn once again that when God calls someone to a particular task which He requires, God doesn't take "No" for an answer. (Jonah is another example). Proof of man's perfidy was in the life experiences of the very people God was saving, *even as He was saving them.* The people of the Exodus challenged God's efforts – and those of Moses, *while in the midst of their exodus journey,* repeating the cycles set and established by Adam. Yet in a demonstration of mercy never, to this day, comprehended by man, God steadfastly stood by them and they remained His people, just as He had promised Abraham.

One more item of prime evidence of God's commitment of absolute loyalty to His plan for using "free" man in the redemption of His people, was that even after at least six experiences of rescues (saving cycles) from the severe consequences of their collective transgression, using individual *judges* chosen by God for that purpose, again chose to decline God's direct control of their lives and called for God to anoint them a human king like their neighbors had. In infinite remembrance of the freedom He had created in them, God *forewarned them* through a prophet, *Samuel,* of the probable unhappy consequences of their demand; then when they stubbornly insisted, had Samuel anoint *Saul* as their first King. And true to His warning, history records that their life as a nation went (cyclically) down hill, from that time on.

The *New Testament* begins with the advent of the Messiah and tells in fascinating detail, the preparation of the People of God for receipt of the "New Covenant" of forgiveness of sin, which is the *only* thing keeping men out of eternal fellowship with God, through the incarnation of God in Jesus Christ, His "teaching" ministry, His suffering death and resurrection in His people's stead and for their transgressions. And the New Testament also records the *passing of the mantle of responsibility* for revealing to all people, the *only* acceptable (to God) means of salvation. And it ends (in the written "Gospels" of the Apostles) with the great command to "redefine" for them, the new People of God, i.e. those who believe that Jesus Christ is the Son of God and Lord of their re-born lives. *Thus* was Jesus' promise to Peter: "...... *upon this rock I will build*

My church." A new Church with a new covenant, constructed with a new cornerstone, using new, re-born building blocks. It was this Church which Christ led to the new world. *"All authority has been given to Me in Heaven and earth"* (Matthew 28:18) in order to regroup and become faithful and strong and to *"Go, therefore, and make disciples of all nations, baptizing them in the name of the Father, and of the Son and of the Holy Spirit, teaching them to observe all things that I have commanded you; and lo, I am with you always, even to the end of the age."*

In 2 Corinthians (6: 16-18) Paul makes it as clear as is necessary that we who have been led to *this* nation, are a very state-of-the-art-proclaimant of the Gospel of Jesus Christ, vested with a new venue (this nation) as he reminds us: *"For you are the temple (Church) of the living God, as God has said: I will dwell in them and walk among them. I will be their God and they shall be My People. Therefore, come out from among them and be separate, says the Lord. Do not touch what is unclean and I will receive you. And you shall be My sons and daughters, says the Lord God Almighty."* To this reminder, add the *Great Command* of Jesus Christ, and Jesus' hope for His reformed Church becomes as clear as any looking glass.

- Thus the Church of God is established – to function as His own Temple, from which the *truth* is to be proclaimed. In accordance with the time scheduled in the planning stage by the Architect, its foundation was formed and the structure was built, and in His own time the structure was re-built and made new by His own Son; the new superstructure developed a need for re-formation from a necessary, long "weathering of the storm" of *human attempts to re-model*, for which the Architect chose inspired men and with great upheaval, reformation occurred, The Church, built for the purpose of *"making know to all people, the promise of eternal life to all who believe, and for monitoring and supervising the "readying" of man for "immigration" into God's New Jerusalem; it is built in accordance with the plan of the Architect.*

It thereby becomes man's ordained purpose to make it possible, by making Him known in all His healing power, love, mercy, grace; His awesome holiness – to the corners of the world – including and from *this* Promised Land (where we are) for God in Jesus Christ, with the help of the Holy Spirit, to prepare His Creation to receive His New Jerusalem.

This is the context in which this "lay" critique of the Institutional Christian Church continues.

PART IV
FINDINGS, DISCUSSION AND
CONCLUSIONS

CHAPTER 9
The Church Of Jesus Christ In This New Promised Land

The Church is built on nothing less ....

First, let us affirm our belief that *all* who believe in the Lord Jesus Christ, who have been *baptized* into His new life, have become spiritual descendents of Abraham – have become, as were those who lived under the covenant which God established through Abraham, God's chosen people. *"But you are a chosen generation, a royal priesthood, a holy nation, His own special people. ...... "* (1 Peter 2:9)

If we are truly His own special people forming a new holy nation, it seems only appropriate to review the instructions which God gave through Moses, whom God had chosen to lead His "first" people to the land He had set aside for them:

"Now O Israel, listen to the statutes and judgments which I teach you to observe, that you may live and go in and possess the land which the Lord God of your fathers is giving you. You shall not add to the word which I command you nor take anything from it, that you may keep the commandments of the Lord your God which I command you. Your eyes have seen what the Lord did at Baal Peor; for the Lord your God has destroyed from among you all the men who followed Baal Peor. But you who held fast to the Lord your God are alive today, every one of you. Surely I have taught you statutes and judgments just as the Lord my God commanded me that you should not act according to them in the land which you go in to possess. Therefore be careful to observe them; for this is your wisdom and your understanding in the sight of the peoples who will hear all these statutes and say – Surely this great nation is a wise and understanding people. For what great nation is there that has God so near to it that as the Lord our God is to us for whatever reason we may call upon Him? And what great nation is there that has such statutes and righteous judgments as are in all this law which I set before you this day?"

"Only take heed of yourself and diligently keep yourself lest you forget the things your eyes have seen and lest they depart from your heart all the

*days of your life. **And teach them to your children and grandchildren** ...... When you beget children and grandchildren and have grown old in the land, act corruptly and ...... do evil in the sight of the Lord your God to provoke Him to anger. I call heaven and earth to witness against you this day that you will soon utterly perish from the land which you cross over the Jordan to possess; you will not prolong your days in it, but will be utterly destroyed ......"* (Deuteronomy 4)

Why critique the Church now?

We, the people of the United States of America attest every time we renew our pledge of allegiance to the flag, that we are a Christian Nation. *"I pledge allegiance to the flag of the United States of America and to the Republic for which it stands; One nation **under God**, indivisible, with liberty and justice for all."* And we affirm, by our Constitution and by our recorded history, that we are a nation of Jesus Christ – a Church.

It is true that a significant number of our "Lay" members of the Church believe that there can be *no separation* the principles and commands of God (taught to us in finite detail by Scripture) and the choices by which we *through our statutes and judgments proffered by our chosen government* go about our daily lives. On that premise then, *"we the people"* of this nation of Christ *need to* from time to time re-examine our progress, or lack of it, in carrying out the legacy of our founding fathers.

But we the people (Lay people) *do not believe* that Christ, in declaring us to be free from the constraints of the Ten Commandments as Go-No Go acceptance into the People of God – which were the basic laws by which God *required* His people to live, but which He freed us from living *in fear of their tenets; we are freed by Jesus Christ TO live them without fear of consequences due us by our past disobedience.*

The questions we would seek to answer in this assessment of the Church's efficacy in contemporary life (in response to the Word of God "teaching" as interpreted by the heroes of the Reformation) are: *"How well are the people of this nation under God, doing today* in obeying the instructions of the *Great Commission* of its "true" Founding Father? How near are we to completing the task He entrusted to us as His People? Do the people of this "New Promised Land, this United States of America, live completely within the values, standards and mores' which He taught us? How effectively is this *Christian Nation* fulfilling *Christ's* purpose in founding this nation, which was to advance the Gospel of Jesus Christ? Is this land, this world prepared to receive His New Jerusalem (Revelation 21)?

Or can the Church we are do more to make the opportunity of salvation by the Body and Blood of Jesus the Christ (who anointed us to the task) known to more people within the boundaries of our Promised Land and to all nations? Can we establish the life on earth demonstration of His proffered "abundant life" by the life we ourselves live and bring into being, using the government mechanisms which He inspired in the writing of our Constitution, in our efforts to "recruit" (proselytize) ALL people into His kingdom, as He has commanded us to do?

CHAPTER 10
Affirming The Nation/church Architect

Recall if you will, our previous discussion of the Theory of Evolution. Evolution remains an unproven theory that enjoys a forced entry into the education of the nation's children; it continues to be *illegal* to teach that there *could be* (there are several) other theories which are equally valid. This errant, *but solely legal* forced entry has already corrupted faithful understanding of the origin of life among several generations of His "new" Church People.

Why the discussion of evolution as a part of a critique of the Church? Let's take a meaningful look at the damage to the mission of the Church, which *is continuing* to be caused by the intransigence of public educators and other "professional champions of skepticism, as well as other, even specious proponents of *political correctness,* that the theory of evolution *must* remain the sole teaching in the public schools, in reference to the origin of the universe or the to life the universe supports.

The "theory" remains "on the books" as a result of the *reluctance* of the Church to undertake action which will persuade the Supreme Court of the United States to *allow* public school students to exercise academic discourse, as a choice for themselves to make from a variety of equally provable theories and from other educational sources such as published "scientific" journals, how they will believe how the universe and all life came to be.

Science (the proof testimony of the mistaken court decision) *now* supports the thesis that the life which the universe harbors *did* come about through a *super intelligent design.* Many of its practicing (and renowned) advocates *now accept* the probability that the designer is a *Supernatural Being.* Many of them have become *born-again Christians.*

But scientist have little inclination or incentive to take the initiative and correct this educational wrong as it affects "lower level" (Public High School) educational circles – which was begun in the first place by one of their antecedents and which they believe can be made harmless to society through the less controversial process of "allowing" those who so choose, to come to their own "understanding" in the classroom of "Higher Education."

One description of the damage to the likelihood of the Church to successfully carry out its appointed mission re: advancing the Gospel of Jesus Christ, (we place it in the context of Christ's Great Commission to the Church) is, as cited by Matthew (28: 19, 20): "......*teaching them to observe all things that I have commanded you ......*"Christ's "teaching" that God created the earth and all life in it. The Church must take positive action to counter the teaching of Public School students that evolution is the only consideration to the question, how did the universe come into being? – If they intend to take seriously the totality of Christ's Great Commission *to it.*

Once more, for emphasis: This unproven theory which has as its bottom line that we can no longer believe that that the earth and its inhabitants came into being by act of a Supernatural Creator, is what our government, through its misinformed legal decision *forces us* to teach our future leaders going through our public schools. In our zeal to live in "full freedom," to grow in capability to enhance the freedoms which we hold to be critical to the pursuit of happiness, (remember the enabling Bill of Rights?) we allow, we encourage and defend without ceasing, *we actually cause* through a manipulated legal system, the *ultimate death* of at least one of those freedoms, which is their combined base freedom: Freedom OF, not FROM religion. And the final nail in the coffin in which "science laden skeptics" hope to bury God through the funeral they call public education (even extended to college level "Liberal Arts"), hammered home by "we don't need a God" educators under the guise of "political correctness" is their pass/fail grading system.

How does it damage our ability to carry out Christ's command? Take a walk in the shoes of a teen-age high school youth who even if he/ she has received Biblical training in Church, Church School *or at home,* find themselves in an arena with their peers (too many of whom have not had that training) at the most vulnerable time of their lives and who are being confronted with a legally mandated, but unprovable teaching, i.e. that *all life just happened to come into being* over several billion (with a B) years of random happenings; that what they learned from family or church is nothing but legend; that 4000 years of Scripture led, generation by generation inspirational teachings and inborn faith that the universe and all living creatures in it, came to be by the spoken word of all powerful, all loving, omniscient, creating Supreme Being who guarantees eternal life for all believers – *is hog wash.* And that the authority for the teaching of their false beliefs is based upon a (flawed, dishonest, imperfect) "science," but is all they can be "taught" but is legitimate because it is imposed upon their "database" by *the U.S. Supreme Court,* which they are also taught to accept as *the authority* of their very lives. Add to their dilemma, the proposition that their *acceptance* of this theory of evolution is a *requirement* of their authority to matriculate into "higher" education.

Can there be any doubt of this cause for the Church losing its influence with the nation's young? Some (in following chapters) of this critique will describe other lost opportunities of the Institutional Church to effectively apply itself to the teaching component of the Great Commission commanded to it by its "Cornerstone;" or to its *responsibility* via a unique form of societal government, to protect its own membership from misshaped life environment. An environment which the Institutional Church could have and should have defined and established in the first place.

We, who are *the* believing members of this Nation/Church, as well as all visitors to our shores, are in the midst of an all-out campaign to change our nation from Christian to a Godless (called diversified) society. The campaign, under the guise of *"political correctness,"* is expertly driven by well;-funded skeptics and non-believers who take advantage of gullible public educators and minor government entities to wage the every-day battle. They force *naive* decision making based upon fear of *threatened* political humiliation or exorbitant legal expenses. Decisions which respond by using *scarce* resources to local, immediate, social issues, rather than looking "down-the-road" to future troubles derived from setting debilitating legal precedents. They have judges whom they have previously "faked out" (brain-washed) on matters of law, whom they have *trained* to render false interpretations of the Constitution.

"They" are lawyers of the ACLU (who have long since abandoned what first achieved popular support for them, i.e. their *Champion of the Underdog* legal services) who now favor making a mockery of the intent of the Founding Fathers to *advance the Gospel of Jesus Christ* through establishing a government that would protect *all* citizens from government intrusion in daily the way they choose to live daily life. They are aided and abetted by a select few so-called "professional of Christianity" who, in a major void of understanding of their *responsibilities* under the Gospel, choose to fight the very government that guarantees religious (as well as the other three) freedoms. They disguise their agenda by "defending" an (recruited solely for that purpose) oppressed minority, at great harm to the majority; the harm being "witnessed to" by quasiprofessional educators or special interest organizations who *naively* use this falsified social agenda as a cover for an even greater harm to minorities, e.g. *they are even unable to teach more than sixty percent of them to read at a basic "able to function" level.*

CHAPTER 11
Building On Our Nation/Church Foundation

Let us begin with the very act of founding this new People of God. Recorded history reveals that the *Founding Fathers* were acting on behalf of the citizens who charged them with the task of defining the covenant (the Constitution) by which we would pursue the mission of our lives. The citizens who so charged them consisted of those (more than 98 percent of them) who professed to be *Protestant Christians.* No other nation, except perhaps the original Promised Land, was ever founded by such a huge percentage of citizens who subscribed to one religion. *Which brings us to the first determination of "how are we doing" re: our Founding Father's legacy?* The present day news media (at least the most assertive of their contributors) opines, and *forcibly* invokes through its "public education" pronouncements that the very idea of one religion being so prominent in America – is *un-American.*

It is highly improbable that there will ever be a *more subversive* statement. And the history of America does not record any official or un-official "changing of the Christian guard."

The *intent* of the Mayflower Compact, the *intent* of the New England Confederation statement, the *intent* of the Framers, has been carefully deleted from history text-books used by the public schools, but those intents *are* faithfully recorded in our National Archives, and are readily available to any citizen who seeks to learn truth. *But the Church we are, by choosing not to confront their false teaching* (2 Peter 2) – *has abdicated responsibility to carry out the very ministry for which this nation was founded.* The Church, *by its refusal to act,* aids, abets and honors" *Political Correctness* – over "truth." More than a few would-be relevant church leaders now actually *side with* and support those who practice "political correctness,"

Patrick Henry, the foremost and historically preserved voice of the American war for freedom, the "give me liberty or give me death" Patrick Henry, who literally triggered the revolution which sent men running for their muskets and for the field, for freedom, said that this nation was not built by religionists. It was built by Christians. It was

NOT built upon religion; it was built upon the *Gospel of our Lord Jesus Christ and thus people of all faiths have found that they could come here to freely worship and not be oppressed by their government as they practice their faith.*

This is not true anywhere else in the world!

This particular statement of Patrick Henry as well as the earlier mentioned compacts is brought out in very few history classes of today's public schools. History as it is taught today, through deliberately omitting cause/effect nuances of historical events because they are personally repugnant to *politically correct* education programmers, is being falsely taught. And the Denominational Christian Church fails to *counter* false history teaching, by refusing to make use of the available legal system *or by teaching the truth in Christian Education sessions.*

The great and public, even if it is fallacious, measuring rod we are held to by very sincere and vocal, albeit grossly mistaken, "Justices" for living under the Constitution which cannot be emphasized too greatly is the original covenant under which we *supposedly* flourish – is *Separation of Church and State.* Failure to apply the word *fallacious* would tend to give this statement a legitimacy that would be absolutely false.

George Washington, who even teachers of *false* history "admit" is uniquely responsible for the success of the "War of Our Liberation – in direct contrast to those who feel that religion and government play no legitimate part together says: *"True Religion offers government its surest support."* And yet present-day secularists, the ACLU and many journalists, even some would-be "Christian Leaders" would have us believe that (the Christian) religion is a threat to "true" American government.

The framers of the Constitution by which all lives in the United States are governed, corrected its framing, a historically perceived "wrong" in all other approaches to "governing" the lives of those *being* governed. i.e. Forcing the governed to accept the oppressive, artificially ritualistic and hardship practices of a government enforced *denomination* of the Christian Church. These framers, in even welcoming absolute un-believers or those who subscribe to "other" beliefs to a new, free, nation home, *in no manner or way implied or directly prohibited* the "Government of the People they proposed, from visibly, *publicly,* honoring the tenets of their Christian faith. Their statement which corrects this wrong tells us: *"The government shall make no law **establishing** a State imposed religion.* The *Bill of Rights* which is so often deliberately and falsely applied to this issue, also assures us that the Congress may not pass any law *abridging* the freedom of religion or *interfering with the free exercise thereof.* False applications take the form off "opinions" of public educators that the rights of one student are abridged and it is more important to prevent "damage" to that student's psyche than it is to teach truth to the majority, or to "allow" majority observance of traditional holiday visuals.

The present day hue and cry to separate church and state had its beginning, *not with Thomas Jefferson* as is so blatantly, deliberately and falsely portrayed; it began when a very smart but apparently un-believing ACLU lawyer (named Leo Pfeiffer) in 1947 who, knowing that there was a case before the Supreme Court, called the Everson Case, wrote a friend-of-the-court opinion. In this opinion, he inserted the phrase "separation of church and state." That phrase had never been used in United States jurisprudence before. He sent his opinion to Justice Hugo Black of the Supreme Court. Justice Black read the opinion and liked it (he was a very "liberal" justice). He ran Pfeiffer's opinion up the flagpole, and the opinion was passed with a vote of five to four. For the first time, in 1947, more than 150 years *after* Jefferson, the idea of separation of church and state entered United States law.

The call for separation of church and state *is* in the Communist Manifesto, *which* has as its basic premise – *there is no God.* The Christian Church in the United States has, apparently deliberately *failed* over the intervening 55+ years to see it as a Christian "Duty" to sue to seek reversal of this subversive decision rendered by the five gullible justices of the 1947 court.

One reason that "The Church" has so far refused to take action, is that many of its "educated" and "professional" proponents have, if not contrary to their vows to proclaim the Gospel, then in direct contravention of the covenant which assures the opportunity to do so, allied themselves with organizations established solely for the purpose of perpetuating enforcement of a law which was *illegally enacted* by the Supreme Court, rather than by the Congress. And their "peers" have done nothing to formally point out to them their error in understanding the tenets of their national ministry.

The results of the 1947 Everson Decision have been disastrous. After having created the bludgeon (wall of separation) the ACLU has for more than 50 years used it to beat Christians into submission and to silence them in the public square. The tactics used by the very well funded, some of the funding coming from public taxes, the ACLU, are simple and effective *and will remain successful* until the Church *recognizes and accepts it as mission, to fight back through member education and the legal system.*

Ironically, the ACLU does not concern itself about - in fact it defends the rights of other than Christian religions to make use of the public form to advance *anti-Christian* beliefs.

The question which *should be* answered by any court, certainly by the US Supreme Court is: What does the First Amendment say about what *any person* can do in the exercise of their religious beliefs? *It says nothing at all about what any* **citizen** *can do.* The *Bill of Rights* talks only about what Congress *cannot* do. But with the very able assistance of the Supreme Court, *"We the people"* are forced to actually *forfeit* the freedoms of protection *from* the government which are *guaranteed* by the First Amendment to our (Governmental covenant) Constitution; action on which (by the first Congress) had to be promised to them before George Washington, Patrick Henry and other would sign on the dotted line.

And the Institutional, Denominational Christian Church chooses to compound this felony by doing nothing of substance to challenge the supporters of political correctness in their constant and successful and destructive (to the mission of the Church) manipulation of the legal system.

CHAPTER 12
Selecting "Quality" Materials And Laborers

Building the Operations Wing:

The cornerstone of the Church (Jesus, its very foundation) declares that those (humans) who believe that He is who and what He claims to be are the "blocks" He uses to build and will always use to maintain His Church. In accordance with His original plan, Jesus appointed all the original builders and delivered the materials and will continue to recruit (call) the *laborers* necessary to maintain His Church, which even the "*Gates of Hades*" will not be able to breach. – this is His revelation of God's Word, God's Way, God's Will. In witness thereof:

- Jesus said to Peter: "*I will say to you that you are Peter and on this rock I will build My Church and the gates of Hades shall not prevail against it. And I will give you the keys to the Kingdom of Heaven, and whatever you bind on earth will be bound in Heaven and whatever you loose on earth will be loosed in Heaven.*

- And Paul, in his letter to the Romans, reminds us what is expected of those who will make this new (nation)Church flourish: "*I beseech you therefore, brethren, by the mercies of God, that you present your bodies as a living sacrifice, holy, acceptable to God, which is your **reasonable** service.*" (Romans 12:1)

- And the *command* we have from Jesus: "*Go therefore and make disciples of all nations, baptizing ......*" Surely it is not too hard a stretch to understand that "all nations" includes those who live in our land, among us.

- All this is tied together for the Denominational, Institutional Christian Church to comprehend it responsibilities by, as mentioned earlier, in his letter to the Ephesians (3: 10,11). Paul writes: "*...... to the **intent** that now the manifold wisdom of God might be made known **be the Church** to the principalities, and powers in the heavenly places, according to the eternal purpose which He accomplished in Christ Jesus our Lord.*"

Application of "Building Code" standards:

Successful arguments that *Separation of Church and State* is mandated by the US Constitution and that the *Theory of Evolution* must be the sole theory of the origin of life, are made possible by the fact that the *Christians* among us have been too busy exclaiming "*I don't want to get involved*" and/or are too busily engaged in *personal pursuits* to do what practitioners of other religions and groups (Muslims, Atheists, Hindus, African Americans, Spanish Americans) have routinely done and *continue to this day to do. They go and make disciples of those around them and they propagate their numbers, while they also finance friends and relatives from their "previous" homeland to come to the US and add to their voter base.* Most notably successful of these is the conversion of some "avowed Christians"- right here in the midst of those of us who are charged by the Lord of our Church to "convert" them.

By far, too many incumbent *Government Office Holders who are* seeking to remain in office "no matter what" are eager to pander to a visible, vocal, well funded voter base, even a base which is pushing pseudo and/or already protected "rights," or special, or solely economic interests, even if they result in severe harm to the common good as measured by *restriction of ability to openly "advance the Gospel of Jesus Christ."* And laws thus concocted are routinely declared to be Constitutional by Justices who were approved to their office by the very office holders (President or Senator) who were elected by these same "other religion" voters and/or by a "mass" refusal of the leaders of Christian Churches to "dirty their hands" be getting involved …… and/or pandering to "attention getting" very vocal, well represented (by "hired" advocates) of pseudo claimants of oppression. The above scenario is equally and effectively played by members of both political parties.

Meanwhile, potential *voter block* Christians, actively counteract the instructions of God (Genesis 1:28) to: "…… *Be fruitful and multiply, fill the earth and subdue it ……* " – the subversion being in the form of (and in a land founded by and for the People of God) legally *killing off* their unborn babies, or by defending the "right" of others to do so. One direct consequence of this overt sin, coupled with the sin of omission which is failure to proselytize neighbors and "aliens" in our midst is that the Christian doctrine, *that from the beginning sustained our determination to advance the ministry entrusted to us by Our Lord*

Jesus Christ has voluntarily given up the political clout which brought this nation into being and sustained it until *the Church relinquished its influence on its partner in mission, this Nation.*

From the time of his original sin, God steadfastly, without deviation, required man to experience on earth, the consequences of disobedience to the Word and Will of his Creator. Those consequences have not always been immediate. The destruction of Sodom and Gomorrah, for example, came only after the people's *repeated* refusal to repent of their wickedness and return to righteous living. Not just some, but all the people. Isn't abortion disobedience to the will of the God who created a means for His people to obey His command to *"...be fruitful and multiply, fill the earth and subdue it ..."* Could it be that God meant to fill the earth from un-believing sources?

Read the opinion of Newspaper Columnist *Cal Thomas,* who until now has been most famous for other than religious utterances. In a column published on January 10, 2003, Mr. Thomas wrote about the hypocrisy of legislative decisions which, with the support of so-called academics, *some* clergy and some journalists, condone and protect court decisions which *approve* a person's right to *kill* a fetus, but work themselves up into a *moral outrage* over any proposal to clone a human. The column states: "...... *Western Culture has told God that we don't need or want Him. It has told history that we will neither learn from it nor care. It worships at the shrine of the Self, and in so doing, it has produced a type of Rosemary's baby that will be impossible to control,* **absent a revival of the things that once mattered most in life.** *After 40 million (and counting) aborted babies in the United States, who, or what is going to stop the cloning, And on what grounds?*

This issue in and of itself poses the greatest danger that the A.C. L.U. will win its struggle to remove God from the official *and eventually the unofficial* consciousness of the United States. They do not have to acquire, equip, train or field an army for a takeover, they have to persuade the "wisest" of its citizens (Trial, Appeal and Supreme Court Justices) and gullible advocates of bogus *constitutional rights* that each prospective mother has a right to *murder* her unborn child, to supersede the baby's right to a life which the mother, *be her own acts of unbridled, undisciplined, careless, personal carnal pursuit of instant physical gratification* brought about; and to do so merely to relieve herself of any "hardship" consequences or "embarrassment" – or personal inconvenience requiring "hard won personal time and resources" to the rearing of the child. In addition to condoning, even by some, advocating direct disobedience of God, the Church – the United States Church, has and continues to give up multi- millions of voter disciples – *by killing them. Sanctity of life is thereby sacrificed to "quality" of life.*

Instead, our Church leaders, especially those of "main-line" denominations have decided to join hands with the ACLU and other secularists, and *tolerate*, if not *celebrate* the diversification of religious beliefs which have overtaken, *but not yet fatally,* damaged the planned (by the Founders) abilities of this *New People of God,* to achieve world-wide acceptance of and allegiance to the Gospel.

God's reaction to *any* diversification within His People is the crux of the history of His People as written in the Old Testament, beginning with Solomon's acceptance of the "gods" of his wives (especially the daughter of Pharaoh) and continues throughout the entire history of the reigns of his successors – portrayed graphically by describing the trials, tribulations and hardships visited upon His People by God' *interventions* into their lives and emphasizing their eventual 70 year exile from the promised and delivered homeland, brought about by Nebuchadnezzar. God sustained the *discipline* of those He exiled, until His pre-appointed time for them to "try one more time." to become His institutional People. And perhaps the most significant act of their beginning again was when the Prophet Ezra, with fervent prayer, led the "purification" of His People be *expelling* the wives and children from their midst which they had acquired, along with the ungodly influences they had exercised over the Israelites.

Since the *purification of His People* through the sacrificial death of Jesus Christ, God and His actions (through the Apostles) to reach out to the Gentiles, no longer distinguishes between people of a variety of those who are brought into His fellowship through repentance of un-belief; by Baptism and the Word – the key "qualifier" is *repentance* of their previous beliefs. Diversification of His People, in God's eyes, is acceptable *not by integrating other "religions" (or sin) into His Church; it is when the Church of Christ 'brings-in" to its folds, those of other nations, races or creeds.*

73

The celebration of diversity previously decried comes through Pastors and Elders of the Church, as they continually urge constant application of Christian principles/values/mores' to "every-day" life by their constituent members *as long as they are not applied to governing the people.* They proclaim that politicians are "by nature" crooked, or liars, so *lets not dirty our hands by going into that lion's den.* In contrast, the factual history of Christianity's re-emergence in Romania is attributed to the Church's presentation of training sessions on their values, standards and mores' to hopefuls for public office in their society.

The church member is thus taught the government which revolutionary sacrifice and blood made possible and defined is no longer necessary to achieve what the People of God need or desire; and that a Christian who aspires to public office is practicing an oxymoron, is really a heretic. Church members are thereby encouraged to join the "Barrabbas" movement. The most common defense of this "*lets not get involved*" practice is: "*You can not legislate morality.*" Never will church "professionals" recognize however, that you *can and should* legislate an environment wherein morality will *more likely* flourish; or that a *true, pract-ising Christian Fellowship* is an environment in which friends and neighbors, (Churched People) can be led to *not accept* immorality as a way of life.

Professional Christians (and legislators) seem to have a knack for confusing the correct, proper, Christian and legal mandate to *tolerate* right to *hold* an errant to the social norm belief and to, in their God-given right to practices it, with a need to tolerate the belief practice itself; and to flaunt that freedom to hold/practice, by *demanding rewards* for their errant practices through legislation or by court decision. Question? Wouldn't such action deny those who do not "tolerate" *their* active erratic behavior, their *equal* right to speak against it? (Isn't that how the Theory of Evolution became legalized, but wrong, fact? The Church thus teaches a naïve if not totally errant definition of "*tolerance*" and thereby fosters and *foments* offensive (to God) behavior.

Professional Church Ministers who teach that kind of tolerance, are teaching that a Christian or Christian Community must live with and honor personal behavior of others which is abhorrent to God, in the *delusion* that God desires His People to live with "*peace at any price*" are also guilty of encouraging believers and non-believers alike that the freedom which Christ brings to His People is the freedom to do whatever carnal man desires, *rather than to understand that God-given freedom means that man is free to live, act and be what God has established as normal, without thus endangering his "God connection."* Not only is that kind of teaching false teaching (as alluded to earlier) but it encourages Christians to *ignore* Paul's exhortation to the Romans: *"What then, shall we sin because we are not under the law but under grace? Certainly not!* (Romans 5:15) and Paul writes in the same chapter (v 23) *"For the wages of sin is death."*

In those extremely rare instances where an announced Christian *does* decide to do his or her duty for the common good and to run for elective office, his/her campaign is (usually) short-circuited by failure of a unified Christian Church to rally to his or her candidacy by *the* adding of competing *denominational* differences to the hyperbole of anti-Christian opposition of the political opponents. In place of becoming involved, even off the pulpit, Church leaders tend to encourage parishioners to *"tolerate"* un- godly attributes of *special interest* candidates, supporting *contrived* concerns. One of the ways they do so is by failing to emphasize the number of (Old Testament) kings of Israel who fell from power (taking their people with them) for leading their "minions: away from their avowed faith in the providence of God, and even going so far as (in the "spirit" of political correctness) to *encourage* their people to accommodate by adopting for themselves, the practices of other cultures.

It appear that all the resulting *confusion* over what is right and what is wrong is the consequence of a *perceived* need (by *some* Seminary Professors and some others who *qualify themselves* as theological academics) to constantly change the as perceived from the time of the early church and its leaders who had been with Christ on earth interpretation of Christ's teachings (which is called Reformed, always Reforming Theology) It is conceivable that much of the need to *reform* theological doctrine is a result of the tradition in "Higher Education" Circles, including Seminary Professors, to either *publish or perish* (academically speaking). Why else, for example, would a Seminary Professor publish a paper for man-on-the-street consumption, asking if Jesus really meant it when He said: "...... *No one comes to the Father except through Me."* (John 14:6) This is about as unequivocal an announcement of destiny as the

Lord of the Church, in Scripture, records. This is also in the face of the Professor's own National Church's Confession that Christ is the only way. (Writing a paper for academic discussion by students is one thing, but producing it for public discourse can cause great harm.

Perhaps if Seminary Professors want to be considered producers of the "bread" of theology, they should begin with Jesus teaching about the leaders of the church who held sway in Jesus' time. The teaching of His disciples that ends up: "...... *How is it that you did not understand that I did not speak to you concerning bread? – But you should be aware of the leaven of the Pharisees and Sadducees;"* Jesus was teaching *disciples* who could be wrongfully influenced by *producers of "theology"* who would contravene His (the Holy Spirit's) teachings.

The history of Sodom and Gomorrah is too often dismissed *from a pulpit* and by public news analysts as an allegorical or a melodramatic, perhaps falsely apocalyptic description of the consequences of God's wrath against His People. So these leaders urge followers to at least *consider* that their proposition that Jesus is not the only way to the Father and therefore should be more willing to exercise more *tolerant* behavior on the part of government leaders (it is, after all, human nature) who, even treacherously promise *materials* betterment of the individual voter, or classes of voter lives.

Lessons from the account of Jonah's mission to Nineveh are seldom, but should be, considered appropriate to today's *positive* to an individual rather than to the societal approach to teaching or *proclaiming* the Gospel of the Word of God as healing to the current state of life in this Nation/Church. This critique assesses why such a lesson should be taught nation-wide. *Contemporary techniques* of the Gospel, from too many pulpits, tends to limit self to the very true *positive* of God's grace while down-playing, if not actually *omitting* the responsibilities of "*If anyone wants to come after Me, let him deny himself and take up his cross and follow Me."* (Luke 9:23) Eliminating or down-playing "born again" responsibilities has the effect of – "I have my salvation, there is no real reason to worry about the welfare of other believers – which is in direct contradiction of Christ's real-life ministry and teachings.

It appears that to the Church, the lesson that the writer of the letter to the *Hebrews* thought was critical to Church leaders is important only to "Lay" Christians: "...... *of whom we have much to say and hard to explain since you have become dull of hearing. For though by this time you ought to be teachers, you need someone (The Holy Spirit) to teach you again the first principles of the oracles of God; and you have come to need milk and not solid food. For anyone who partakes only of milk is unskilled in the word of righteousness, for he is a baby. But solid food belongs to those who are of full age, that is, those who by use of reason have their senses exercised to discern both good and evil."* The most often *discounted* (by today's Church leaders) lessons for strengthening individual and corporate faith *and capability for effective ministry,* are those they bring to us about the need to *sacrifice our "private" interests* for the purpose of preserving and building the Kingdom (on earth) of God. (Hebrews 5: 11-14)

We are the appointed *Body of Christ: "... for the sake of His Body, which is the Church."* We remain His Body on earth until He is satisfied that His ministry is complete. His ministry is: *" ... Because He has anointed Me to preach the Gospel to the poor, He has sent Me heal the brokenhearted, to preach deliverance to the captives and the recovery of sight to the blind, to set at liberty those who "are oppressed ...."* and are we to totally ignore the promise of Jesus (in Matthew 25: 31-46) that *if you do these things you will be accepted into eternal life. If you do not (do them) you will go into everlasting punishment.* The work of spreading the Gospel and of bringing all people into His Kingdom is not accomplished by those who limit themselves to "I believe, I am saved, therefore I need do nothing else re: His ministry to all people.

CHAPTER 13
Hiring Skilled Workers

Then He said to them: *"The harvest truly is great but the laborers are few; therefore pray to the Lord of the harvest to send out laborers into the harvest."* (Matthew 9: 37, 38)

For this purpose (the hiring of skilled workers) we now remind ourselves that the project for which we seek workers is to restore this Nation/Church to its Architect and Chief Builder. It would seem logical, from a labor coordinating standpoint, to designate the worker pools we would build – one for the Church half, the other for the Nation half.

The laborers we seek are pre-qualified. They receive their "wages" before they are even aware of their "call" to the project. This is called by Reformed Theology, *election to eternal service (or fellowship)* with the Architect. They never "apply" for the job they are called to do, some even say they are not called to "a job" at all. Some say that since the worker's wage was paid at the Architect's initiative, all with the same "premium" wage, because all are equally unqualified (depraved is the term used by the Reform Community) *and is paid without regard to whether or not they will labor.* Terms described for prompting laborer participation in the achievement and/or maintenance of the project, used heretofore in this treatise, as well as world-wide by many who are subscribers to *Armenian Theology,* or who never understand *Reformed Theology,* such as duty or responsibility, or *"obedience to His commandments"* (the 1st & 2nd of the Ten Commandments) are viewed and taught differently by the two theologies mentioned and are subject to much "you are not being Biblical" debate. *That debate is the primary cause of the schism between denominations of the Body of Christ.*

The Apostle Peter strongly urges members of the Church to become able and ready to: *"......and always be ready to give defense to everyone who asks you a reason for the hope that is in you ......"* (1 Peter 3:15)

There is little evidence that Reformed Denominations are "effective" in equipping their disciples to make an effective defense of their beliefs. This writer has belonged to two different denominations of churches proclaiming "Reformed" theologies over a seventy-nine year life-time of "cradle-to-the-present" being preached to, and only once in that time did one of the "churches" ever present for hearer edification, the five points of Calvinism, either as a single sermon or as a series – and that was not from a pulpit, it was an "extra-curricular" event. Even in that forum, the presentation was more of an *assertion* of beliefs than it was an "educational" happening.

There are serious questions in the minds of too many lifelong members of Reformed congregations (and all the members of the Armenian congregations) over the theology of the disciple's *freedom to choose* either *to* or *how* he/she may most effectively become involved in the ministry of the Church. These questions, in either case, do not revolve around "am I saved?" The questions, or many of them, revolve around a lack of clarity in Reformed teaching about a need for *scriptural admonitions that a "saved" person must" persevere"* in applying one's self to what-ever God had "called" that person to, which according to Reformed belief, that person could not refuse. e.g. How do they respond to Solomon's fall from God's grace as a result of his later life decisions to worship "other" gods, *after being "elected" by God to the throne of Israel before he was even born; whose call he could not deny or resist?* And why did Jesus and the Apostles use words like *rebuke and admonish* as the exhorted believers to "straighten each other out" if they strayed from the "narrow" path?

Why did Paul find it necessary to teach that it might *become advisable to forego a freedom,* if exercising it would destroy another's faith and cause him or her to sin? Why does Jesus tell John in Revelations (3:20): *"Behold I stand at the door and knock, if anyone hears my voice and opens the door, I will come in to him and dine with him and he with Me?"* And what is the purpose of Luke's discourse in his Gospel (18: 1-8) about the persistent widow? How does Paul's assertion *"So then, faith comes by hearing and hearing by the word of God* affect the call of those members of the "fellowship of believers' who are not preachers?

There is no attempt here to *refute* Reformed Theological beliefs. There *is* an urgent call to clearly educate by answering *from the pulpit,* honest and sincere questions about the part that these and other teachings play in the over-all revelation of God's Word, His Will, His Way. Otherwise, the church will never, on this earthly plane, become united.

The issue for this discussion is not what individuals are or how they are "saved." The issue is how are the laborers necessary for the continuing functioning of His Body, the Church, to be rallied to the specific tasks that will make it function? Christ provides the faith to endure the in-built hardships of service and He speaks to those who provide the "brainpower" of the Body which makes it do the specific tasks He assigns to it. But He leaves it up to those disciples "in charge" of all the members of the Body, to identify, to describe, to rally the servants (even those whose vocational joy is in doing "some other" task) to make the requisite "calls" to initiate and then to actively support those doing those specific tasks.

And it is the *desirability* that certain tasks which are "appointed unto" mortals to whom *Jesus* delegated the "work" for the enhancing His earthly ministry to achieve His announced end and aim, to which individual members are "called" by His Church. Using God's call to Moses as an example, there is little Biblical assurance that an individual's call *will* be to perform *his* favorite task. The *joy of serving God may appear* as the task is "worked" but not necessarily as it is appointed by the Church. There is sometimes no way for the members of a small congregation to reserve for themselves their *favorite* task. There is no Biblical assurance *readily seen* by participants in a planned act of ministry that *every individual* has the *right or the call* to perform the same task.

A major paradox in relation to the how you are saved and how you are called to ministry debate is that "Preachers" belonging to denominations holding to either side of the debate, share the privilege of preaching from the other's pulpit. Some of them even switch denomination affiliation by having the "receiving" de- nomination "wave" a preacher's "deficiency" in theological education. The result is that the "man" (or woman) "in the street" laborer in evangelism becomes extremely unsure of what to say to a "lost" seeker of eternal life. Prospective laborers *for the harvest* find it too confusing or too difficult to "take the Church's call." Yet Jesus, in response to a concern of His Apostles about someone doing "miracles" in His name even though he/she was not a follower of Jesus, taught: *"...... do not forbid him ...... for he who is not against us is on our side."* (Mark 9: 39, 40)

The point is: No matter how it may be described, Jesus hopes and expects that those who are "called" to discipleship - to *take up his (personal) cross of reluctance and to apply himself to the tasks that enable the Institutional Church to function!*

Laborers and Leaders – Church half:

A long and loudly heard lament of frustration from those "in charge" of those Christian Denominations known in the United States as *mainline* is: *We are losing members right and left, how are we going to keep up our ministry? There are so few young people" interested in" a Pastoral ministry. Even most of those who do enter Seminary opt for career fields other than a Pastorate.* The concern seems to be more on "quality" (as defined by a denomination of the Church) of leadership than it is on the genuineness of the *spiritual drive* of the remaining laborers of the harvest.

At the same time, there is hears a joyous proclamation of accelerating growth in membership of the evangelical and/or independent congregations.

All Christian congregations publicly proclaim and evangelistic ministry that reaches out to "lost" sinners or to those who "want to" nut are too preoccupied with preservation of self and/or family to seek a spiritual life. When it comes to "proof of the pudding" however, too many denominational congregations who qualify themselves as *true Church,* routinely place evangelism on the "back burner" while they over-cook liturgical or governance disciplines and ritualistic practices to something called "good-order" in worship or in Church life, while limiting *outreach* programming to *special offerings* in support of more *politically correct* originated charities. They never realize that the recipients of their largesse, sometime deliberately, disguise their need, even when the recipients are local, *and never learn that they should relate their "gifts" to the hand of a loving, caring, benevolent God.* The Denominational Church is strangely reluctant to make it known that the gifts were given *to the glory and in the name of the God who thus is watching over those in need …and politically correct organizations are not going to tell them.*

Usually, those Christians who "hate" government welfare programs which are funded by what they define as excessive taxation, also fail to recognize that much of the genesis for government "relief" programming is related to the reluctance of Christian Church members to *tithe (or better)* the income from jobs which they also refuse to recognize as having come to them from the providence of God – the original "I don't need God anymore" syndrome, and to reach out in the name, to the glory of God, to those who by their personal *misfortune* might thereby be fertile ground for the planting of Gospel seed. The attitude of these "reluctant" *tithers* seems to be "I just don't see any need to get personally involved." (Apparently they also do not relate themselves to the church in Laodicea, described in Revelations [3:14])

There *are* two "major" Christian congregations and undoubtedly many more which are perhaps not quite as visible within the Christian Community called the United States of America, which have achieved world-wide recognition as being visibly *above the norm* for contemporary ministries. Both of them are Denominational Ministries. They are worthy of note for the purpose of this critique, so their "Ministerial "Bio" is included, with apologies in advance to them, for the injustice to them that is sure to occur.

If there are two, one must be described before the other. So without rank, the first begins with a young Pastor who in 1955, accepted a "call" from the Classis (Governing Board) of California of the Reformed Church in America (not one of the three normally recognized as "main-line") to establish a new church in Orange County of that state. The story of the struggles of this *missionary* Pastor, who opened his first Mission Church from the roof of a concession stand of a rented "Drive-in" Theater, and now stands with world-wide recognition as an *American* Christian pasturing the Garden Grove Community Church of the Reformed Church in America, which in turn sponsors the *internationally* viewed and participated in world-wide ministry, *The Hour of Power,* from the also internationally acclaimed *Crystal Cathedral,* is nothing short of *inspirational evidence* of God leading, cajoling, guiding, counseling and assuring step-by-step success of effort of man (or woman) involving himself *totally* in the ministry of *Jesus Christ* to which he had been called. *This ministry has achieved world-wide recognition as an American monument to faith, hope and love, (which is) the very first fruit of the Gospel of Jesus Christ.*

The mission, that its Pastor, *the Reverend Doctor Robert A Schuller* himself is reluctant to call complete, reaches even the very top level of world leaders. The acceptance of his Gospel message by millions of those (including leaders perceived by "the world" to be evil as well as those who are perceived to be immoral) can easily be traced to his call to them, *not* to become Christian, but to become followers of Jesus Christ and to put into practice the call of Jesus to live, act and be *"as I have commanded you."* Even *recognizing* their temptations to (including actually doing it) "stray from" *the straight and narrow path"* of the daily *taught* direction that these world leaders were now committing themselves to, Pastor Schuller counseled them with a verse of Scripture which they could (and did) accept as the *tiller* by which they could steer their ships of state. The verse: *"Those from among you shall build the old waste places; you shall raise up the foundations of many generations; and you shall be called the repairer of the breach, the restorer of the streets to dwell in."* What better "political" recognition could one aspire to?

More evidence of the universality of the acceptance of the Gospel of Jesus Christ as it is proclaimed by Doctor Schuller and his son and many fellow ministers of the *Hour of Power* ministry is in the record of testimonies from the Crystal Cathedral and/or written, published memorabilia under signatures of global leaders like *Mikhail Gorbachev, Boris Yeltson, US President Gerald Ford, Jack Kennedy, George H W Bush and William Clinton; Armand Hammer, Actor John Wayne,* as well as (from among hundreds) such great and world-caliber spiritual leaders as *Norman* Vincent *Peale, Billy and Franklin Graham, Corrie ten Boom, Mother Teresa, Shaykh Ahmad Kuftaro* (the most prominent of the only six Grand Muftis in existence, of the Muslim religion) among thousands of (not named here) others.

In a moment of questioning of self (as Paul advised the Church in Corinth to do) about the significance of the tome, energy and resources expended in his ministry to the overall effort to make Christ "real" to lost seekers, compared to her ministry of healing, Mother Teresa assured Dr. Schuller: *"I heal their physical bodies you heal their spiritual beings."*

According to this Pastor of the largest Christian congregation in this world, all this recognition was achieved not by him, but by *Christ* through him, based upon his conviction that *"There are infinite possibilities in little beginnings if God is in it"* Dr. Schuller, in his published biography (the latest of more than 30 books with Gospel assurances) attributes the mass acceptance of his *preaching* ministry to his "inspired" efforts to make his sermons a therapeutic outreach to "hurting" seekers of new lie. The constant theme of the total ministry (at some risk of errant assessment) is: Be a Positive Thinker; believe in a God who believes in you. Dt Schuller is, lives and preaches *Possibility Thinking*. He speaks to each individual who is listening, urging him/her to *receive* the healing which can come only from Jesus Christ.

Doctor Schuller's ministry is not without its detractors, (who are) usually second guessers or those unwilling to *"come to the edge"* with dreams of efforts to *"Proclaim the Gospel and teach what I have commanded ......"* thereby reaching people (in staggering numbers) who would have otherwise - no hope of hearing the Gospel.

In reaction to his project of building the Crystal Cathedral, (financed by acceptance of contributions from around the world) some of the most vociferous and hurtful of these detractors, are members of the denomination which gave him his call; and includes so many skeptics who like Judas Iscariot at the meal at which Mary anointed Jesus' feet with expensive oil, thought and critically said: *"This money would be better spent of the poor."* Per- haps even defenders of denominational rubrics should review: Mark (14: 6, 7) in the context of establishing the priority of *the Body of Jesus (the Church)* in our lives. Jesus responded to Judas' complaint: *"Let her alone. Why do you trouble her? She has done a good work for Me. For you have the poor with you always and whenever you wish, you may do them good."*

The multi-million dollar *Crystal Cathedral* complex, the chosen subject of scorn by those who fail to understand or "agree with" is now viewed world-wide as the most famous addition to the important role played by *Great Monuments of Faith* throughout the history of the Church. The cathedrals at Chartres and Notre Dame, along with Westminster Abbey and St. Peter's in Rome (as examples) continue to inspire *the faithful* even centuries after the last workers set the last stone in place and inlaid the last stained-glass window. And as for helping the poor, these nay-Sayers fail to recognize that the millions of dollars they say should have gone to the poor, really went into the wages of the laborers who did the building, and the truck drivers, even to iron ore miners - keeping *them* from becoming poor.

And this new, visible, Christian center enables the ministry to serve as the distribution center for as many as seventy-five hundred charities meals ach week through *World Opportunities International*. It allows ministry to specific relief as needed for particular populations in particular regions such as the children of Chernobyl after the nuclear disaster that occurred there. It sustains a prison ministry, a psychological counseling center, a suicide prevention center, a Hispanic American ministry, a self-worth program called Confident Kids, an annual youth gathering, the *International Conference on Care and Kindness;* and Dr. Schuller has for many years hosted the *Robert Schuller Institute for Church Leadership,* the first formal education for Pastors of any denomination, which dealt with leadership responsibilities *for* Pastors, and which has been attended by many Pastors and Church Elders who have in turn, built up "failing" congregations into large, "fruitful and effective ministries.

This *Garden Grove Community Church of Orange County* ministry is some-what unique among Positive Thinking ministries, in that in addition to delivering the "milk" of the Gospel to untold millions around the world, it is also engaged feeding the *solid food* of teaching and initiating programs of the "call of the Gospel" for *believers* to mature in faith in their Savior, by the practice of *involving members of the congregation and "visiting firemen" who Pastor other congregations, actively,* in "obeying" the command of Christ to Peter: *"If you love Me, feed My sheep."*

There is no way that this description of this ministry, culled from its own history, has been here justly treated. A complete, accurate and informative description is readily available and is invaluable to any struggling congregation and/or Pastor seeking guidance as to "how far can I go" in carrying out the *Great Commandment* to the Church. The book, *My Journey,* by Robert A Schuller tells the whole story to date (it will never be over) in readable, compelling and inspirational language.

It is recognized within this critique that the light of the Gospel that emanates from Dr. Schuller's ministry (and many other ministries known world-wide, including those begun by Dr. Norman Vincent Peale, "Billie" and Franklin Graham; Bishop Fulton J. Sheen; Dr. D. James Kennedy [whose ministry will be discussed more *thoroughly* later]; "Jim" Cymbala [also high- lighted later] and thousands of Pastors of smaller *localized* congregations which do not achieve nation or international visibility) is so visible to those who hear their proclamation *because the candle power they use comes directly from emphasis on Jesus Christ and His revelations of the mercies of God over and above the "confinement of denominational traditions and practices.*

Thus has spiritual "milk" (and perhaps a little baby food) been given to tens of millions of people who (some of them) never before knew that "food" was available.

Acquisition of "many" Laborers: (Matthew 9:38)

How far will the "milk" of the Gospel go in motivating believers to do what God's Word calls for them to do – i.e. the *Great Commission?*

Unfortunately *and unnecessarily,* the enlistment of congregation leaders of local ministry is severely curtailed by the reluctance of the Denominational Churches to recognize by members of the Body of Christ, (as advocated by Paul to the Church in Rome) – thereby denying them opportunity to apply their *Christ awarded* skills or talents to the ministry to which they *would* commit; thereby failing to the *most effective* use of both ordained and lay participation in the larger mission of this Nation/Church. Paul urged Roman followers:

"I beseech you therefore, brethren, by the mercies of God, that you present your bodies a living sacrifice, holy, acceptable to God, which is your reasonable service. And do not be conformed to this world, but be transformed by the renewing of your mind, that you may prove what is that good and acceptable and perfect will of God. For I say, through the grace given to me, to everyone who is among you, not to think of himself more highly than he ought to thin, but to think soberly, as God has dealt with each one a measure of faith. For as we have many members in one body, but all members do not have the same function, so we, being many, are one body in Christ, and individually members of one another. Having then gifts according to the grace that is given us, let us use them; If prophesy, let us prophesy in proportion to our faith; or ministry, let us use it in our ministering; he who teaches, in teaching; he who exhorts, in exhortation; he who gives, with liberality; he who leads, with diligence; he who shows mercy, with cheerfulness." (Romans 12: 1-8)

Now let us take a look at the whole, the "big" picture. Lets look at it from the *truism* (and it is a truism) that the Denominational, or for that matter, the Institutional Church as we now know it, *cannot survive* without the presence of the scholars, theologians or teachers we now identify as *Ordained or teaching professionals,* who are the "members" that enable us to build, update, protect and strengthen the institution. And *the institution* is the Church envisioned by Christ (and the Apostles) to be the most effective "Body" to complete the ministry of salvation for His people. *Does that mean that persons who are not Seminary trained are by definition, not capable of the Office of Word and Sacrament?* What about those persons whom God ordained and made responsible for establishing God's People – like Abraham, Isaac, Jacob's son Joseph, Deborah and the other judges (not all of whom were trained by the existing "schools") or any of the prophets recorded in what we revere as *God's* Word – or King David or Josiah, *who was able to postpone Judah's destruction by leading his people back to God?*

Or in the New Testament: It is a blessed truth that the Apostles had highest quality and on-the-job training (which did not guarantee Judas' fulfillment of the Pastoral role). But what about Stephen or Timothy or Titus or Philemon or Priscilla and Aquila (whom God used to clue in Appolos to the full Gospel)? And there are many who are alluded to but not named in the Bible. There is no record of *any of them* having experience Seminary education, yet together with *"those who believe in Me through their word"* they built a (known) worldwide Church that rocked the Roman Empire off its very foundation.

Are we to assume that God will never again call a believer to a given task (as He did Moses) who has not been "recommended" to Him by a professional churchman? Are all evangelistic or "independent" churches really illegitimate in God's eyes?)

These "Lay" people could do no more than to apply the understanding of the Gospel (which was not yet written to encourage repeated or widespread referral), as well as their faith-inspired insight, plus the "gifts" given them by the Holy Spirit- albeit they were trained, counseled and mentored by the Apostles. Again: These were servants of God (who are even today) recognized as being the *instruments* which God used to build His Church. Most of these people worked with and were mentored by Paul, generally accredited with being the most successful evangelist of the Gentiles and who, himself, received only a few days of "education" after being "hit between the eyes with a two-by-four" welded by Christ as he traveled the road to Damascus. And was Ananias, his teacher, really a product of Seminary?

Many of the Ordained Elders of the "Main-Line" Churches have heard the Gospel proclaimed, taught and explained for 30, 40, 50 or more years. Could it be true that *none* of the preachers they heard were able to communicate the Gospel to them with sufficient clarity that *not one of the elders* could assimilate the message of hope sufficiently to "hear a call" from the Church or from God, to "lead" (Pastor) a small congregation (whose members have also heard the same quality/quantity of "preaching") in their already defined and functioning ministry? *Are we to no longer believe the theology that whom God calls, God qualifies? Or do we simply exempt from that theology any who have professionally served society in "other than Church" capacity, but have never undergone three or more years of Seminary training?*

A paradox is that according to "visiting" professors from old, revered and hallowed Seminaries (Princeton, Pittsburg and Philadelphia) have very strongly stressed that if the institutional church is to survive, *radical changes* in the existing function and structure and mode of operation would have to take place. One of those "visitors" gave a life expectancy of sixty years for the institution. He gave that estimate fifteen years ago.

The most debilitating spin-off of continued failure to effectively "employ" *lay congregational leaders* is that neither those who *have a call to serve in that capacity* nor *those who need their leadership* will long "persevere" (Paul's word) in their determination to answer God's call. And not only *that* disciple or congregation will discontinue their contribution to *"advancing the Gospel of Jesus Christ,"* but the world-wide ministry of the Church will diminish by the amount of the "refused" contribution as well.

Before going any farther with this discussion, it would be not only *unfair* but extremely *inaccurate* to not note that national organizations of the three "main line" denominations *have urged and made possible through legislation* for their "subordinate" organizations and congregations to make effective use of *all* the talents, skills and abilities given by Christ to "lay" members of the Church. And also to be accurate, *some* so-called subordinate jurisdictions *do* (with measurable success) avail themselves of these "innovative" opportunities.

The problem is that too many *pockets* of local level "professional" disciples, who can't bring themselves to "go-along" with national level decisions to use disciples who have not "benefited" from a *Seminary* education, organize themselves at the next (district) level and devise *seemingly* rational reasons to "defer" or otherwise forestall the "commissioning" of lay disciples, in so far as utilizing them as primary and *on-the-scene* leaders of very small local congregations. In one "district" level organization of a main-line denomination, e.g. in central Pennsylvania, *Commissioned Lay Pastors* who must already be an *Ordained Elder* of a local congregation in order to qualify for training in Preaching Skills and Reformed Theology, who have been functioning as Elders in their local church ministry (and ministry program planning), have staffed *and chaired* committees, even the district organization itself and have been filling vacant pulpits in many leaderless congregations for many years, *have been judged to be incapable of being "the" leader of a small (40 to 70 members) congregation "because they (to a person) need two more years of "polity" training, and at least two more training experiences "outside" the local district.*

In the meantime, within that district, up to thirty congregations located in communities for up to (many of them) 150 years ministered to their "host" community and have been the *source of laborers* for all three levels of their denomination which are (jurisdictionally speaking) above them in terms of the wider ministry, have been "making do" with guest preachers and appointed (by the regional entity) governing board (local) chair persons, who, in turn, have to sacrifice attention otherwise required by "full-time" responsibilities to the congregation which pays them for full time services, or who are retired from full-time ministry. But in either event, they are not intimately attuned to the interests and concerns of the local community which is their "part-time" concern, or to the talents, skill or abilities, nor will they be able to identify, let alone recruit a disciple who could (and would) serve local or wider ministries.

There really is method to their tactics. Many of the disciple "recruiters" at the intermediate level or higher, in a frustrated attempt to see that every congregation has an "Ordained" Pastor have determined that existing small congregations should be, in the interest of efficiency and "good order" – be close out and their members "urged" to join a large congregation (to be) built in the middle of the territory which is currently being served by this cluster of widely separated smaller ministries, or in a "new" location. "After all, their thinking goes, with the state-of-the-art of transportation available today, travel won't be a problem." Even if there is a study somewhere that suggests this to be a viable option for *filling pulpits,* it sacrifices the life-long involvement in the carrying out *Great Commission* by the targeted "small Church" disciples to the convenience of less trouble for those charged with seeking out disciples to lead them. And there is little, even no evidence that the *Advancing of the Gospel* would be better served. If a cost-of-benefit analysis of a "super-church" to replace a cluster of small churches was ever made, it *might* address the *material* resources required but it would not likely address any loss of already functioning discipleship. In fact, their pre-formed parameter of such a study is "some of these small churches should be closed down." It is apparent that they have *given up* on the young adults of childbearing age and the youths of those communities whose parents were unable or unwilling to teach them the *Gospel of Salvation.* (Apparently they do not hold with the *Lost Sheep* or the *Lost Coin* taught by Jesus in the training of His Apostles.

On another plane, is the evidence that one small congregation located in a rural setting conducted an every member study (done by a specially appointed committee) of how the strengths and weaknesses of *their* congregational ministry should "pattern" their plans to "grow" in ministry, was shut off and the findings to date buried because some of the elders and a majority of the members were *less than confident* as to whether their very popular Pastor of fifteen years was a "leader" capable of shepherding the flock to "new" pastures, and the Pastor was never made aware of their lack of confidence. The solicited input of the disciples who would do the work of rebuilding was ignored. That congregation has shrunk from a membership of 80 to 40, and now has little or no recognition in its host community.

Equally troubling was the statement of a *Bishop* at an intermediate level of Church organization, that if the organization would raise the minimum salary for Ordained Pastors, more young people might be attracted to the pastoral ministry. Even giving credence to the *absolute truth* that those who effectively fill the *Office of Word and Sacrament* are seldom paid their worth, any contention that a higher minimum is necessary for any one to "accept" a "call" to a pastoral ministry, raises a legitimate doubt as to the spiritual quality of the one holding out for that pay-scale *as a decision determinate.*

Laborers and Leaders – Nation Half

The people who formed the convention which authored the Constitution of the United States were Christians. (in response to those few "critics" of general statements) Actually two of the framers were Deists, meaning that only 94+ percent were Christians. About half of them had some king of formal theological education. Many of them held "high" church positions such as head of The American Tract Society and the head of The American Bible Society.

One of the founding fathers, *Thomas Jefferson,* along with *Benjamin Franklin,* was considered least religious of all, in that they were not *evangelical, born again Christians.* It is noteworthy, that they are practically the only two founders that today's secular media and public schools ever tell anyone about. Many of the others did remarkable things in founding the nation, *but they are totally ignored by the media and the textbooks because they were Christians.* As mentioned heretofore, what the educators and the ACLU lawyers represent to be the founding father's lack of Christianity in their deliberations and formulating of a society, *are deliberate and absolute lies!*

Way back in our history (when this writer went to school) it was taught that the role of *Supreme Court Justices* was to apply the *intent of the law,* (the Constitution and its amendments) to any issue brought before it. What has happened, especially since the Henson Case brought to Justice Black, is that the ACLU and the *Separation* forces have convinced the sitting justices that their role is to apply the *letter* of the law - as the appellants respond to it and as it is presented by false (or "urged") testimony and/or "intellectual" persuasion – or as an opportunity to *impose* their personal political agenda through *court wrought* and illegal legislation. *The Supreme Court itself thus becomes the most blatant violator of the US Constitution!* And the Institutional Church's failure to "become involved" in the governance of this Nation/ Church is its primary protection.

There is no evidence (or historical or otherwise reason to believe) that the founders of this nation or the writers of its Constitution ever *intended* to take God or His values, principles or mores' away from its government – their stricture was for the *sole purpose* of preventing government from *establishing by legislation* and "official" church or denomination thereof. Welcoming practitioners of "other" religions and guaranteeing their right to "practice" *was not intended to be tantamount to removing from the majority of its citizens (Christians) their religious rights, nor the right to be governed by their beliefs.* The intention of the writers was to welcome to this haven any who might come in the hope of a "better" life than they were experiencing in their homeland and bring their beliefs and (non-harmful) practices with them; *it was not the framers of the Constitution's intent to substitute "guest's" beliefs for their host's beliefs and practices.*

Whether all agree to the above assertion or not, one thing is certain. The authors of the Constitution wrote into it that although a given act may be legally right, *it is not always right to do it.* Supreme Court Justices should be able to and are by function description expected to dispense justice using that "wisdom." *Otherwise, legal questions not resolvable at the local or appeals court level would have been authorized to be settled by popular ballot.*

The Bible teaches that same approach to life! E.g. Paul's admonitions to the Corinthians (1 Corinthians 10:23 - 11:1) about exercise of personal freedom, *even freedoms brought to them by Christ's teachings.* Paul's lesson makes the point that exercising even God-given freedoms is appropriate *only if it does not damage a "lesser" faith in Christ, in someone else and that when that becomes the case, not exercising it is to the glory of God.*

The Institutional, Denominational Church does a miserable job of educating its followers that this is the application of freedom that Jesus brought to them through His Apostles, - *and that this is what the writers of the Constitution had in mind when they wrote the First Amendment.*

The hue and cry of *un-believers* aided and abetted by some who have achieved and are quick to exploit to their own *anti-constitutional and anti-godly agenda*, who have received worldly recognition as "Church" Leaders have succeeded in effecting a take-over of national and local governments by those vociferous un-believers.

The tactics they use are to threaten costly court action on anyone who mentions God or Godly values as their decision determinates in "running for" public office, or even more successfully in operating the office they succeed in winning. These "secularists" (or more concurrently, humanists) succeed because they have also scared or convinced judges at all levels of the bench that *their* interpretation of the Amendment is correct. (In addition, they have spent two generations of force-teaching this interpretation to those who eventually become judges, through the pass/fail processes of "higher" education)

The result is that there are few "practicing Christian" office holders; and those who do confess to be Christian are elected *on their promise to not involve God in their decision making.*

And the Denominational, Institutional Protestant Christian Church refuses to *"waste"* resources by searching out and nominating and campaigning to elect candidates who promise to "hold to" their Christian beliefs.

The availability of laborers who will pledge to carry out the pre-announced ministry of this Nation/Church, at home or abroad, is severely curtailed for the above reasons, as well as for other reasons which will be discussed in succeeding chapters of this critique.

CHAPTER 14
The "Now" Condition Of The New Church Structure

We can be truly thankful that within and from this Nation/Church millions of "lost" people all over the world have received and have drunk of the milk of the Gospel. Perhaps it would be appropriate to see if the baby is growing and if it might be ready to advance to solid food. The appropriate evaluation criteria is (surely) that which God established as identity for His People, i.e. How do His People rank the priority of their activities of *survival* of their exile from Eden and are the teachings of His Son whom He sacrificed to give them new life, being *lived* by His People? For this critique, we focus on those who reside in this Nation/Church.

There is an almost universal feeling of the contemporary *laity* of this Nation/Church that this nation is *right now* perilously close to the way of life that infuriated God as *He judged* life in Sodom and Gomorrah; certainly as God instructed Isaiah to warn Israel (which the people did not heed) and for which Israel was destroyed even as the people (except for a remnant few) were taken into a new, 70 year, exile. The prayer of the laity is that God will *give us another chance as He did Nineveh.* Lets evaluate the record of that Nineveh happening:

The fish story aside, this record of Jonah's very, very reluctant obedience to the call from God – a call which Jonah vehemently *argued* (with God) against, even to the point of running away from the very presence of God (attested to by Jonah's written statement) – this record is a witness to power and mercy of God *and of His willingness to change His mind if certain pre-established conditions are met to His (God's) satisfaction.* Nine- veh was the capital city of Israel's arch-enemy, whose wickedness had come to the attention of Almighty God, Israel's pro- tector. But God, with a mercy not only not understood but was severely, vociferously resented by Jonah, decided not to just go ahead and wipe out the city and its people as He did Sodom. He would *warn them* and give them an opportunity to *be delivered from His wrath.* God sent Jonah to Nineveh with His warning. Jonah's resentment, *disagreement* and active rebellion against God's decision of mercy to the people of Nineveh, and his fuming inner turmoil at the *success* of the warning which he did eventually deliver on God's behalf, is what Jonah records for us in his four chapter book of the Old Testament. The witness of Jonah, the record of his unsuccessful foolhardiness of trying to say no to God – of *his* deciding that God was not being *fair* to His loyal and life-long servant by *forgiving* the servant's archenemy, is well worth reading and meditating thereon. But that is not the point of this record of God's mercy (which is) most appropriate to this discussion.

Many Gospel milk-drinkers have never even heard of the *good news substance* of the story of Jonah. It is most meaningful when accompanied by the description of the society of Ninevemites (if that is the correct way to refer to its people) and the biography of its king. They may not even know how to spell Nineveh. After reviewing the description of its society and of its leader *several times* within the framework of the news being widely publicized in *today's US media, they might want to spell Nineveh – U N I T E D   S T A T E S.*

The Bible commentary on Nineveh and its king reports: The king of Nineveh was a cruel and idolatrous leader of a proud and ruthless people who were notorious for inflicting viscous punishment on its own "less fortunate" citizens as well as its conquered foes. Nineveh's society was what we are told by civil-rights activists (the ACLU and those who deliberately misread the Constitution as *guaranteeing* separation of Church and state) is what our society should be – *"normal."* It was *immoral, oppressive and violent – and officially denied God.*

Then wrath of God against Nineveh was as surely as much against *a people* who basked in (who indeed greedily wallowed in) the "perks" of the king's leadership and the society he thus provided them, as it was against a king and his government. With "perks" and benefits of a lifestyle reflecting *idolatry, violence, oppression of the weak including slavery of conquered foes, and rampant, deviate immorality.* Is it hard to imagine that Nineveh's lifestyle was the ultimate example of the kind Paul warns Timothy against as he exhorted him to be aware of what he is facing as he pursues his ministry in the name of Jesus the Holy Christ? Paul writes to Timothy: *"You must understand this: That in the last days, distressing time will come. For people will be lovers of themselves, lovers of money, boasters, arrogant, abusive, disobedient to their parents, ungrateful, unholy, inhumane, implacable, slanderers, proligates, brutes, haters of good, treacherous, reckless, lovers of pleasure rather than lovers of God, holding to the outward form of Godliness but denying its power ... ."* Surely that's enough for us to get the picture.

Our Inheritance – the Nation/Church - 2006

If you read any "today" newspaper, look at *any* TV news program, follow up on *any* political campaign, pay any attention at all to any Judge's decision (including, no *especially* the Supreme Court of the United States) or watch any day-time or prime time YV entertainment, read any current (so-called) literature or just listen to friends and neighbors, many, if not most of whom could not find a Bible in their home or in church they list as *their* church, even in the case of a life-threatening emergency; if you listen to them discuss *any* current worry or concern, societal or personal, *it would take very strange quirk of mind to see any difference between Nineveh of Jonah's - time and "the good Ole US of A.*

One of the many lessons we could learn is that one of, perhaps the most insidious life-style concepts we are called upon to endure by secularists/humanists (and supported in the interest of peaceful co-existence by "peace at any price" Church leaders) calls for *absolute, unlimited tolerance* toward active, society destroying, personally harming (of self or loved ones) and the greatly *mistaken* belief that the Constitution which guides, guards our daily life really permits our fellow citizens to *inflict* their personal ideology upon us, *our* ideology not-withstanding. Insidious because *tolerance* is one of the easiest words in English vocabulary to abuse, to use in disguise of an attitude of *no opposition appreciated or allowed.*

No controls appreciated or allowed *tolerance* is too often called for when the issue is (as Shakespeare might have said) *to obey or not to obey* the tenets of Almighty God in legislative, executive or judicial decision making. This in the face of one of our *most revered* historical facts, i.e. the document that spells out the basic premise of our freedom, indeed which justified our armed rebel- ion against a king (who might have held the king of Nineveh as his personal idol) and which in turn led to the substance of our Constitution begins: *"We hold these truths to be self evident, that we are endowed **by our Creator** ....with certain inalienable rights ......"*

96

Doesn't sound much like the *framers* of our Constitution advocated life, a total society *to become free form God,* does it? It appears to, to members of the ACLU, who have in turn convinced supposedly wise but greatly confused (in their application of their "wisdom") Public Educators and *some* "Christian" clerics as well as "Justices" at all levels of our Justice System to shout (or in the case of judges, *declare*) *unconstitutional* ANY display of belief or faith or trust in the teachings of Jesus Christ. And that is *any!* Not only are *posters* spelling out the Ten Commandments of God banned from Public Schools, but also in courthouses where the proceedings are usually about infractions of "civil" laws which interpret them; or even in the private offices of public officials, Town Squares – you name it, they are banned there.

And search it for yourself! *Nowhere in the Constitution* and *nowhere in any of its amendments* can you find *"separation of Church and State"* either stated or implied. All – that is – all decisions adjudicating such separation are results of judges being persuaded by the aforementioned educators and lawyers, usually using trumped-up and/or false witness testimony that to mention *"God"* or to allow private or individual prayer, or oral or pictured references to God or to Jesus Christ is to *cause anyone who hears or sees such a reference to believe that the government entity which allows it, is forcing belief in God on the hearer.* Meanwhile, under these same Constitutional definitions, "they" are permitted to loudly and publicly announce the *"there is no God"– no matter what that announcement does to another "hearer's" belief system ......* but according to those who champion *separation*, it is unconstitutional to debate the *No God* advocates, even by saying "I believe you are wrong and here is more than four thousand years of witness (the Bible) as well as the majority (80%) of those attending the debate to counter their argument. Debate *used to be* for the purpose of unearthing truth. (It does appear to be constitutional to allow the Armed Services of the United States to *require* organized Satan worship on base – if it so much as request by only *one worshiper."*

Jesus Christ, through Paul, teaches us in 2 Corinthians (6:14- 18) *"Do not be unequally yoked together with unbelievers. For what fellowship has righteousness with lawlessness? And what communion has light with darkness? And what accord has Christ with Belial? Or what part has a*

*believer with an unbeliever? And what agreement has the Temple of God
with idols? – for you are the temple of the living God, As God has said:*

- *"I will dwell with them and walk among them. I will be their God
and they shall be My people. Therefore, come out from among them
and be separate says the Lord. Do not touch what is unclean and I
will receive you. I will be a Father to you and you shall be My sons
and daughters, says the Lord God Almighty.*

One paradox of the "separation" debate is, that every office holder,
every legislator, every judge is installed in his/her office by taking an
oath *to the God they would free us from,* and they do it in an official
and public ceremony – *which the Supreme Court has declared to be
constitutional.*

Getting back to the comparison of Nineveh's Pre-Jonah society with
contemporary society in the United Sates:

It is alleged that the "leader" of the United States, not a king, who
derives power from the consent of the governed *is not* idolatrous or
cruel, or immoral or corrupt or hypocritical and does not encourage
nor lead the man/woman in the street to live (*in a tragically warped
interpretation of freedom*) to live as if they had no need for ethics or
rules of behavior. Does recent election history really substantiate that
kind of electorate innocence? *Does not history record* that latter-day
major election campaigns are won or lost on *"character is not an issue,
vote for me on how much I can get for you from the trough of government
taxes?* What "decision to vote for" criteria *are* routinely applied by the
majority of the electorate in selecting a candidate for office *at any level*
(local, state or national)? Most public debates of candidates, or of their
supporters, *openly* revolves around whether or not *personal character* is
a criterion which *should be* applied against a political promise that that
candidate will make the decision maker's life more "abundant" – usually
defined as providing the means for the voter to become personally more
affluent. Public sentiment indicates that no "religious" candidate can be
elected unless he/she promises *to not let his/her beliefs* color their decision
making. *What greater nectar can there be to appease the ACLU gods?*

Another paradox is that many of the people who vote for a popular
candidate because they give the candidate credit for an economic "boom,"
do so because their so-called boom is really built on an opportunity for
both parents to earn family income, even though it requires that they

call upon someone else, an "outsider" who is not necessarily trained or familiar with the parents' values, to take responsibility for instilling *"wholesome" standards and beliefs* their children should have and rely on to then through mortal life. All this effort just so they (and their children) will have enough *material "things"* for them to feel "superior" to their neighbor, or to pay their personal stand-in.

It is also denied by our "educated" consciences that the United States is cruel or vicious to our conquered foes. Maybe that could be explained to those to whom we refer as *native* Americans or others we call *African Americans,* or a Mexican field laborer who is *:invited"* to do work which *"we"* cannot be expected to do. Or, within our own society, explain it to the forty-five million aborted fetuses (which is a Latin word meaning *person*) or to the 35 to forty five percent of the wives who are battered, many of them *killed* each year, or to the *hundreds of thousands of children* living under our Constitution who are daily injured or maimed or murdered by parents or siblings or neighbors or strangers entering into a *parents away from home working* house.

Or let us meditate on terms of *"official" societal Guide Lines.* Consider the Federal Government (tax) financial support of the ACLU even as it abandons its original purpose (a good one – to protect citizens from governmental abuse of personal rights) and using legal *steamroller tactics,* applies lies, innuendo, deliberate exaggeration of immaterial "facts," false witnesses, and trained though not "educated" judges against specifically chosen for not being able or willing to expend scarce resources for a courtroom defense, *manage to destroy the very Constitution they have sworn to defend.*

Speaking of social amenities, it is not that long ago when *Pot* was used for cooking, *grass* was what covered a lawn, *coke* was what drunk from a little green bottle (now a collector's item) *aids* was something you gave people in need, a *closet* was a place to hang your coat rather than from which people with abnormal life-styles emerged and *obedience to parents or to righteous and constituted authority* was normal; or *marriage* was something one did in preparation for acquiring a family? In order to discover contemporary meanings of long tested, tried and true words, it has become necessary to look into police records or *politically correct* classrooms or listen to the jargon of the streets or *just ask any present-day school age "good" children what the current definitions might be.*

In the morality frame of reference, it is not hard for those who grew up "in the Church" to remember when Elvis Pressley was photographed only from the waste up on the Ed Sullivan show because of the way he gyrated his (fully clothed) hips as he sang. And they can remember when TV producers edited out certain scenes from drama shows because they were too explicit in their portrayal of murder, or mayhem, or "so-called" romantic events. The real "irony" is that in those "good old days" – superior acting managed to convey a story line to discerning audiences *without resorting to visual demonstrations.* One can also easily remember when there were "unwritten" taboos" *even in TV commercials* (such as false teeth, people modeling lingerie, long drawn-out kisses, household commodes, or showing intimate body parts being enhanced by this product or that, *because children* might see them or because *John Q Public* was respected for bring clean-minded, sensitive, moral *and smart enough to figure out what the product would do for the purchaser* without having to see specific examples? Have "educators" (secular or Christian) who rail against public display of *Christ in Christmas* because of it "influence" on children *or a minority of "offended" adults* ever been asked (in court) about the possible effect of denying them their 1st Amendment rights, would have on the majority they are railing against?

It is not really that long ago that quality drama whether in movies or on theater stages or on TV, focused on ethical, moral or religious values, standards and mores' leaving to the watcher's imagination (and therefore not *neglecting* the truth of) violent, sleazy, odd-ball weird or other than normal aberrations of life in a Christian society – before talk shows ever came onto the scene.

Today's presentation of *realism* on those same media is actually *dishonest* in that their producers are just that. They get a group of would-be "brain-stormers" together who dream up the most bazaar or violent and/or immoral happening they can imagine; recruit untalented (but money-hungry) actors; produce their product; and then market their product to today's "people of Nineveh" within this nation and world-wide. Much of the rest-of-the-world never sees any demonstration of American culture other than what these dishonest representations bring to them. "Reality" as it is being seen today in movies and on TV even by our own impressionable and jaundiced youth, and by those of other nations, *whom we would impress with our righteousness,* is not an accurate representation of the fabric of American society – *it is a spot of stain or a hole torn in that fabric.*

This is, of course, (and remains so) because *the People of God* have decided to turn their collective backs on or a deaf ear to those who seek out the *lesser percentage* of the population who *are* perpetrators of violence and immorality, obviously because the (the Church) don't want to get involved; most ridiculously, as a result of being taught *"you can't legislate morality."* – Apparently also meaning that it is to *teach morality* (with anything like a reward/punishment technique) to their offspring. And once more, the Christians, in exercising their tragically errant view of *toler- ance* actually *encourage* these evil and wrong depictions of American life.

According to Matthew and all the original Apostles (except Judas) and according to Luke and according to the last Apostle whom Jesus called, Paul, *the Body of Jesus Christ (the Church)* was created for the specific purpose of *"...... go therefore and make disciples of all nations, baptizing them in the name of the Father, and of the Son and of the Holy Spirit, teaching them to observe all things I have commanded you and lo, I am with you always, even to the end of the age."* This, the "Great commandment," is repeated several times in this critique because it *appears* that today's Institutional Church believes, at least it acts like, the *proclaiming* half of the commandment is all that is important to Him who initiated, defined and set into motion the New Covenant Mission and then *entrusted* it to the Church, i.e. (to these defeatists) *it is a waste of time and effort to do the teaching half.*

From the time God established His People through Abraham, God's followers, in exercising the freedom He simultaneously gave them to choose His or *worldly pursuits,* have cyclically chosen to live the abundant life provided by the God they "followed" until they managed to "forget" that God, not they themselves, had provided the abundance *which they eventually corrupted* and then set their sights on the idolatry of comfortable affluence as they entered into disobedience of His criteria for remaining *His People* then finally abandoning altogether His way. They usually did this by interpreting "His Word, His Will" to favor easing their earthly existence by removing concern for others of His People and eventually turning violent, evil and immoral. Each time they did so, and God decided they were in danger of forever destroying His hope for them to "return to Eden" – God gave them another chance to repent and to turn back to His Way. But when they *refused* to repent, turning more and more to *destruction* of His plans for them, *God decided that His personal intervention in the mortal lives of His People became necessary.*

Of such were the records of Sodom, the 70 year exile of Judah (Jeremiah) the eventual destruction of Israel, even Jonah's warnings in Nineveh. The cycles continued even after the ultimate intervention of God, which was the sacrifice of His only begotten Son Jesus, for the purpose of freeing His people from oppressive and *misinterpreted religion.*

Witness the corruption of His teachings which eventually resulted in the *Dark Ages* (with their crusades) and in destroying the "catholic" response to a call of men to ministry and then brought about the *Protestant Movement.* The most recent intervention being when the Protestant Movement in turn, became so oppressive that God brought a homogeneous group of *righteous* followers across a much wider Jordan, allowing them to *refurbish* His Church. Typical of God's wisdom in testing the mettle of His "new" People after taking them safely through the *Revolutionary War* which brought about their opportunity to fashion a way of life which reflects obedience to His Word, His Way, through the vetting process of the war between the states and perhaps, the "war to end all wars," God "allowed" the *great depression* as a, perhaps the final tempering of their faith and loyalty to Him, ending the tempering process by establishing the new nation's might through the process of taking His People safely through another (truly) world war and a "cold" war which saw the destruction of a nation which had *officially* denied God to be sovereign over all peoples.

In the process of His People's efforts to carry out His plan for the building of His eternal Kingdom, God also established this new nation as the most prosperous of nations, with sufficient "leadership" and material resources to become the ultra-benevolent presence of God to *all* people. And typical of man's propensity to disabuse their Creator's benevolence to those who committed their trust to Him, His People of His new Nation/Church persevered in their faith during the tempering process, then with new generations coming to maturity, in the 1960s, once more the people of the nation credited *themselves* the material prosperity He *allowed* and declared any no need for, even the existence of a Creator – God. This Christian Nation in response to the Institutional Church's decision to *not remain involved in, fact to discourage member involvement in the political arena" is in extreme danger of losing its Christian Nation status, if not in the eyes of its Creator, certainly in the eyes of "all nations.* God's criterion for remaining His Nation/People is spelled out for our assimilation in Moses' instructions to the Israelites just before they went into the original Promised Land:

"Now this is the commandment and these are the statues and judgments which the Lord your God has commanded me to teach you, that you may observe them in the land you are crossing over to possess: ......that you may fear the Lord your God to keep all His statutes and His commandments which I command you, you and your son and your grandson, all the days of your life, and that your days may be prolonged. Therefore hear O Israel and be careful to observe it that it may be well with you and that you may multiply greatly, as the Lord God of your fathers has promised you, a land flowing with milk and honey." (Deuteronomy 6: 1-3) And verse 12 warns us: *"...... then beware, lest you for- get the Lord who brought you out of the land of Egypt* (and from England/Holland) *out of the land of Bondage."*

Peter reminds us: *"But you are a chosen generation, a royal priesthood, a holy nation, His own special people, that you may proclaim the praises of Him who called you out of the darkness into His marvelous light; who were once not a people but are now the people of God, who had not obtained mercy but now have obtained mercy."* (1 Peter 2: 9, 10)

Moses and Peter were speaking to how God wanted His People, a separate people, to individually and collectively, to live their "every-day" lives.

How does the "contemporary" Church fit into God's plans?

This Nation/Church seems determined to give to those who have elected to become unbelievers (so that they could "freely" pursue material gain or personal, privileged glory) the "help" they need to discredit or destroy what the Lord taught through Moses and *through Jesus Christ in Peter* who came to us so that God's law would be fulfilled and that we would be free to live in accordance with God's Word, with God's Will, with God's Way:

"...... that you may live and multiply and go in and possess the land which the Lord swore to your fathers ...... for the Lord your God is

bringing you into a good land, a land full of brooks and waters, of fountains and springs that flow out of valleys and hills; a land of wheat and barley, of vines and fig trees and pomegranates, a land of olive oil and honey, a land in which you will eat bread without scarcity, in which you will lack nothing, a land whose stones are iron and out of whose hills you can dig copper."

"When you have eaten and are full, then you shall bless the Lord your God for *the land He has given you. **Beware that you do not forget the Lord your God by not keeping His commandments, His judgments and His statutes which I command you today. ......***then you say in your heart, My power and the might of My hand have gained me this wealth ... then it shall be, if you by any means forget the Lord your God and follow other gods and worship them, I testify against you this day – that you shall surely perish."* (Deuteronomy 9)

Has this Nation/Church succeeded in self-destructing?

Let's take a lesson from Jonah: This Church seems to be reluctant to live by faith that God *can and will* keep His word. So from his experiences with the Almighty and Merciful and Benevolent God – let us learn a lesson from Jonah; and then let's make that lesson applicable to life in this Nation/Church, today!

Let us pick up Jonah's report on his experiences in resisting God as he finally acquiesces to God's command to take the warning to Nineveh. – as he finally makes the effort to ward Nineveh's King and the people of God's wrath, *and of the promised consequences of that wrath if Nineveh fails to repent of its wickedness.*

Jonah took off on a three-day tour through Nineveh, proclaiming that if *the people did not repent,* in forty days God would destroy the city as He did to *Sodom.* Jonah began at the outskirts of the city and addressed God's message to every man and woman he saw on the streets first, foremost and exclusively, before any audience with the king. In fact, he most likely got his audience with the king because the king had heard from the "grass roots" and knew that his minions *believed* the message which Jonah brought, even to the point that they were already wearing sack-cloth and ashes in repentance of their sinful, evil lifestyles. The King and the people of Nineveh *officially, by decree, repented,* accepted God's sovereignty – and God, in his mercy, repented *His* judgment with penalty, and Nineveh was spared the threatened total destruction.

A rational conclusion to our findings and discussion of the "now" church:

We, the Institutional, Protestant Christian Church *have* succeeded in getting all people (to include all nations, even our own) to hear the Gospel of Salvation, we have Baptized those who were unbelievers but became believers through the message they heard from us. We are well on the way to accomplishing *the first half* of Christ's Great Commandment to us. But we have had little success in on our responsibility to perpetuate the capability of the People of God to *complete* the ministry which He entrusted to us. We have reverted to looking after the agenda we define (self and congregational preservation) and have *in effect* abdicated interest in preserving the *"holiness"* of the fellowship of believers by *teaching* (through living and demonstrating) *"all that I have commanded you."*

But we have not yet self-destructed! Jesus himself in Smyrna, as well as the writer of the epistle to the Hebrews, *both of them,* urge us to persevere in attempting to complete the mission we have undertaken. Succinctly, the attitude toward perseverance they urge from us is:

- *Perseverance to the end is a mark of those who know Christ. Jesus, through John, told the Church ay Smyrna: "Be faithful, even to the point of death and I will give you the crown of life.* (Revelations 2:10) *Such character sets apart Godly leaders and enables them to continue trusting God in difficult days.*

Our present difficult assignment (brought about by our own sins of omission) is to bring this Nation/Church which He established for us, back to Him – and to complete the assignment He gave us in its founding,

Let us consider a warning effort (similar to Jonah's); let us take it to *our own people and our government.* With absolute faith in Paul's teaching that I (we) *can do all things through Christ who strengtheneth me"* – let us organize and implement an all-out project for that purpose; we can call it *Sackcloth and Ashes.* (The name being in recognition of the Old Testament tradition of wearing sackcloth and ashes in public as an announcement of confession and repentance and as a commitment to change.)

The beginning step of *any effort to* carry out the Will of God, to assure *ourselves* that what we are about is *His business*; to achieve success in completing His mission, is that we must follow the leader, *Jesus the Christ* – appointed to that post by God the Creator. Studying the Gospel according to Mark (1:35-38) reveals the *how, when and why* we can thus trust our calling to *this very project:*

- *"...... Now in the morning, having risen a long time before daylight, He went out and departed to a solitary place, **and there He prayed.** ......But He said to them, let us go into the next town that I may preach there also, because it is for this that I came forth."*

PART V
SPECIFICATIONS AND BUILDING MATERIALS

CHAPTER 15
To Refurbish This Nation/church

"Reading" the Architect's Original Design

As we are Baptized by the Holy Spirit of God, which is what Jesus promises to all who believe that He is the Son of God and that He took the death penalty in our place for our sins, we are changed from being *of* this world into becoming a temporary resident *in* this world. The Apostle Paul states that *with* our Baptism we have been recreated to newness of life. We have been adopted as His son or daughter. He is our Heavenly Father; which means that we have accepted the *responsibilities* of being in His image. *God therefore reasonably expects, in fact God commands us to live, act and be like His first-born Son, Jesus.*

It is true that we are still, figuratively speaking, in the womb of eternity. We are, again figuratively, as an embryo, a fetus, *coming* to full term, born (more accurately, reborn) into eternal life, into the family of God. We are still developing, completing our gestation period as we "take on" the genes of our very Creator. ***We are re-born to emulate the "first born" of God – Jesus.***

One of the qualities (genes) that made Jesus what He was when He lived in this physical world, was His self-declared need to pray; and the word He left with us (the Gospel according to John) as He was being transformed into His Spiritual (eternal) Being, was that if we are to have any hope of a capability to obey His command to us, believers through the message which the Apostles brought us, i.e. *"if you love Me, keep My commandments"* – **We have to pray too.**

Prayer is the communicating channel between us and our Heavenly Father who is the source of our new life, the teacher through The Holy Spirit; the Designer of the Utopia we long for. He it is, the *Architect of this Nation/Church* we are, who *alone* can approve any recovery or refurbishing of its tattered being.

Apropos of the Constitution being a Christian document establishing this Christian Nation/Church: There is the record of Benjamin Franklin (notably one of the "least Christian" framers) in an effort to bring order out of several months of rancorous disagreement among the writers who were charged with "coming up" with the basic law of the land, diluted the rancor among the members enough to prevent a premature dissolution of the conference (several of the states' delegates had threatened to "quit" the convention) by a motion on the floor, that from the time of the motion's passing, every daily session would begin with prayer to the God they served. Franklin is credited in history with thus "saving" the new Nation/Church.

The *Word of God* to which we cling as our hand-book of gestation, cite *many* experiences of mortal life which prompted Jesus to pray. The scripture cited earlier, the Gospel according to Mark, in it *first chapter* stresses the need Jesus felt for the sustenance of prayer. (See a detailed discussion of the attitude of Jesus toward prayer, both for His need as a human and ours, yours and mine, in Appendix B to this dissertation.)

The original sin was Adam's own personalized decision, *and the actions he took,* to undertake to improve what God had provided and promised, *and to hide both from his Creator.* It would be just as foolish, to say nothing of evil, to begin a project like *Sackcloth and Ashes* before obtaining the Architect's input and approval. And make no mistake, the *Architect* of this Nation/Church and the hope for its recovery from an accelerating movement to a disastrous, self-inflicted end, is *Jesus the Holy Christ.* The Holy Spirit is, by original design, *His* voice relaying to us *His* response to our prayers.

Why "first" the Architect?

The Deity of Christ - the Architect, the designer of the Church: *"In the beginning was the Word, and the Word was with God, and the Word was God. He was in the beginning with God.*

The Pre-incarnate Work of Christ: *"All things were made through Him, and without Him nothing was made that was made. In Him was life, and the life was the light of men. And the light shines in the darkness and the darkness did not comprehend it."*

The Word of God is nothing if it is not the history of the Creator's effort to preserve and protect and provide the where-with-all for His creation, humankind, to be and to enjoy what He envisioned it to be. He started human life out on the right foot - not even bringing into play those conditions of life that eventually caused Him to sacrifice the very life of the Son He begat for the specific purpose of guaranteeing eternal fellowship – humanity with its Creator. God sees fellowship between man/woman and God to be that perfect "fruit" which comes only from the branches that sprout from the vine which "grows" them, and He alone is that vine (John 15: 1-5). The vine He is, is unique (the word *holy* is reserved to describe it) among fruit bearing vines, in that the vine itself "prunes" those branches which bear no fruit. (John 15: 6), but for those that do bear fruit, much is promised and delivered.

The Architect of the Church He "made" is as described by His beloved recorder of the origin of His building (the Apostle John) the *Chief* Architect, the designer and superintendent of builders of His Creation, *the Church*. As Superintendent of builders, the Architect trained His building "carpenters" (first, the Apostles, then you and I) by the use of illustrations, *parables and/or allegories* which by their personal understanding of that which He spoke, aptly demonstrated the lessons He taught. The lesson of the vine and branches mentioned above applies equally to the Church He was leading them to build and the "members" of which it is built.

To those whom He blessed who came to believe through His builders and to dedicate their life to Him and His Church, that would be you and I, *there can be no doubt that the Architect of the Church and of this Nation/Church is Jesus the Christ.* (Remember, "without Him nothing was made," including this nation!

And in order to dissolve any lingering doubts as to who is the Architect we serve, or doubts generated by the a "yes, but what have you done for us lately" syndrome, let us add to the history of God's Holy Word, the product of a well-known, and famous witness of the Architect's work in contemporary times – even today. The witness being the senior Pastor of the member of His body known as the Coral Ridge *Presbyterian Church of Fort Lauderdale, Florida. The Reverend Doctor D. James Kennedy,* Theologian (and a whole lot more which we will get into in more depth, later) of the Coral Ridge Ministries, as he witnesses to the world the work done by the Holy Spirit through the Church he pastors. Pastor Kennedy relates that achievement of contemporary times to the timeless (Old and New Testaments) *involvement* of the Architect whose leadership we (separately) seek for the project *Sackcloth and Ashes:*

In lesson form, (extracted from a sermon delivered to the nation and to the world over television and radio) this is Dr Kennedy's witness:

According to *A.W. Tozer,* one of the great saints of the last century, one's spiritual future is discernable if that one expresses exactly what he/she "automatically" thinks about God, *because a person rises no higher than their concept of God.*

The disciples of the first century had an *exalted* view of God. The God they served and proclaimed could do anything. Their faith was: *O Lord God, Creator of Heaven and earth, nothing is too hard for thee."* And so, in response to their Lord's final command (Matthew 28: 19,20) they set out on a huge and glorious task. They were eleven men whom God had told to do a little, simple thing. *Go change the whole world!* They set out to do it; they have in great measure *succeeded.* These men, who abandoned their master at His arrest, after their first-hand witness of His having *overcome death – became so trusting in the characteristics and attributes of God that they became unafraid to undertake fantastic things.*

The Apostle Paul instructs us to remember always, that as believers in *Jesus* Christ, we are to live *supernatural* lives. We are no longer ordinary people, our lives are joined with the One who *spoke* and worlds were framed. By our Baptism we belong to the One to whom God has given all authority over Heaven and Earth and He has come to dwell in our lives with *all* His resurrection power.

It goes without saying. Living a supernatural life begins with thinking supernatural thoughts. Our "teaching" witness asks: Do you think supernatural thoughts? Are you making supernatural plans, plans that you cannot possibly bring to pass *yourself?* Are you praying for supernatural results and *expecting* God to work in supernatural ways?

E.g. one of the true heroes of the past is *William Carey.* Not too many latter-day Christians know who William Carey was, so a little "pertinent" bio would be in order" Carey was a poor, *uneducated* man who did nothing but fix shoes – but he had a dream. On the wall in front of him in his shop, he had placed a map, a map of the world. He would sit at his bench fixing shoes *while dreaming of millions and hundreds of millions of lost souls that needed a Savior; and he dreamt of a world won to Christ.* And he was not afraid to tell his fellow worshipers of his dream.

William Carey was laughed at. He was told to shut up and sit down. But he wouldn't shut up or sit down because there was this dream. And so he set out on along trip to India.

William Carey launched something two hundred years ago, that came to be called *The World Missionary Movement.* To use words of the late Winston Churchill which he spoke to the Royal Air Force, and apply them much more accurately than what Churchill was referring to when he spoke them, we can certainly say: *"Never did so many owe so much to so few."* With little support and help, *missionaries* have done the greatest work in the history of the world. Today, 200 years after William Carey set out for India, the work he dreamt of, has been planted in *every single nation on earth; because William Carey had a dream and believed that God could/would enable him to do it.*

Carey learned a number of languages. He wrote a dictionary in Indian. He became a scholar; he became one of the greatest men who ever lived, all because he believed what the Apostle Paul also believed: *"I can do all things through Christ which strengtheneth me."* (Philippians 4:13)

The witness Kennedy asks: Do you believe that? Teacher Kennedy *says*: If we could get *Christians* to really believe that, we could change the world, not merely this Nation/Church, in a much greater hurry.

It was said by a Professor of the University of Glasgow some thirty years ago (James Stewart): "If we but show the world that being committed to Christ is *not a tame, humdrum, sheltered monotony,* but the most exciting adventure that the human spirit could ever know, then those standing on the outside looking askance at Christ would *come crowding* to pay allegiance and we would be well see the *greatest Spiritual revival, since Pentecost."*

It all begins with a dream. Do you have a Godly dream? (The dream of *Sackcloth and Ashes* is such a dream.) Many people don't dream dreams. They don't have visions. *They don't lay great plans for God.* The reason they don't *could be* they feel they can't do it. *They apparently do not accept God's charge to humans to be stewards of His Kingdom.* They don't think of the condition that if God wanted to do it himself, maybe He would have foregone all the trouble to himself, coming from His Creation of humans. And in the human arena, whenever we *do* come up with some kind of a plan, *immediately* we will experience from other

113

people, comments such as: *"I wasn't able to do that before, or Oh you can't do that, or Don't be ridiculous, that will never work,- You can't, you can't, you can't."* But Paul assures us: *"I can do all things through Christ, which strengtheneth me"* – and the hand of omnipotence is placed over ours ...... We *can* do it, by faith. Making dreams come true is a matter of believing I can. By the grace of God, I can do it. That is called *positive thinking.*

Even secular world people have discovered the power of a positive attitude. It is called PMA (Positive Mental Attitude). There are some people who say it (PMA) is the *whole secret* of life. It does work wonders. But there is also a warning to be written into the motto of PMA and that is that *you can't do all things through your own strength.* There is limitation to our own ability, our knowledge, our strength, our power. *Beyond that limit* we run into things like overconfidence, delusion, cockiness and self-harm. But we *can do all things* through Christ, because *there is no limit* to His wisdom, power or ability. E. g:

Recall if you will, in the battle the Israelites had with the Philistines, how the Philistines paraded *Goliath* out and challenged the entire Israeli army. He was a huge man, a giant. All their courage, their PMA ran out. Their self-confidence reached its limit; they had ended up in despair.

Here were all those brave soldiers *cringing* in their trenches. Then along came this young *stripling* (named David) who went out to take on Goliath, saying I come in the name of Jehovah. There *is* such a thing as *God confidence*, which is infinitely better than self-confidence and with Christ, as David demonstrated – *We can do all things.*

Now let us understand that *does not mean* that anything we might attempt, even in His name, is necessarily going to instantly happen. Jesus did say: *"If ye shall say to this mountain, be thou removed and be thou cast into the sea, it shall be done."* (Matthew 21:21) That does not necessarily mean that you can speak to the mountain, furrow your brows, close your eyes, concentrate for sixty seconds and the mountain will do a swan-dive into the ocean.

It doesn't often work that way. It may, in fact, *take an awful lot of work on your part;* but it *will* come to pass. E. g. considering the experience of sailing through the Panama Canal; there *was* a mountain there at one time. But someone had the faith to say "that mountain is going to be cast into the sea." That mountain is not there any more. It didn't happen overnight, *but it did happen.* It began small, with a first shovelful of dirt; it continued through the work of many, many laborers who were attracted by the dreamers, it reached a crescendo (overcoming many troubles, even disease) – now water flows and ships sail where the mountain was *before the dream.*

The reformation dream started with a thesis was added to by people such as John Calvin, Ulrich Zwingly, John Knox, and others who, over a prolonged, troubled and even violent time, *shepherded by Jesus Christ, reformed and rebuilt His Church.*

Try it, you'll like it! If you have never dreamed a Godly dream, please do so. God has given you a mind to dream such dreams and God has entrusted to us, His believers, continual reformation of His Church with the promise that *"lo, I will be with you always, even to the end of the age."* Which brings a question: If you had a written guarantee that you could not possibly fail, what would you attempt? Go ahead and dream a dream of returning America to the Church of God, because *you do have just such a written guarantee – from The Lord God Almighty.* ("I can do all things through Christ, which strengtheneth me")

Now for a "today," a right now testimony:

Pastor Kennedy says: "Forty years ago, I dreamed a dream." That this property where now rests Coral Gables Church and other buildings used for its ministry, was a field of sand-spurs, thistles and weeds. The same was true across the street (where other buildings of Coral Ridge Ministries now stand). But I dreamed a dream of a church where multiple thousands of people would come to glorify God; where the music would lift up His name, gloriously; where they could learn the Gospel of Grace – that Christ *can* change a human heart; that He loves us *in spite of ourselves*; that He died for our sins and rose again, and is *willing to come and live in our hearts **if we will repent and invite Him in.*** I dreamed that dream (says Pastor Kennedy) and opened my eyes – and there before me was a field full of sand-spurs, thistles and weeds.

Many years have gone by but the dream persevered. By the *strength of Christ,* I continued to pursue that dream. And this day, *forty years later,* through the hard, constant work of many, many people called to that dream, *God has answered it and brought it into fruition.* "I can do all things through Christ, which strengtheneth me."

That is the word that Christ has for us today!

If that word is true, isn't it absolutely, positively, totally tragic that there are many Christians who are not trying to do *any- thing* for Christ! They have no dream, no goal, no desire, no plan, no vision, *nothing*. All they have is a guarantee that *if they did, they could not fail.* How does one explain that lack of a dream, *to Christ?*

(Doctor Kennedy made that statement as the Coral Gables Church celebrated its fortieth anniversary. In the Fellowship Hall for the celebration, there were over 1000 people {Coral Gables membership now stands at approximately 10,000, with a peak attendance of over 12,000}). Pastor Kennedy says: "and as I look back on this, there is just one thing that comes to mind:"

Doctor Kennedy's fortieth anniversary confession: "We have seen what God has done. This is *The Lord's* doing, and it is wonderful in my eyes, because most certainly I (alone) could have done *none* of what He has accomplished. I have often thought that if someone had given me a list of things He has brought to pass over the past forty years, and I read it, and if that someone had said – here is your job description for the next forty years, I would have said: you've got to be kidding, I quit. *Nobody can do that.*" Well, says Doctor Kennedy, no body *except Christ. He is the one who has done it – this is the Lord's doing and it is wonderful in our eyes.*"

Doctor Kennedy continues: "But looking ahead to the future, I continue to dream, to *another* 40 years. I won't be there, but some of you will. Here is the text of the continuing dream (from II Chronicles 25): *"And the man of God answered, The Lord is able to give you much more than this."* Much more than this is a frequent phrase in God's word.

- *"Shall He not much more clothe you, O ye of little faith"* (Matthew 6:30).
- *"How much more shall your Father which is in Heaven give good things to those who ask Him."* (Matthew 7:11).
- *"... if we were reconciled to God by the death of His Son, much more, being reconciled, we shall be saved by His life."* (Romans 5:10).

- *"For if ...... many died ...... much more the grace of God and the gift ...... Jesus Christ ......"* (Romans 5:15)
- *"Moreover, the law entered that the offense might abound. But where sin abounded, grace abounded much more."* (Romans 5:20).......... and on and on the texts go. "Much More" *God is the God of much more. "God is able to give thee much more than this."* Doctor Kennedy goes on to list eleven more and new components to his dream, including: A Church of 35,000 members; A full-fledged Christian University; The completion of Westminster Academy; A full summer camping program; A retirement complex for older ones; A home for the homeless; Facilities for expectant unwed mothers; A medical clinic for the indigent; 100 million trained witnesses for Christ, worldwide – through Evangelism Explosion which he has already founded; and, he concludes, *"I see through the mists, right here in America, a nation which has been brought back to God."*

Not every dream, of course, has to be of a feat of gigantic proportions or an "ultimate, heroic accomplishment. Using the Panama Canal or the Coral Ridge Ministries as examples, a "heroic" acc*omplishment* will more likely be achieved through the realization of many smaller, coordinated dreams.

Do you dream of the Kingdom of God to which you have been called? Do remember – Christ created His Church for the purpose of building that Kingdom on earth, while He did His part in Heaven, leaving us with the Holy Spirit)One with Him) to guide, counsel, direct and strengthen us in its building. The Church, in the form of *all the people we are commanded to proclaim salvation to, or as many as will accept Him, is the realization of His dream.* That is the purpose, that is the promise of "I can do ... "

If Sackcloth and Ashes is to have any hope of success, it must have a plan (that' our dream) *and it must have the full participation of its Architect* (that's our prayer).

CHAPTER 16
An Approach For Receiving Architect Approval

The Project Objective:
A project objective is its very reason for being. Project *Sackcloth and Ashes* is no exception. The statement of its objective is proposed as: *To return the Nation/Church called the United States of America to its founding purpose, i.e." We all came into these parts of America for the same end and aim, namely – TO ADVANCE THE KINGDOM OF OUR LORD JESUS CHRIST."*

This Nation/Church was founded and established with great and heroic effort by people called by Jesus Christ for that purpose. *Jesus Christ and He alone was is and always will be the head of this Nation/ Church.* All authority in Heaven and Earth has been given to Jesus Christ by Almighty God (Matthew 28:18) who raised Christ from the dead and set Him above all rule and authority, all power and dominion and every name that is named not only in this age in that which is to come. God has put all things under the Lordship of Jesus Christ and has made Him head of His Church, which is His body.

Christ calls the Church (including this Nation/Church) into being, giving it all that is necessary for it to achieve its mission to the world, both for its building up and for its service to God. *Christ is steadfastly present with His Church in both Spirit and Word.* The Church belongs to Christ alone to rule, to teach, to call *and to use the Church as He wills.* And He exercises His authority by using the men/women to do the work of establishing and extending His Kingdom.

The great ends of this Nation/Church are the proclamation of the Gospel of salvation of humankind; the shelter, nurture and spiritual fellowship of the children of God; the maintenance of divine worship; the preservation of truth; the promotion of social righteousness; and the exhibition of the Kingdom of Heaven to the world.

These arguments stated above are not in any way new. They are taken from the constitution (Book of Order) of the Presbyterian Church

(USA) and are proclaimed by that denomination of Christ's Body, the Church to be the "principles" under which it constantly functions. Other denominations operate under very similar tenets.

Typical of the historic cycles of the People of God when they are experiencing *trials and tribulations,* they personally (or if the tribulation is widespread enough, as a "People") submissively align themselves in "loving obedience" with God, and then when their lives begin to reap the benefits of His *blessing,* they turn away from Him and *attempt to once more go on their own.* Today's people of the Nation/Church are fast allowing themselves to be drawn away from Him who brought it into being and who has blessed them more than any people have ever been blessed. *Sack-cloth and Ashes* should be an "independent" commission, in the sense of its members being led by a Church Member who is not presently *spending an inordinate amount of time* in the higher echelons of the governing of the Church. It should have authority and resources enough to do its work. This would perhaps, equate to God's promise to Moses to send Israel a Prophet.

As prayer is made for guidance in response to the *suggestion* for this project, recognition should be given to a ministry already underway and is already attracting some exceptional, high caliber "laborers." The second of the two ministries mentioned in Chapter 13 as almost (but not quite) uniquely contributing to the intended success of its founders, those who gave their lives and fortunes to their leader, *Jesus Christ,* of fulfilling their charter, its God inspired Constitution/Covenant, is the ministry of *the Coral Ridge Presbyterian Church of Fort Lauderdale, Florida.* This ministry, which over the forty plus years of its existence has grown from seven- teen members to approximately 10,000, is led (and Pastored) by *the Reverend Doctor D. James Kennedy AB, M Div, D.D., D. Sac Lit, PhD, Litt. D, Sac Theol, D Humane Let.* Its Gospel Message is heard via Television and Radio and in printed form in more than 40,000 cities and towns in the United States and 156 foreign nations.

This ministry is well worth singling out because it involves so much more than "Preaching the Gospel" to those who "care to" listen. Doctor Kennedy founded *Evangelism Explosion International,* which is even now training laymen in evangelism in every nation on earth. Doctor Kennedy has also founded a school, *Westminster Academy,* which "allows" God into the classroom, and a Christian Radio Station which broadcast 24/7. He is the Founder and Chancellor of *Knox Theological Seminary* and the *Center for Christian Statesmanship* in Washington D.C., a spiritually based outreach to men and women in positions of authority and influence in the nation's capital. He is the founder of *The Center for reclaiming America,* a nationwide network of concerned Christians (who are) seeking to restore God's virtues to American Culture. Doctor Kennedy has authored a variety of works, including the landmark textbook *Evangelism Explosion* now in use in many languages to train *laymen* in the art of witnessing. And Coral Ridge Ministries is also a stewardship vehicle for the raising of funds necessary to wage legal warfare in reference to specific actions against those who try to force the nation, some-times even the Church half, to remove God from its decision processes.

Most of the previous discussions in this critique, in reference to the *fact* that this nation was founded to be a Christian Nation, reflect (not very well perhaps) Dr. Kennedy and Coral Ridge Ministry's pronouncements on the issue over a period of years. Doctor Kennedy gave the keynote speech in the year 2000 to the annual *Reclaiming America* conference. The title (of this message) – *Nation/Church* is an unintended, perhaps, by-product of what was learned from the ministry just described. A "write-up" of Dr. Kennedy's address is included in Appendix B to this dissertation. It will be very evident from a perusal of that speech that Dr. Kennedy and the Coral Ridge Ministry clearly view any hope of successfully proclaiming the Gospel of Jesus Christ, and of that Gospel being "heard" by those "seeking Christ with all their hearts" convincingly, as resting squarely on the ability of the Church to *demonstrate Christ's love and mercy and grace,* **by being substantively involved in the daily life and culture of God's People, including in their governance.**

It is also great news that if the political climate is ever to favor being able to reassert lost Christian *involvement* in our national government, that time is here. By the grace of God, the current president is an vowed and practicing Christian who has already begun to swing government processes and practices and appointments back our *constitutionally established* Christian doctrine. He has already made Christian appointments to key offices. It was very difficult to achieve, but by choosing Christians (who were) eminently qualified to perform the duties to which he was appointing them, he persevered against (sometimes) severe opposition and won their approval. It was necessary for those charged with approving the appointments to "hear" from their constituents before his getting that approval, but he managed it. There are still many (judicial) to which he must find qualified candidates; anti-Christian forces, even *before* any candidate is nominated, are loudly and publicly "fighting" those nominations, but with the help of fellow Christians (who are also church members) these "enemies to righteous government" can be defeated. But – if there is to be any reasonable expectation that vacant "benches" will be filled with judges who will rule on the basis of law rather than use their unique forum to *circumvent the law and illegally legislate* by their decisions, *The Institutional, Denominational, Protestant, Christian Church must become involved in the process by communicating their desires to the appropriate Senators - -* and by keeping abreast of votes on any issue which are rendered by their Representative of Senator with the idea that if any elected official *fails* to perform overall (not necessarily issue by issue) for the common good (not for special, ungodly interests) the incumbent official will not receive continued electoral support.

A suggestion:

The Coral Ridge Ministry *must* have a cadre of exceptionally qualified disciples from which could be formed a nucleus of "leaders: ministers (Ordained and/or Lay) around which the Institutional Church (combined denominations) could build a *Sackcloth and Ashes Project team.*

On the assumption that *Sackcloth and Ashes* will want to *refurbish* this Nation/Church, some basic building material will need to be made available.

CHAPTER 17
Recovering "Slightly Damaged"
Building Materials

The value of *refurbishing* rather than *rebuilding* an invaluable but deteriorated possession is in utilizing by cleaning, restoring and/or reshaping from its unacceptable condition, as much of its revered original materials as possible. So it must be that we *laborers,* who have been entrusted with its maintenance and success, undertake the refurbishing of this Nation/Church which now as always belongs to its Creator, *Jesus the Christ.* In preparation for the project *Sackcloth and Ashes,* each of the original *building blocks* will be examined, "cleaned up" and restored to original condition.

The Cornerstone:

Our "examination" affirms that the original cornerstone, *Jesus the Christ of God,* must continue in its original place and that there is no other aspirant able to replace it. *And Jesus Christ needs no restoration!*

The assertion posted above is the result of an in-depth examination of those who would, in this Nation/Church, aspire to or be nominated by unbelievers of Jesus Christ to become a new cornerstone to a vastly different (if more popular) Nation minus the church. The results of that examination were eloquently proclaimed to the congregation of the Coral Ridge Presbyterian Church in session and to the world via Television and Radio by Doctor/Pastor Kennedy. The substance of his proclamation is de-livered in Appendix B to this dissertation.

The *Founding Fathers,* following the leadership of the Holy Spirit of Christ, the Cornerstone, led the members of this *Congregation of Believers, relocated to a New World,* to risk all their worth, including life and limb, to establish this Nation/Church, defining *rules of order* (the Constitution) in order to guarantee you and I *the* freedoms which would enable us to *take to conclusion* the responsibilities they bequeathed us.

Jesus told John on the Island of Patmos to write to the Church in Ephesus: *"......Nevertheless I have this against you, that you have left your first love. Remember therefore, from where you have fallen; repent and do* *the first works, or else I will come to you quickly and remove your lam- stand from its place – **unless you repent*** (Revelations 2:4-5); to the Church in Laodicea write: *"Because you say I am rich, have become wealthy and have need of nothing ...... and do not know that you are wretched, miser-able ,poor, blind naked ...... as many as I love I will rebuke and chasten. Therefore be zealous and repent ...... if anyone hears my voice and opens the door, I will come in to him ......"*

The *cornerstone* of our Nation/Church is as He has always been, alive and well and ready, willing and able to take us through *Sackcloth and Ashes.*

But those of us who as the blocks with which He will refurbish His Church, who would respond to His call to open our very own door, *certainly do need to be re-shaped and retrained.* We, all of us, need to *trait by characteristic,* by prayerful recommitment to our acceptance of His grace and by the tempering which can only come as we re-engage in the ministry, to which we are pledged, take up our personal and corporate crosses and *zealously* pursue His goal of *salvation for all mankind.*

This reconditioning of "building blocks" has two dimensions which are both individual and common to all. Individual is, of course, between each "self" and Jesus. "Common" is where congregational ministry comes in. *The Institutional, Denominational Church, through its many congregations,* is the designated actuator of the elements of reshaping and retraining. To be successful, we must all, actuator and re-trainee, in our Jesus bought and paid for liberty, agree on the "shape" and texture of all building blocks we are expected to attach to the cornerstone.

The Building Blocks:

In any refurbishing project, if any of the old material, if any of the original specifications, if any of the time honored and traditional allure of the old is to be restored, the materially usually has to be *cleaned up and repaired* before it can reclaim its contribution to the whole. In the case of the building blocks to this Nation/Church which we reasonably expect to attach to and validate this Creation with its cornerstone, such a *cleanup* must deal with the natural substance of the blocks. That substance is *sin – personal and corporate sin.*

"......... For when you were slaves to sin, you were free in regard to righteousness. What fruit did you have then in the things of which you are now ashamed? For the end of those things is death. But now, having been

set free from sin and having become slaves of God, you have your fruit to holiness and the end, everlasting life. (Romans 6: 21–22)

Since Adam of the Garden of Eden, ALL have sinned and come short of the glory of God. The logical conclusion then has to be – if everyone in a given group, read that as a congregation of the Church, is short of His glory, then the group is no more free of the stain of sin than the most "sinful" of its members. That is a truism because in any group, the product is greater than the sum of all its parts. Or can that be true of sin?

The purpose of any *fellowship* is to build on its available strengths. We are called into eternal fellowship with our Creator. And we are called to be His presence among His people on earth. We are called to complete His earthly ministry, which is to bring salvation to God's *fallen* people. We are slaves to Jesus Christ! Can we truly free others from the consequences of their sin if we live as we did before were freed, before we were cleansed from our sin? If we are to become of any value whatsoever to Christ in the refurbishing of His Church, *we must remain free of the sin from which His death in our place, cleansed us.*

Human tendency, *and as long as we wear this earthly body, we remain human,* when we accept the freedom He brings to us, we respond with an infant-like attitude to the discipline and authority which our new *slave-master* applies to our *re-born* life.

Human infants begin early in life to test the waters of *individuality* for themselves. They probe and stretch, a very little at first the self-interpreted as very vague guidelines, not only of their parents (or if they are newly "saved" Christian adults, "Ordained" Elders of the Church) but those of "school" or society or Christian Doctrine or *"new life"* strictures as they are placed on their lives, until they (in their own mind at least) have a definitive understanding of whom or what they are or have become and in the case of physical infancy, what they want to do with *their very own life.* Note: It is in this point in their disciple maturing that the Church can best apply its developmental responsibilities.

The very real truth is, however, that testing, molding, probing, changing, trying does not really stop when we reach that "all wise" age of maturity. For most of us, *it never really stops while we are on this earth.* The "human" inner turmoil brings us into conflict with God's remaining active commandments – *love me (God) first and always, love your neighbor as yourselves and obey with all that you are these commandments.* Failure to do so is to sin.

This is what Jesus was teaching when (in John 14:15) He said to His Apostles: *"...... if you love Me, keep my commandments."* As He taught throughout His ministry, these two commandments make it a requirement to apply His teachings about believer's relationship with each other with each other and with the world.

This is the primary purpose of weekly, even *special event* congregational worship services involving those who have responded to *evangelistic outreach* of the Institutional Church. This responsibility for sustaining and/or enhancing the faith of those experiencing confusion on how to apply the eternal Word and Will of God to whatever situation has arisen to try to mold his Word to fit the situation, is what brought the Pharisees, Sadducees and Scribes into conflict with Christ. *There is a constant struggle within the contemporary Church* to justify Paul's teaching in his letter to the Corinthians (3:16) *"Let the word of Christ dwell in you richly in all wisdom, teaching and **admonishing** one another in Psalms and hymns and spiritual songs, singing with grace in your hearts to the Lord."* Hence – Jesus' parable about the lost sheep. (Matthew 18: 11-14).

The confusion over scripture comes in the name of *reforming theology by way of excusing and thereby promoting the exercise of "human" or sinful behavior,* and in effect, putting leadership zeal to work in the building up of their congregation and their denomination above the command of the Lord of the Church to make "fruit-bearing" disciples by *"teaching them all I have commanded you.*

There is no vagueness nor is there any possibility of misunderstanding God's guidelines for developing our own individual or congregational or Church identity in God's Kingdom. It is *to love God, love your neighbor love yourself.* To live, act, be or do what does not reflect love of God, love of neighbor or love of self – *is to sin!*

And God gave us the life and teachings of His only begotten Son, and will sustain us always by the counsel of His Holy Spirit, so that there *will be no misunderstanding* of what it means to love with all our being.

The institutional Church and all believers should *"salute"* and revere those "good" parents and teaching disciples and Pastors who "suffer" the trials, the seemingly constant disappointments of their offspring and/or "infant believers" who choose to ignore what opportunities for participating in Christ's ministry have been presented to them and thereby elect a totally different avocation or lifestyle of their own. I.e. Vocations or lifestyles that *"lay waste"* to the resources, time, talents and abilities of those who have sacrificed a lifetime to declaring to them the values, standards and morals that Jesus taught and *demonstrated* would be essential to those who aspire to eternal fellowship with his/her Creator. But it is also a significant part of the Church's ministry to lead those "good" parents and teaching disciples around the nooks and crannies which need to be detoured in order to bring their "lost sheep" (or lost coins) into the sheeppen, which is the Kingdom of God, all because they lack the communications from the *Body of Christ* which is inherent in the *Fellow-ship of Believers, in their gentle loving admonishment,* which Paul is calling for in his letter to the Colossians.

The sins of disobedience to the instructions of Jesus, manifested in the conduct of His ministry on earth, *are as tempting to the Church as they are to the individual.* In the Church it takes the form of "My responsibility is to Preach the Gospel, after that they're on their own." The congregation can be as immature or as childish as *any* individual. But with Pastoral involvement and training, a congregation can become that fellowship *and society* which is most likely to be successful in adhering to the teaching of the brother of Jesus, James – the first Bishop of the Jerusalem Church, which is: *"Brethren, if any of you wanders from the truth and someone turns him back, let him know that he who turns a sinner from his (sinful) way will save a soul from death and (thereby) cover a multitude of sins."* (James 5:9).

Paul witnesses to us: *When I became a man, I gave up my childish ways as I come to understand that to love God, to love our neighbor, to love our self, is to live and act and be like Jesus."* And to live, act and be like Jesus is to *give up* our now, our comfortable routine lives in order to dwell constantly and completely -- *in His Word.*

What makes Jesus unique among men is that He lived – *as a human* – in the midst of all the trials, tribulations, trouble, evil that you and I as sinners, prompted the Father God to bring upon His earth; *without any sin of His own.* Sin is the total difference between the Lord of the Church and the "building blocks" which He uses to build the Church.

He, the cornerstone, is without blemish, we the building blocks He has called to the task, are use-less to Him until we are clean-up, *but only as we persevere in our striving to remain free of sin.* (If we falter in our striving, He is our advocate before the Father to forgive us; if we fail to persevere. He is powerless to help us) *we are cleansed and called to refrain from sin.* There is a more in-depth discussion of the ravages of sin and how to stay "clean" to be found in Appendix B to this critique.

The "damaged" building blocks having now been restored to their created "mint" condition by their Creator himself, it becomes the task of the Nation/Church to whom He entrusted the completion of His personally appointed *end and aim*, to assure the perpetuity of the mission (until He states by His return visit defines it as such) by acquiring new "quality" building blocks to add to the structure.

CHAPTER 18
Supplying "Quality" Building Blocks

Specification of Need:
Jesus the Christ created perpetuity of His ministry, which is to seek out and recover all who have become lost, *"even to the end of the age."* He did so by recreating His body to the form of His Church. It is the appointed purpose of the Church to *complete* Christ's redemptive ministry. And He "upgraded" the Church's capability for successful completion, after the need arose, by founding this Nation/Church. (which is) designed to give its citizen members *all necessary freedoms* to act, without fearing destructive consequences from its government *as long as the designed structure of the Nation/Church is preserved.*

The *Institutional, Denominational, Protestant, Christian* Church started out – and continues to be – the primary source of new building blocks for its maintenance. It has the responsibility of assuring the stability of structure by assuring the quality of the blocks, which is accomplished by devising the application of God's consistent Word, Will and Way to *contemporary* life. Quality is certified by self-examination against the criteria *revealed to us* by the ministry of earth of Jesus and recorded in His inspired Word and by the *disciplining* of those individual members who show signs of veering off the appointed way – and by disciplining its corporate self.

The writer of the epistle to the Hebrews teaches:
"...... Therefore brethren, having boldness to enter the holiest, by the blood of Jesus, by a new and living way which He consecrated for us through the veil, that is, His flesh, and having a High Priest over the house of God, let us draw near with a true heart and in full assurance of faith, having our hearts sprinkled from an evil conscience and our bodies washed with pure water. Let us hold fast the confession of our hope without wavering, for He who promised is faithful. And let us consider one another in order to stir up love and good works, not forsaking the assembling of ourselves together as is the manner of some but EXHORTING ONE ANOTHER and so much more as you see the day approaching." (Hebrews 10: 19-25)

Assuring Quality Content

In the fall season of each year, a new school year begins. Parents will once more be *tempted* to pass off to "professional" educators, responsibility for passing along to our "future" – our children, whatever those "professionals" consider to be appropriate knowledge. "State-of-the-Art" in social practice, is the way too many educators describe appropriate, or perhaps more definitively: *Politically Correct.*

Why begin a discussion of assuring the quality content of the building blocks supplied by this Nation/Church for *Sackcloth and Ashes?*

One of the most open "secrets" of the cultural war which is the genesis of the severe concern of the laity of the Church that this Nation/Church is in more danger from the degeneration of the society that we depend upon the Constitution to "guarantee" than it is from the War on Terror, is the known fact that terrorists, the fanatical and "false" Muslims who are their warriors, perpetuate their ability to wreak havoc on civilization by "educating" their children from infancy in the rationale of hatred for all who believe other than what they espouse, by sponsoring schools that teach their hatred, all over the world, many of them in this nation that protects them from this nation's citizens and government; and that the society they so viciously revile is being rapidly destroyed because it is in the process of removing from its schools and its government decision processes, all that the God who brought them into being ever used to make them the formidable foe they have reason to fear, meanwhile:

We, Christian religious leaders (Pastors and elders) as well as parents, who currently function as the building blocks who are now the Church have, in effect, abdicated to educators (who are "officially" practicing as unbelievers) the shaping and the quality control of the building blocks that we are entrusted to pro- vide for the continual refurbishing, the perpetuation of the Nat- ion/Church which is our heritage. And we do so in response to the false feeling we have allowed to be implanted within us by the humanists we have also allowed to become our governors, that many, too many people in today's world believe that the *Word of God, more specifically the teachings of Jesus Christ as presented by His contemporary Church,* have become irrelevant to the "circumstances" of life as we have "advanced" them.

The very real hardship in countering the apparently prevailing feeling of irrelevancy is that first the baby boom and then the "X" (now some of the "Y") generations who are today's parents and grandparents, have gotten so far out of the "mainstream" of the followers of Jesus Christ, that it might be beyond the capability of those of us who remain in His flock, to convince them otherwise, or *so say the handwringers and doomsday prophets* among the so-called faithful, who look more to tradition *in form* of worship practices than they do to innovation in ways of developing communicating the *good news of the presence of God* in today's society, and of *salvation* being offered even to today's "lost" generations. One would have to assume that they don't believe Paul's assurances communicated in Philippians 4:13.

There is no criticism intended in the above statement to imply contemptuousness of traditional worship practices. Tradition is a very real strength in sustaining the faith of one who has already accepted Jesus Christ as personal Savior and as the cornerstone of the Church. There is indeed, *inspiration* in experiencing a traditional worship service. *That does not, however, mean that others who are caught up in "state-of-the-art" advances in the life style they are living, must be locked-out of any opportunity to accept the grace of God,* just because the "traditionalist" is unwilling to speak to them *in a language not too out of date -- for them to understand.*

The point of all this then is, it is up to *all* who accept the stewardship of the Gospel, to adapt the method of the *proclamation* of it to a form as well as a language which *they* will stop, hear and be challenged enough by that they will want to explore it themselves, under the auspices of The Holy Spirit, just as he/ she who proclaimed it to them have done all of their lives, and should continue to do. It might be well to review Acts 2:1-12, the account of Pentecost, for a reminder of how important *Peter* felt it to be to proclaim the Good News of Jesus to His people, in a language which they understood. Please note: you are urged therein to *adapt the method of the proclamation* of the Gospel to their lifestyles, NOT to adapt the Gospel itself to their likes and dislikes. *The goal of proclaiming the Gospel is to amend existing circumstances of life to God's Word – not the reverse.*

The Gospel is, of course, relevant in and of its self; it states the fact of and the means of every person ever born achieving eternal life. But the true relevance of the Gospel message is lost if those to whom it is proclaimed do not "hear" it; the *history* of God's efforts to "save" His creation from absolute destruction is nothing if not a 6000+year record of man's intransigence in *"those who have ears to hear "* Appendix B to this dissertation will present a more in-depth discussion of the need to, and the ability of the Church, *which has been entrusted with doing so,* to make it relevant to contemporary humanity.

It is an appointed responsibility of this Nation/Church to identify quality building blocks to its steadfast growth.

CHAPTER 19
Assuring Quality Input

The Apostle Paul's call for and definition of quality Ministry:

As extracted from Ephesians 4: 1-29: *"I therefore, the prisoner of the Lord, beseech you to have a walk worthy of the calling with which you were called ......<u>endeavoring to keep the unity of the Spirit in the bond of peace.</u> There is one body and one spirit just as you were called in one hope of your calling; one Lord, one faith, one baptism; one God and Father of all, who is above all and through all and in you all ...... and He himself gave some to be apostles, some prophets, some evangelists and some pastors and teachers for the equipping of the saints for the work of ministry. for the edifying of the Body of Christ that we should no longer be children tossed to and fro and carried about by every wind of doctrine, by the trickery of men, in the cunning craftiness by which they lay in wait to deceive, but speaking the truth in love may grow up in all things into Him who is the head ... ... Christ ......This I say, therefore, and testify in the Lord, that you should no longer walk as the rest of the Gentiles walk, in the futility of their mind. But you have not so learned Christ, if indeed you have heard Him and have been taught by Him, as the truth is in Jesus; that you put off concerning your former conduct the old man which grows corrupt according to the deceitful lusts, **and be renewed in the spirit of your mind,** and that you put on the new man which was created according to God, in righteousness and holiness ......Therefore putting away lying ... be angry but do not sin ...nor give place to the devil ...let him labor, working with his hands what is good that he might have something to give him who has need. **Let no corrupt communication proceed out of your mouth, but what is good for edification,** that it may impart grace to its hearers.*

Inserting Values, Standards and Such into the Building Blocks

All authority to define and describe the elements and/or the characteristics of the materials that make up the *quality of* all components of an edifice being constructed or refurbished, rests with the Architect who creates and initiates the project. The edifice of this discussion is the Nation/Church called the United States of America, an edifice in two equal parts which are described by its title; the Architect is *Jesus Christ*, who designed and through His Holy Spirit supervised its original construction.

The elements which Jesus has chosen, according to His Holy Word, are the values, standards and morals which He has communicated in a firm, consistent and straight forward manner in the whole of His dealings with His people from the time He (in His Mercy) "trained" Adam as He exiled him from the Garden of Eden. And He has consistently affirmed those values, standards and morals by the rewards He provided to His people for observing them and by the "discipline" and the punishments He delivered to those who refused to abide them.

The values, standards and morals He chooses are succinctly listed for us as the Ten Commandments which were given to Moses by God the Father, and which were validated by Jesus the Christ who taught that to obey the first two (to love God above all and neighbor as self) will automatically put us into obedience to the other eight.

We who are the Body of Christ today, have no excuse if we fail to impart them, and the "right" understanding of them, to those who will follow us as we are "relieved" from our tenure of exercising responsibility for their efficacy both in the fellowship of believers and in the society which we erroneously consider to be separate from the "Church." We tend to (or at least we act as if we) limit our interests to "within Church" life and evidence little or concern about our also God-given responsibility to create a society which lives the values, standards and morals we proclaim from our pulpits. Did not those who initiated what we now call the Reformation, at least those who fought the established Church to change – Zwingly, Calvin, Knox, et. al. – fight for a Church which would define *all* of life for those who believe?

Did not the writers of the Constitution, led by the Holy Spirit of the Architect who designed it, deliver to us a covenant by which social as well as religious life is shaped in these United States, and does it not *guarantee—**as long as Christians interpret, legislate and judge** its application to our daily lives—to the <u>Body of Christ</u>,*- ample opportunity and the means to be the dominate supervisor of its building and the appointed manager of its continued maintenance?

And let us not delude ourselves. Let us not pass the buck back to those who tempt us to qualify our quality elements. The trials, tribulations, hardships, anguish and suffering that we endure can *usually* be traced to our own resistance to the values, standards and morals which. *if we do not turn our back to them,* God assures us will attain for us the peace and spiritual prosperity and the self-fulfillment we so desperately seek in our own lives; which will provide the permanence we also seek in the Body of Christ we are. But before we go any farther, let's come to agreement as to what we mean by *vale.*

According to Webster, a *value* is something of *primary importance to us.* Not really hard to understand at all. If it is *important to us,* it qualifies as a value – *to us.* A *standard* is, for our purpose, a life action or factor by which a value receives its worth. E.g. the Feeding of the 5,000 assigned a worth to the value – compassion.

God's Plan for Perpetuating His Values in the Construction of His Church:

Now let us begin our obedience to Paul's call for the Churches he organized, to produce new building blocks for the building of a world-wide Body of Christ. We begin with an examination of the basic building blocks of the *New Jerusalem* that Christ revealed to John on the island of Patmos. (Revelation 21) It remains true that Christ is and always will be the Cornerstone, but the basic blocks which are to be attached to it, *according to any reading of God's word,* is the product of *the Believing Family.* In Genesis (2:24) God says as He completes creation of human kind: *"Therefore a man leaves his father and mother and clings to his wife, and they become one flesh."* And we profess as we participate in a wedding ceremony that *we accept God's standard* – "Till death us do part." We do this in our wedding vows, which are made to God *before making them to each other.* In Genesis God also commands us to be fruitful and to multiply – *to bring forth a family.* More than 250 times in succeeding chapters of God's Word, the *family* is brought to the forefront. The product of man and wife, according to God's plan is family, either by birth or by adoption, or even if a given "one flesh" has no child, by involvement with Church ministry re: children of another family.

God's plan is for believers to "raise" their children in the "ways of the Lord" – spelled out in detail by Moses during the Exodus from Egypt and throughout much Scripture following – thus becoming a perpetual source of quality blocks for the building.

With an extremely rare exception, most Christian congregations resident in this Nation/Church do preach and support as a high point of ministry, the strengthening of "the family." But many of them, too many of them, dilute their own ministry to families by their "libertine" definition of *tolerance* when it is applied to divorce or other than orthodox behavior of one or both parents in a (usually) vain attempt to provide "normalcy" for the children of that family. The result is that in the society that the Church is charged with (by Geneva type Reformed theology, at least) the family as a God created unit of the People of God, is seconded to *salvaging the individual members thereof.* The Church is anything but *bold* (as was Peter in "governing: the People of God as they became the first congregation of His new body on earth.) (Acts 5: 1 - 11) One of the very debilitating (to the preservation of Nation/Church) results of the Church's seconding groups (families) to the in-need individual (rather than to address both concerns at once) is the deteriorations of the entire fellowship, i.e. "civilian" society.

It is true that most congregations preach, support and encourage through "special worship observances" what is commonly called *patriotism* re: the Nation, but all except a very few of them *fail to* tie civil life into the values, standards and morals which are what made the Nation/Church into the last remaining "super- power" on earth; and it started out as a potential superpower (in its beginning) which came to be around a common (to all its sub-divisions – states) end and aim, to *Advance the Gospel of Jesus Christ, the Kingdom of God.*

There is a more specific and substantive discussion of God's concerns about a deteriorating society which He brought into being included in Appendix B to this critique of the Nation/Church He established through His dedicated followers some 250 or so years ago. The discussion revolves around Isaiah's tenure as the prophet of record who was called to reveal God's growing anger with the "free-fall" of the citizens of His first Promised Land.

CHAPTER 20
Appointing The Supplier

The Bottomless Reservoir:

In the context of the sermon *"A Family Affair:"*

All if Scripture testifies to the Creator's plan to use human disciples, guided by The Holy Spirit, to complete the work that God began in Jesus the Christ.

Spiritual writer *J. M. Nouwen,* author of more than 40 books, puts it perhaps most succinctly and clearly as he writes: "Jesus *needs* us to fulfill His mission. He needs *people* to carry the cross with Him and for Him. He came to show us the way to His Father's home. He came to offer us a new sense of belonging, to point us to safety. *But He cannot do it alone.* The hard, painful work of salvation is a work which God *chooses* to be dependent on human beings. Yes, God is certainly full of power, glory and majesty, but God *chose* to be among us, *as one of us,* as a dependent human being. Jesus is the way of dependence, of passion. He who *became a child*, dependent on the love of Mary, Joseph and so many others, completed His earthly ministry in total dependency. He becomes a *waiting* God. He waits, wondering what others will do."

Jesus came to us as a baby, was taught the tenets of the One God, the only True God way of life by His earthly father (Joseph) and His mother (Mary); was dedicated to God by the sacrament of Circumcision, as the first born *child* of Mary and Joseph. *The earth shattering world changing ministry of Jesus, whom we look to as Savior, took its first step as a human family.*

This Nation/Church's Official Human Family:

In 1992, at one of the national political conventions, the nominee for the office of President of the United States said in his acceptance speech: *"I am sick and tired of all the weeping and wailing over deteriorating family values."*

That nominee's election campaign made fun of any need for *personal character* in the most powerful office in the world. He was elected by the majority of those voting in this *Christian* nation. History has revealed how little regard he really did have for family values, as he flaunted unreasonable popularity because he is given credit for a supposed general prosperity, *which history also reveals began two years before he took office,* and which in reality, actually tears families apart by making it necessary for *both parents* to work in order to "afford" other material "blessings' – which those among us who worship worldly "things" have decided are *primary* values. President Clinton was elected by and retains an *unreasonably* high "after office" popularity with men and women of the electorate who put the *American Dream* above dreams of a perfect, everlasting kingdom, made possible for us by our Heavenly Father.

Believe it or not, I *am not* singling out President Clinton. Unfortunately, a promise of *material prosperity* will get *anyone* elected, who can convince a majority of *luxury seeking* voters that he/she can deliver on those promises, and *both political parties* pander to those who vote for personal, not necessarily over-all prosperity. Makes one wonder how the Church teaches members to obey the "pick up their cross and follow me" Christ taught in Matthew (10:38)

Three short years after the Clinton inauguration, the District Attorney of Dauphine County (Pennsylvania), in a reply to a media question about five murders in five days in Harrisburg said: "The root cause of violence in the streets, in the schools, in the homes for crimes of theft, sexual crimes and even vandalism by *younger and younger* perpetrators is *the almost total elimination of personal values.*

Within another couple of years following the District Attorney's remarks, the event where a young mother confessed to drowning her two sons was set in the tragedy of a broken family. Not only was she divorced, so were her father and mother. *No one had set for her an example of family love.* Even more, some more recent violent events, like at *Columbine High School, those in Mississippi, Georgia, California and in a Texas Church,* at the very *least* indicate a wide-spread *deterioration of family kept and taught personal values and standards.*

Values, standards, morals have been mocked, derided, decided, scorned until even the young among us *who would like to live by them, grow afraid to,* or they are shunned by their peers until they begin to wonder – *what's the use?*

And let's face it. Establishing, teaching, setting living examples of the values about which we speak, are *not* the responsibilities of schools or social groups, churches or governments, although the Church *should be* a major contributor. Since creation itself, responsibility for teaching, shaping, learning to apply *learning to apply circumstances of every-day life to God's values* has been vested in parents, older siblings, in family. Created so by God Him- self, *nothing,* not two parents working, not single parent hardship, not lack of education, not banning prayers in school, not court decisions, not TV programming, not freedom of speech, *nothing,* absolutely nothing relieves *family* from (at least the) responsibility for preserving, for building young lives on basic values such as hope, piety, morality, patience, compassion, justice, loyalty, kindness, hard work, faithfulness, love. The abundant life which Jesus promises will result from the exercise of these values. To Jesus, *the abundant life does not speak to material comfort.*

One basic that we parents (church elders are a form of parent) often forget or choose as an immediate (albeit temporary) solution to problems of children discontent is that cash allowances, or new clothes, or a new house or car, or "keeping up with the Joneses, will *never* be as worthwhile a gift or legacy as is the values which *guarantee a* satisfying and meaningful life to our off- spring. We do not *need* to be but we do *seem* to be on an accelerating to family, to national, to *belief* self-destruction. And the one institution willed to all of us by our Creator i.e. the Church, appears to be also trying hard to self-destruct. It is true the gates of Hades cannot prevail against the Church; the Scriptures and the personal word of Jesus so assures us. But any institutionalized congregation *can destroy itself,* through congregational suicide. Learned Presbyterian Theologians *warn* us that if the present trends continue, the Church *as we know it* will cease to exist by the year 2050, little more than one generation from now.

Read what Christ himself revealed to John on the Island of Patmos about first century churches - in Revelations 2 and 3.

But now, *having described the worst case,* let us look forward with some hope, with faith, with renewed resolution, to reversing what we have allowed to happen in the building of His Kingdom, the building of which God *entrusted to us.*

First, those same chapters (2 and 2) of Revelations that we cited above, *also* provide us with insight into how to renew and to build up, to strengthen Christ's Body, His Church. In that insight, let us here and now resolve to go back to the basics that brought us, *and can return us* as the People of God, as a "society" which includes in its motto "*In God We Trust*" – which can return us to the top of the heap.

Here is how those basics we would return to, originally came about.

The "Human" Family: (Remember, we are in sermon context)

Chances are there was a time not too long ago that this congregation was made up primarily of several generations of several families. A family of families, you could say. That may still be true of course, but perhaps not like "the good old days." Today, with the state-of-the-art we enjoy in travel, communications, education, technology, each succeeding generation has before it a wider variety of opportunities, in more places, sooner rather than later, than did the generation that spawned it. But truth be known, those opportunities *need not impede nor destroy family life.*

Family life may need to accommodate state-of-the-art, but it *can* still exist. Family members can still stay in touch, can still visit each other either physically or by (e.g.) E-mail, can still tolerate, support, encourage each other, can still remain "*close*" in spite of the fact that they might live hundreds of miles apart. All it really takes is, as the song goes, *a little bit of love* on everyone's part. My daughter, who is adopted, drives eight hours one way at least four times a year to visit family and retain relationships with friends; and she invites my wife and I to visit her two or three times a year. We talk to each other every week. True, sometimes it becomes necessary for us parents to *initiate* a call when it is really her turn, but that is insignificant to the fact that *we talk to each other every week.*

Basics can still apply, but they may have to be exercised under new and different conditions. They *can*, that is- IF we raise our children to understand that freedom means *that we are free to do, not free from* family values. In the "good old" days, the several generations within families *shared* their time, their dreams, their ambitions and often their work, their daily lives, as well as their church affiliations – their worship experiences. If technology *is truly* so far advanced, why discontinue the tradition?

Each family thus formed its own "dynasty." Each generation had some member, usually the eldest son (although in my family, when the sons went off to war, my eldest sister stepped in), who would take over the "patriarch's" role. This line of succession carried with it a very important set of responsibilities, i.e. to teach and preserve and to build on the family heritage. Family heritage was not delivered, *it was entrusted.* Young people learned early in life, the beliefs, the life practices of the family heritage. And they learned that those values far, *far* outweighed *personal priorities,* that even where life work did differ, *care and nurture of home base* was a *family* affair. Each generation was trained and *reasonably expected* to and to add to their heritage. The individual's wants and needs were, wherever possible, integrated into the family precepts. And it worked – at least until the ball was dropped by the family *and the family church leadership, which assumed rather poorly, the role of the Holy Spirit as counsel to families who were confronted by "prodigals" mimicking Adam and Eve in the garden,* hiding behind the guise of "*love compels me to untie the apron strings.*"

And they were required to work at it! They put their know-how and energy into building more and new successes. If their "home-stead" was a farm, the younger generation, from the time they could physically handle them, were assigned chores. After all, *they* were the ultimate beneficiaries of their heritage. They were never to be *given* the benefits. Like Smith/Barney, they were to earn them. If they were not farmers, as in my case, the patriarch in training, my sister, handed out household chores to be done while she went to work to earn money for our collective "keep." Repeating, this all worked, until families, *with church leader "compassion" and support* became discontented with the work which God assigned them i8n order to "keep" themselves and their family. They developed the "emotion" that "I want my child to have it better than I do." *The Church dropped the ball of stressing within its membership, the desirability of "working for a living" but make it secondary to Christ's Ministry.* The lessons of the congregation form after Peter's sermon at Pentecost was apparently lost to those "teaching elders."

What you and I hand out so liberally today to our "beloved' children, pleasures like movies, or TV time, or sports events, or peer activities, or trips to vacation spots were *then* awarded only after or if the assigned work was done *and* if their was money *not otherwise* earmarked for improvement of the heritage (higher education for example). YMCA and Church Camp were the biggies (more value for the money). More importantly, *real* pleasures were taught as those recognized by the family as derived from actively, effectively, importantly, contributing to life with-in the heritage. Everyone had an opportunity to be a "hero" to those who were important to them.

As *members* of the family dynasty, they took care of their own, as long as their physical capabilities permitted. When their capabilities lessened, they applied *experienced wisdom* to the well-being of their family. Their own security was in the assurance that if or when *they* could no longer look after things, the "clan" would close ranks and they, in their turn would be taken care of among loved ones *who cared*.

Each generation, having confirmed the allegiances to the family by contributing to its welfare, having been accepted as bone-fide members, responded to their own good fortunes by raising their "next" generation in the same tradition.

But then came the 1960s, often called the *rebellious* generation. Instead of *reaffirming* family values by tying them to a transfer of the qualities of their heritage *and to their Christian beliefs,* when the "baby-boom" generation became, in many instances, the first of their family to acquire "higher" education, in a misinterpreted spirit of "their education makes them smarter than me" – parents *effectively, and sometime overtly, abdicated* their responsibility to *bring them up in the ways of the Lord,* and those (many of them church elders) who claimed that *intellectual superiority* was the new hope for success, took over *and destroyed* previously learned values and standards, called "a Godly life." Those students who *had learned and practiced* "Godly" values, were scared *or "conned"* (by self-styled social scientists) into *refuting* them.

The real shame of this transition to "new" values was that many of the "name" institutions of "higher learning" were long-standing Church sponsored, whose "new age" teachers had apparently never heard of the Tower of Babel event.

Family tradition and its heritage was torn apart, destroyed rather than strengthened and built upon as a response to traumatically changing times. And, once more – along with government aided by self-styled social *experts,* in the forefront of *the agents of change,* were "respected" Church Leaders, many, too many of whom were *self-serving* "seers" of theology.

Let us now look at today's Epistle Lesson, Romans 8: 12-17:

"Therefore bretheren, we are debtors – not to the flesh, to live according to the flesh. For if you live to the flesh, you will die; but if by the Spirit, you will out to death the deeds of the body, you will live. For as many as are led by the Spirit of God, these are sons of God. <u>For you did not receive the spirit of bondage again to fear, but you received the spirit of adoption, by whom you cry out, "Abba, Father."</u> The Spirit himself bears witness with our spirit that we are children of God, and if children, heirs – heirs of God and joint heirs with Christ. <u>If indeed, we suffer with Him</u> that we may also be glorified together."

Paul is speaking to a much higher, longer lasting, permanent and infinitely more rewarding dynasty. In fact, the dynasty to which he speaks is the only frame of reference in which *any* family dynasty can prosper. *The ultimate dynasty, in which all mortal dynasties have meaning, <u>is the family of God.</u>*

You and I and our previous generations, through Baptism, were born, or more accurately *born again,* into a family older than time itself, and yet, a family that has no age. It is a family that goes on – forever. Your branch, my branch, *will forever belong.* Through the Baptism of The Holy Spirit and the resurrection of our Lord; you and I, whose brother is Jesus, will live, will honor our true Patriarch, forever.

This eternal genealogy, founded through Abraham's trusting obedience to God the Father, *affirmed and guaranteed unto perpetuity* by the sacrificial obedience of God's first-born, His only begotten Son, is the *lifeblood* of the family of God; and His family is *not* a do-nothing, rest on the laurels of the Father family. *This family, beginning with Abraham, became a People, the people became a nation*

Individual man and wife begat offspring and they together grew in numbers until they required being organized into groups of families, with leaders appointed to solve and effect solutions to interrelations problems, with rewards and penalties, with discipline and encouragement requiring participating individuals to observe commonly beneficial values, standards, morals, ways of life. And that leadership, which engendered harmony among those who followed and became its combined strength, was called government. This Nation/Church was envisioned by its founders and constructed on this pattern of governance that was given to Moses by God; was intended by the Constitution which is its "way of life" – to be governed by Christians, on the basis that its Christian populace must actively do what is necessary to appoint (elect) Christian Governors, giving them the strength they would always need in order to maintain the values, standards, morals and way of life they founded.

WE were adopted into this family because God so loved us that He searched us out by the active, very active, extremely active ministry of that love. The blood that makes us members of this eternal family is not *our* blood contained in our own veins. It is the blood *of our own Christ – transfused into us by Baptism.* The transfusion takes place as we confirm, as we come to believe, as we are, to quote John the Baptiser, *Baptized with the Holy Spirit of God.*

Our patriarch, the head of the family into which we were adopted, *actively sought us* and, without any merit of our own, received us into the only family that has absolute value. We have accepted, we are now *members of the family of God.* We *now* have all the rights and privileges and security we seek, and we *did not* have to earn them by works like we *rightly* must do in our mortal family. We are called to apply our talents, skills and energy which He imbued in us while we were still in the womb, to this supreme heritage because He made us a member of it. *We are assured:* In our re-birth into the family of God, we can constantly discover peace, indescribable joy and personal fulfillment/ contentment far, *far* beyond what we, in our materialistic short-sightedness can ever envision or attain "on our own." And in our membership, we have also been given; we have been *entrusted* with and by our acceptance have taken onto ourselves, family responsibility.

To each other, we close ranks and we nurture, support and take care of our own. We are called to new *and even greater* successes for this dynasty into which we are adopted (John 14:12). On behalf of our Patriarch we live, we strive, we *work* for success as He defines success, which is the offer of adoption to *all* His Creation into the bosom of His family – *and we do it to His honor and glory.*

God gave the blood of His incarnated veins to adopt us, you and I, into His family; when we had no merit at all. *Would we dare to assume that His interest is limited to only us?* God's Word tells us: *"God so loved **the world** that He gave His only begotten Son, that **the world** might be saved."* All the active ministry which was undertaken by this Patriarch of this everlasting family, was to bring into His dynasty *all whom He created, all whom He loves.*

God's plan, His recipe for the successful completion of that mission, calls for His Son, His agent of reconciliation, to "go" and prepare a place for us, a permanent, secure and everlasting home-stead on His ground. But before He went, He created a *new Body* to complete God's outreach to "not yet" members of His family. Christ re-created His Body, the Church, for the specific purpose of continuing *until completed,* the earthly part, the very active part of God's adoption plans for *all* His people, until He decides that all that can be done, has been done; until He returns to earth to take us to the home which He went to prepare.

It is the appointed responsibility of every one who accepts membership in God's dynasty to expend their energy at first, their lives if necessary, towards delivering in substance, His promise of eternal membership in His family, to all corners of the earth. That is the only chore of our heritage. That is why Jesus healed the sick, fed the hungry, comforted those in despair, *and charges us to do the same.*

Success of Christ's mission hinges, present tense, on *our invitation in His name* for adoption of all people into the family of God, into the very family into which you and I were re-born, with the assurance to them that all who accept will be redeemed. To paraphrase the Apostle Paul: "How are they to respond if they do not hear this "saving" news, and how are they to hear, *if we do not tell them?*"

You and I, the Church, this earthly Body of Christ, are *entrusted* to deliver this promise of God. By the way, any "success" of the message we deliver is not left to us, it is between those to whom we deliver it, and God.

If message delivery takes *all* our time, that is what any family member is called to contribute – *all* his/her time. If it takes all our energy, all our "wealth," even all our physical health – *that* is what we contribute. There is no energy, no wealth, nor health, worth the effort, *except that which honors our Patriarch.* All that we are; all that we can produce – there is no less – that will honor our God!

And to be effective, we must depend on the basics, the values, standards and morals taught us by our elder brother, Jesus. *With Him,* we all share the *responsibility* to bequeath those same basics to all people *in our nation – even to the ends of the earth.*

How do we perpetuate those values? Moses describes for us how, in his farewell instructions to the *original* People of God as they were poised on the banks of the river Jordon to enter their Promised Land:

"Keep these words (values) that I am commanding you today in your heart. Recite them to your children and talk about them when you are home and when you are away, when you lie down and when you rise. Bind them as a sign on your forehead and write them on the doorpost of your house and on your gates."

(Deuteronomy 6: 6-9)

Solomon, whom God made the wisest of all men, teaches us in Proverbs: *"Raise your children in the way of the Lord, and when they are old they will not depart from them."*

Jesus says: "If you love me, live these values I have taught you – for all of your days, for all your generations."

We, the People of God, have been appointed "supplier" of all "quality" materials with which He has chosen to refurbish His Nation/Church.

We have the Cornerstone, we are to supply the building blocks; we now look to producing a proper mix of "mortar" for the refurbishing project called *Sackcloth and Ashes*.

PART VI
DOING THE WORK

CHAPTER 21
Mixing The Building Block Mortar

Rallying the Mixers:

The Architect has fully designed this Nation/Church into which we have been called. His ministry described the building blocks of the highest possible quality, which He will accept only as *He cleanses them* and as they are *presented* to Him through *Baptism by the Holy Spirit*. He taught by actual demonstration, the process of their acquisition. He has entrusted to His Body, in the form of this Nation/Church the active building. *He has prepaid the cost of our labor.* The first construction "foreman" gave us his interpretation of the Architect's job expectations. The Apostle Paul began the "recruiting" activity in the labor pool to which we belong; it is open-ended, continuing without change to this day.

The construction *Superintendent* whom Christ left to train and to guide the mixers and builders is His Holy Spirit. The standards which He set to be employed in the building are:

"I beseech you therefore brethren, by the mercies of God that you present your bodies, a living sacrifice, a holy, and acceptable to God, which is your reasonable service. And do not be conformed to this world, but be transformed by the renewing of your mind, that you may prove what is that good and acceptable and perfect will of God .... Having then gifts differing according to the grace that is given to us, let us use them. ...... " (Romans 12:1-2, 6)

Selecting Ingredients for the "Ultimate" Mortar:

The Architect has seen to it that we have written instructions, the Bible, which identifies the ingredients that He requires, as well as those He *does not want* to mix into the "ultimate" mortar that will affix the building blocks to the Cornerstone and be the strength of His building. The specifications are such that this Nation/Church will be able to stand against any onslaught brought against it by any enemy of His mission to recover *all* mankind from the "fiery pit." The Architect identified the ingredients He will use; *He has entrusted to us their acquisition.*

The *emulsifier* which transforms the ingredients into the mortar contains two interdependent elements, neither of which can provide sufficient bonding without the other.

If one of the two can be recognized as primary, it is most ably identified within the first two of the Ten Commandments:

"...... *You shall love the Lord your God with all your heart, with all your soul, with all your strength, with all of your mind, and your neighbor as yourself.*" (Luke 10:27)

The other element is tied to the primary as if it is one and the same: Love is primary *in that it brings about the second,* which is *forgiveness,* even as it (love) goes about the task of searching each of the building blocks out of its "lost" position in the waste-heap of *potential* blocks, and "calls" each to *qualify itself* by *believing and trusting the Architect's desire to accept it, and by demonstrating that "faith" (by a complete renunciation of the failed "I'll take care of it myself syndrome), is accompanied by repentance; which results in death to worldly existence and in re-birth to new life.*

One of the very serious weaknesses in the substance of the teachings of present-day denominational Churches as they try to mold understanding in the hearts and minds of believers of a doctrine of forgiveness, is that whether they intend it or not, their presentations are burdened with more of an aura of *erroneous political correctness*-than with accurate interpretations of Biblical utterances, to wit:

Christ taught the Apostles (especially Paul, Peter and John) to include in their organization of congregations of His Church, instructions for believers to remind each other when one of them strays from what has been described to them as WWJD or if someone offends their "brother" - using language like admonish and rebuke. In (this writer believes) a misinterpretation of Paul's second letter to the Corinthians (2:18) "... *If it is possible, as much as it depends on you, live peacefully with all men*" the Church tends to substitute the word *tolerate* for *forgive.*

No-where in God's Word is there any sign, real or implied, that God advocates that sin be tolerated! Beginning with the exile of Adam and Eve from Eden, God has promised forgiveness of sin *if* the sinner confesses the sin and actively repents. That theme is carried steadfastly and consistently throughout both Old and New Testaments of Scripture. No where in Scripture is it said or imp- lied that the consequence of death for sin would ever be abolished. One of the greatest attributes of God is that He does not, once declared, change an edict, a "value." God's *Grace* is that the announced penalty of death for sin is *transferable* from him who is guilty to His only begotten Son – because as a human on earth His Son had no sin of His own – *but only if the sin is confessed and repented by the confessor.*

And the importance of "*forgiveness*" as a quality to be desired in any building block of Christ's Church, is that there is no greater evidence, nor strength, of the existence of the primary quality ingredient *which is love.* God, one with Jesus Christ and the Holy Spirit *is love.* How can any building block be more securely attached to the Cornerstone, than by the application of the same substance as that to which it is attached; the act of forgiveness is a prerequisite to the pleading by any sinner to God for forgiveness of sin: In the prayer He taught us, we know it as the Lord's Prayer, Christ phrased our plea: "...... *forgive us our debts **as we forgive our debtors.**"*

A more comprehensive discussion of the theology of forgiveness is included in Appendix B to this critique.

The Primary Element of the Mortar Emulsifier:

God is Love! The Primary element in the emulsifier that will transform the ingredients into mortar which will be the strength of the edifice called *the Church, the Temple of Our God,* has to also be – love!

As mentioned above, God reduced the statement of His required allegiance to Him by His People (the Ten Commandments) to love Him with all one's heart, soul and strength and love neighbor as self. Love is what God's People are all about. We are the manifestation of His love to all mortals, thus His Body becomes the reservoir from which His Grace flows to all who "seek" Him by name or by hope of overcoming the hazards from the very debilitating evils of this world. So it seems appropriate that we agree on a definition of love:

Webster says: 1) Love, a noun, is an emotion of affection, a state of being. *God's word* says (so does Webster 2) *Love is a verb. Love is self-sacrificial action.* In God's holy word, to love is to give!

Webster brings us to how we humans are prone to misunderstand what God's own word tells us about His loving interventions into our lives. With God, love *is always action.* The very foundation of our faith is our belief that God (Jesus) willingly, lovingly died in a terrible, horrific way for our sins; and the basis for our hope is that God, as He created man out of His love, *pre-destined* each one of us to be His, even while we were still in the womb. Our *misunderstanding* is that our predestination means that whatever happens to us is God's will for us. That erroneous belief is, un- fortunately, *double* predestination, which is *not* what God, or Jesus, or the Holy Spirit teaches, or what the holy Word of God implies.

An in-depth examination (and a theology) of God's revelation of the value *love,* is also presented in Appendix B.

The ingredients being called for in tow separate but equal categories will *only* form into the ultimate mortar with the above specified emulsifier, validated by a demonstrated test called absolute faith (i.e. how righteousness is defined); and the two categories must work in tandem for *Sackcloth and Ashes* to achieve its announced purpose.

Category One – The Evangelistic Mandate:

"Go therefore and make disciples of all nations (including this Nation/ Church) baptizing them in the name of the Father, and of the Son and of the Holy Spirit, teaching them to observe all things that I have commanded you, and lo, I am with you always; even to the end of the age." (Christ's Great Commission)

Making disciples requires that the proclamation of the Gospel be done in such a way and in a substance that is understandable by its hearers, in order that the hearer's natural reluctance to change from his/ her status quo can be overcome; and that he who proclaims recognizes that opposition to change happens as much in those who have *learned to live with less than "desirable" conditions of mortal life,* as it does with who are "convinced" that committing to Christ can only decrease their *self-made* security. Natural reluctance to change will not usually be over- come with-out firm but gentle prompting. It is axiomatic that forswearing militancy *does not necessarily eliminate* firmness in proclaiming or defending Christian beliefs – or in executing the teaching half of the Great Commission. Paul's letters to the various "infant" churches more than illustrate a need for *gentle but firm* admonition, on more than one occasion. Christ's letters dictated to John on Patmos reinforce that need.

Many of the ingredients to be mixed into the mortar apply to both categories even though they may be mixed differently in each.

The ingredients are all unique and *equally necessary* in the sight of the Architect, so they are discussed herein in random order. The laborers who are called to do the missing are also unique. They are in the image of the Architect and of the building blocks. Like Him (and them) they are called to mi the mortar, then attach new building blocks to the Cornerstone thereby becoming His product, this Nation/Church. Their mantle of uniqueness is acquired by their labor of mixing the mortar, attaching the blocks and forming the structure; becoming final and permanent as each personally stands before the Architect when the time of their task is finished.

The Ingredients:
Transformation "By the Renewing of Your Minds:"

Each aspiring laborer is "hired" by through the Sacrament of Baptism. All are accepted as, and will always remain equal in the sight of the Architect. But each is given different tasks in accordance with his/her abilities or the then present situation. All of the tasks require a process of "renewing of your mind," some of them more than others. For some, the process is called "higher education" – some are processed through "on-the-job-training (such as the Apostles, Moses, the Prophets, etc. received. All of them contain Christ's admonition to repent, be baptized by the Holy Spirit and to carry one's personal cross, the beam of which is repentance; i.e. abandonment of previous lifestyle – the mainstay being *complete trust in His Lordship.*

"Renewing of your mind" is a process of changing personal thought and attitude from "normal" human, to Godlike:

"...... Therefore gird up the loins of your mind, be sober and rest your hope fully upon the grace that is to be brought to you at the revelation of Jesus Christ; as obedient children, not conforming yourselves to the former lusts, as in your ignorance, but as He who called you is Holy, you also be holy in all your conduct, because it is written, be holy, for I am Holy." (1 Peter 1: 13-16)

Contemporary teaching by some Seminary Professors as they were leading seminars for aspiring "lay" preachers, many debaters on the floor of national and regional assemblies of Denominational Churches, sermons delivered across many pulpits, have the effect on "want-to-be" laborers, some elders, certainly candidates for ordination is that Jesus Christ *may not be* the only way to God. Such assertions rank right up there with the theory of evolution as a candidate for *false witness of the year.* Those who make such arguments, buttress them by citing the times that Christ "mixed" with known sinners, but they ignore or play down His declarations about coming to save those who are lost as well as His teachings about the weeds being consigned when they mature, to the fires. It is, apparently, their way of taking part in the Reformed, always reforming approach to interpreting the Word of God. These would (like to) be reformers of theological thought should make *some* attempt to validate their *supposed re-form* by answering, of their own "internal wisdom" some (at least these) pertinent questions:

- Could it be that the point I publish or otherwise advance is from a current need for "publish or perish" defense of my tenure, or maybe a need to make myself visible and/or a champion of a "special; interest" group which complains that Christians are being less than fair or loving, when they exclude me or my practices, which I will not give up or trade for theirs, from obtaining leadership positions in their churches. Perhaps Paul's letter to Titus also had these teachers in mind:

"......*For there are many insubordinate, both idle talkers and deceivers, especially those of the circumcision* (sounds like "nominal" believers who might believe in the *idea* of a God but have never known Jesus personally) *whose mouths must be stopped, who subvert whole households, teaching things they ought not, for the sake of dishonest gain ...... they profess to know God but through their works they deny Him, being abominable, dishonest and disqualified for every good work.*" (Titus 2: 10-16)

- Does my participation in reformation "studies" sincerely hope for finding some nuance in the presentation of the Gospels, or in the teachings of Jesus, which all the scholars who precede me in applying he original languages and their "time of Jesus" word meanings or colloquialisms to the Scriptures they interpret "just had to have missed" in their review, allowing me to communicate more clearly than does the Bible, to contemporary disciples, the message they bring. Or am I trying to enhance my ego by being credited with a believer shake-up equal to Martin Luther's discovery of Grace?
- Will the theory of the "real" meaning of Scriptures which I am putting into the hoppers of explaining Jesus' ministry, His

teachings and His commandments to all who would follow Him as a teaching preacher or as a "field laborer" really improve the likelihood of success in advancing the Gospel of Jesus Christ; or would it "sour the milk" being fed to *potential* laborers?

- Does Paul's call for "Renewing of Your Mind" address itself primarily to erroneously dissecting the words Jesus used, precisely as did the Lawyers, Scribes, Pharisees and other leaders who would not "understand" His declarations and teachings, or is the call addressed to a need to *faithfully* "take up your cross (of forfeiting the "comfort" of misguided, "permissive" theology) and (obediently) follow His teaching and commandments?

- Could my proposed thesis of theology be more in tune with adjusting traditional interpretations of Scripture in order to tolerate or excuse certain patterns of behavior, rather than require the adherents of those patterns adjust their life patterns, all of it in a misguided hope to get "sinners" to "join the Church?"

- And a final question, perhaps the most important one: How does this "Reformed Theology" point I am making publicly affirm Jesus Christ as the Lord of the Church and attest to the truthfulness of His statement: *"No one comes to the Father but by Me?"*

In the interest of providing objective and "unbiased" answers to these and other, perhaps more poignant questions:

There should be immediately conducted, by a sub-committee of the independent *Sackcloth and Ashes* "parent" commission, an evaluation of the envisioned "benefits" of public "free-will" brainstorming what the Word of God (the Bible) really means as it reports the teachings of Jesus and/or the Apostles, versus the possible harm it can do to the commitment to His ministry of those among us who are eager to accept what 2000 years of analysis of the use of the language in which they were originally written; or those among us who are *convinced* that the information which was (popularly identified as) begun by Martin Luther and affirmed by the teachings of people like Calvin, Knox, Zwingly and others of that time.

This evaluation should include the efficacy of all curricula for the education of Christians, not omitting those in Seminaries, of the curricula's contribution toward enabling them to: *"Most assuredly I say to you, he who believes in Me, the works that I do he will do also, and greater works than these he will do ...* " Educational items needed for the sole purpose of enabling all levels of "laborers" in His ministry to proclaim and to defend the Gospel, to "weather the storm" of worldly counter-attacks and to teach and admonish one another (who wander from the fold) include (again, in random order):

Church Teaching on Abortion:

In a very recent debate on the floor of a Presbytery meeting of Elders and Pastors of the Presbyterian Church (USA) concerning a call to submit an overture dealing with governmental sanction of Partial-Birth Abortion, to the upcoming National Assembly of the Denomination, those who opposed the overture did so because *"we are not qualified to determine when life actually begins."* That kind of argument within the Church not only refuses God's Holy Word. but also directly supports the Justices of the Supreme Court who refuse to now consider scientific evidence not in existence when the original Roe v Wade decision was rendered, meaning that they (the Justices, supported by the Church) believe themselves to not be bound by God's revelation of knowledge, even to correct a grievous wrong. It is tantamount to both parties living in the petulance of "since God won't reveal to man His secret for "activation" of life, we will either prevent life from occurring for those caught in the consequences of their lust, or we will authorize and encourage the destruction of the product of His creation process.

It is painfully evident that if the Church's position is to oppose abortion (at any stage of development) *it has not made the Scriptural references to "unborn child" generally known or very important to those who form and validate Church polity* (the Pastors and Elders mention above) to say nothing about someone who might, for personal reasons, be tempted to abort an unborn child. *The Church is sinfully remiss in not challenging* (using legal processes) *the Supreme Court's decision* (based on false science re: when life begins) *that murdering an unborn child is Constitutional,* E.g. Both John the Baptist and the Prophet Jeremiah were sanctified or consecrated from "their mother's womb." *"Before thou comest forth out of the womb, I* (the Lord) *sanctified and I ordered thee a prophet unto the nation."* (Jeremiah 1:5) And we are all familiar with the story of when Mary visited Elizabeth, the "babe" in Elizabeth's womb leaped for joy ...... when Mary came to her *bearing Jesus in her womb.*

(Luke 1:44). And David, in Psalm 139 (13) confesses: *"For thou hast possessed my reigns, thou hast covered me in my mother's womb."*

We seem to be reluctant to understand that God calls for man to fill the earth with his progeny, that He created woman primarily for that purpose (not here denying woman's capacity to be an equal, sometimes superior partner in man's stewardship of all creation) *and that if/when God decides enough is enough, the birth process will be suspended.* God created a propagation process (we humans call it sex) to enable man to perpetuate his work of stewardship – at his own initiative and discretion *within the bounds of God's counsel man's right of discretion.* Which means that life begins at the moment the process begins, at the moment of egg fertilization, of conception.

The combined denominations must be induced to unify (re: this issue), organize, implement and vigorously pursue educational programs aimed at people of child-bearing age and their families, designed to produce Biblical responses to the apparent public attitude that abortion is the prospective mother's choice to make. The public attitude was engendered in the first place (with church tolerance of it) by women, and men supporters, who were willing to commit murder as a means of dodging the undesirable consequences (having a child to raise) brought upon them by *sexual revolution* indulgence of *"nature at work;"* or that "pregnancy may wreck my marriage" by becoming evidence of (husband or wife) adultery; or "this is a legitimate method of population control in China (which makes no claim to be a Christian nation). Does not Biblical history record that God's instructions to the Israelites to wipe certain people (the Amorites and the Canaanites for example) off the face of the earth, which was God's response to those people's "culture" of sacrificing their own children to their idols of self-indulgence or "convenience?"

The Church, by its failure to "get involved" in public education or in the political arena, in this so-called *"between me and God"* issue in effect at least, makes a major contribution to the ability of these same civil libertarians to take away other legal freedoms such as public displays of the Ten Commandments, or Christ at Christmas, or even the practice of teaching school children to have pride in their nation through recitation of the Pledge of Allegiance.

In addition to the psychological harm likely to occur to those committing abortion *and to the family involved* and the death of the unborn citizen of the Kingdom of God, is that abortions over the last 30+ years have reduced the likelihood of people who would preserve and protect constitutionally guaranteed freedoms and rights, and in doing so to advance the Gospel, to be elected. The paradox is that the loss of personal or pet freedom is highest to those who subvert other "equal rights" to *immoral or sexual freedom.*

True Personal Freedom:

Paul wrote to the Corinthians (1 Corinthians 10: 23, 24) *"All things are lawful, but not all things are beneficial. All things are lawful, but not all things build up.* **Do not seek your own advantage, but that of the other."**

The Church evangelizes by proclaiming to "the lost" that if they but accept *Jesus' sacrificial death* in lieu of their own punishment for their sin; eternal life will be theirs for the asking, *without any necessity to earn it by "obedience to the law."* They are thus set free at no other cost or action to or of themselves, of eternal consequences of their sin.

That is a true proclamation! *But that is only half the story.* We, the Church, have become pretty weak, some "lay" persons say we are failing, at stressing what all who proclaim the Good News of Salvation, beginning with Christ himself, and emphasized by those who formed the earliest of the Christian Churches, as they added themselves as building blocks to His Cornerstone, finished their proclamation with: I.e. (To them) to believe is to *give up* (become free of) any need for continuing to be preoccupied with sinful pursuits, in order to provide for their own ultimate security. God's Word, as expressed through those early church founders, very clearly requires that *to give up (become dead to) "the world" is to place all their eggs in the one basket brought to them by Jesus.* Their key word was: *repent.*

Paul says it best: Paul says in his letter to the Romans that to experience salvation from God's wrath, you must *"… present yourselves to God as being alive from the dead….for sin shall not have dominion over you, for you are not under law, but under grace. And having been set free from sin – you became slaves of righteousness."* (Romans 5: 13, 14, 18)

It is incumbent upon the Church to continually stress within its sermons, Church conducted education programs, by involvement in daily life of members and society and by "gentle admonishment" through fellowship, *all of the responses* called for in Scripture which are part and parcel of "*believe in the Lord Jesus Christ and receive eternal life* (including actively applying Christian Values to "other than church" daily life). The freedom brought to us by the death and resurrection enables us to *completely obey the most important of the Ten Commandments: Thou shalt love the Lord thy God with all you heart and soul; and "if you love Me, keep my commandments." The love of God is satisfactorily (to Him) expressed only be each believer's involvement in the carrying out of His Great Commandment by this Nation/ Church, established under His guidance for that very purpose.*

The Church is delegated by its Architect to admonish its laborers that *freedom, true freedom is God given.* One instrument of that admonishing (Paul says to Timothy, rebuking) is the Constitution of the United States, the *covenant* by which this nation is governed. The Bible and the Constitution teach: True freedom is a matter of choice; the Church must teach that every choice which a believer makes *established the condition of his/her life on earth.* The Church must begin this teaching at the earliest possible age of the believer, because it has allowed *unconstitutional* definition of rights and freedoms (wrongly enforced by Supreme Court usurpation of legislative responsibilities to permeate public school instruction.

If a believer's choice is to enslave his/her self to Christ, contentment, God's peace (of heart and soul and mind) as well as joy, will be the conditions of his/her life. If the choice (the only other choice available) is to turn away from Christ, in the phrase used to warn the elected radical President of Iran, *serious consequences* will be the prevailing probability. E.g. If a laborer chooses to live immorally, a tarnished reputation, or social; ostracism, or a debilitating disease, or personal unhappiness, oppress- ion, horrific (sometimes a "living") death can be the consequence, and even involuntarily, the "precepts" established by God for His creation to live on earth can fail to apply e.g. even a decision to drive a car faster around a curve than is considered safe by learned engineers, can result in injurious circumstances – *But God doesn't cause an accident.* God created "natural" laws, but He gave mankind the power to reason and the freedom to decide whether or not to abide by those laws; and e.g. God "allows" a man to decide whether or not to commit a murder, or to steal, or to commit false witness, - *He also allows man to live the consequences of his (man's) decision as to whether or not he will he will "obey" the "laws" He created.*

One of the most debilitating weaknesses of Church instruction revolves around Christ's teaching: *"......if a man wants to follow Me, let him take up his cross* (of pre-born again lifestyle) *and follow."*

Celebrating the Sabbath:

God, through Moses, taught the Israelites that a very vital facet of life as God's chosen people was their *constant recognition* of His participation in their daily "comings and goings." For this purpose, God established three annual, multiple-day holy feasts to be held as a means of refreshing, reconciling, reuniting (Genesis 19:1-3; 31:54-55; 43:16-24) and the restoring of His people (Luke 15:23-24) as they encountered the *"discipline"* of experiencing life as His own People, but are still required to demonstrate to Him their faith, trust and reliance on Him as Governing Lord of their lives. This practice of annual festivals has been translated into Christian practices in the form of Advent and Christmas Day, Lent, Holy Week and Easter, Thanksgiving and Pentecost – to name some of them. All of them established specifically for the purpose of renewing the believer's relationship with God.

But *before* any of those feast were "appointed" by God, He established a weekly opportunity for His people to renew/refresh ties with Him – He was even the first to practice the weekly celebration – *" ...... on the seventh day, He rested."*

Like too many individuals from our "cohort" of Christians, the Institutional Church, or many of its denominations, has relinquished the blessings of celebrating the *Sabbath* to "modern," fast-paced, state-of-the-art," *corruptible of this world's "necessities"* for "personal" renewal. Again, by its reluctance to highlight God's promised abundant life virtues, (most likely because "we can't compete with what is "available" to modern man) the Church has corrupted God's intended blessing to man via a recuperative Sabbath; and in the process, tarnished man's "picture" of his Lord and His God. Perhaps this is one of the reasons that Shop- ping Mall parking lots are much more crowded on the Sabbath than are the Church's. (Recognizing that non-believers will never "allow" reinstatement of *Blue Laws,* the Church must simply *discourage Sabbath Day Shopping* by its members.

In order to prevent man's "burning out," the Church must reintroduce those fellowship practices, perhaps a more modern version of them, which kept a believer's eye focused on his/her relationship with God and his fellow believers, placing in plain sight of all believers evidence, of God's mercy, love, care and grace. Practices (which can also be enjoyed on week-days) such as Communal Meals, Quilting Bees, Discussion Groups, Prayer Groups, Outdoor or indoor Picnics, Hymn Sings, Peer Group Gatherings in the Church Fellowship Hall or at private homes, Hobby Meetings, or any of the other activities (surely there are many more) *which are dedicated to the glory of God and in thanksgiving for the abundant life, delivered by God.*

The Stewardship of God's Believers:

Jesus Christ and all His Apostles focused a major portion of their "Disciple teaching/equipping" time in laying out for all would-be followers and advocates of Christ in the arena of God's practice of appointing "man" to do the work of establishing His Eternal Kingdom – describing the qualities and characteristics, the necessary virtues such a disciple of the Church must have. One point stands out above all others as Jesus and the Apostles teach stewardship of "the Body of Christ. That point is that stewardship is total commitment of all that is a steward's life, not merely money or possessions, but the time, talent skills, the very life of the "steward."

Especially when added to his call for followers of God, in Ephesians 6, to put on the full armor of belief, perhaps the most eloquent of such teachings re: "steward" members of the Body of Christ, is Paul's, as he writes to Timothy as his mentor, after he appointed Timothy to "Pastor" the Church in Ephesus, concerning who he should *avoid* in seeking men to appoint to the offices of Elder, Deacon or other "principles" of his Church building ministry, as well as the qualities/ virtues Timothy should try to implant into all whom he will convert to the Way of Christ:

"......*he is proud, knowing nothing, but is obsessed with disputes and arguments over words, from which comes envy, strife, reviling, evil suspicions, useless wrangling, of men of corrupt minds and destitute of truth, who suppose that godliness is a means of gain. From such, withdraw yourself.*

Now godliness with contentment is great gain. For we brought nothing into this world and it is certain we can carry nothing out ...... But those who desire to be rich fall into temptation and a snare and into many foolish and harmful lusts which drown men in destruction and perdition. For the love of money is a root of all kinds of evil, for which some have strayed from the faith in their greediness and pierced themselves with many sorrows ...... Command those who are rich in this present age not to be haughty nor trust in uncertain riches, but in the living God who gives us richly, all things to enjoy. Let them do good (with their material gains) that they may be rich in good works, ready to give, willing to share. ..." (Extracted from Timothy 6)

He who "prepared the way" for our Lord, (John the Baptist) told us how important it is to God that we share our material wealth. He did this as he was preaching "repent and be saved" in his wilderness "church," even *before* he ever came face-to-face with his cousin – Jesus: *"So the people asked him, saying, what shall we do then? He answered and said to them, He who has two tunics* (Notice he did not say two coat-racks full) *let him give to him who has none, and he who has food, let him do likewise ...... do not intimidate anyone or accuse falsely, and be content with your wages.* (Luke 3: 11-12, 14)

Compare John's teaching on sharing your wealth with the almost universal reluctance of today's preachers to stress to those who would be Disciples of Christ, the Biblically stated demand of God that all believers tithe of the fruit of their labor. And please note that the definition of John if the wealth your must share, is very different than is the definition in vogue today, where much of our teaching, even within our Christian Fellowship, is don't forget to put enough away for a "rainy day." Contemporary teaching seems to forget or at least down-play the teaching of Jesus about the rich man who was going to build bigger and better barns to hold his abundant harvest. (Luke 12: 16-21)

The damage of foolhardy reluctance to teach tithing and overall stewardship as a method for carrying out the Church's responsibility to proclaim the Gospel by making the loving providence of God *tangible* to His People and to His enemies, can be measured by the extreme amount of taxes demanded by governments and dedicated to the *glory of the" head of government"* or to other than Church benevolent organizations in place of *to* the *Glory of Almighty God.*

There is no naiveté here. Of course the government, as well as some secular "relief" agencies have already established infrastructures for caring for those in need. But those infrastructures became much more than "obstructions" to Nation/Church ministry, as the reluctance of "disciples" to share their wealth causes the Church to abdicate "in the name of God" out-reach to secular efforts to save the "poor and destitute" from suffering and pain. there is a paradox in relying on these other infrastructures, and that is that the major portion of "personal wealth" that would be otherwise allocated by taxpayers for that avenue of relief, is exp- ended for the paying of inflated wages of "professional" administrators, leaving so much less available for those who are doing the suffering; in turn *deemphasizing* worshipful and loving thanksgiving in the hearts of those who give, and most surely in the eyes of those who might be inclined to glorify God as they receive these "blessings." A Case in point would be the upheaval in disbursement of funds by the American Red Cross and the "mismanagement" of funds by the exorbitantly overpaid executives of the United Way.

The Institutional Church can enable its member disciples of "the Way" to *experience* the love to which God calls His followers, and can at the same time *reduce individual tax burdens* by firmly calling for *and implementing* an efficient ministry of tithing and can enhance its proclamation of the Gospel by an on-going, continuous *Public Relations* (not merely publicity) program which makes known to all what Christ *through His Body the Church* does directly for recipients, in the name and to the glory of God – including what the Church does in support of those "secular" help agencies that become expedient in response to disastrous happenings.

A key to God's attitude toward believers giving from their "hard-earned" treasure can be discerned in Jesus' teaching on discipleship in Luke (14:44): ...... *So likewise, whoever of you does not forsake all that he has – cannot be My disciple.*

And stewardship, as taught and practiced by Jesus and the Apostles, is not limited to sharing material wealth by believers!

If the Church is, as Jesus defined it, His Body, and if as is widely believed, the Church of this Nation/Church is, *by electing to not get involved* in governmental struggles to protect its ability to function and to *advance the Gospel of Jesus Christ* in the every-day lives of its present-day believers, then this "congregation" of believers is in very real danger of *self-destruction of this member of His Body!* The need for tithing *includes* the contribution of time, talent, skills and energy to the ministry for which this Nation/Church was brought into being.

There needs to be a nation-wide, all Church participation in a legal defense *and/or political campaign fund* for use in combating a very real and unbelievably effective, organized and on-going campaign to *eliminate God and the teaching of His precepts,* not only from all governmental decision processes, but from the hearts and minds of our daily lives. The battle is already begun, it is being waged in the courts in front of Judges who are being persuaded by "professional" educators and *self-acclaimed intellectual* theologians who use false witnesses and fabricated scenarios and faked privacy and "culture" issues, sustained by contributions from "patrons" with illicitly gained (in terms of ethical business practices) wealth. This on-going battler is against the only realistic, dedicated, current efforts of the leadership of this Nation/Church *to safe-guard the four freedoms guaranteed by the Constitution for its citizens by which they are to live in peaceful obedience to their calling.*

The "good guys" who are bringing this battle to "the enemy" in the name of Jesus Christ are those participating in the ministry of the Coral Ridge Presbyterian Church and the programs it supports to that purpose (discussed earlier). The "enemy" warriors in this battle for survival of this Nation/Church are organizations like the ACLU and pseudo religious organizations which espouse separation of Church and State by the removal of God from governmental deliberations, citing *false* historical evidence of the Founding Fathers intent and an absolute lack of understanding of Jesus' and the Apostles' teachings. (Legal use of such funding for political campaigning is discussed within the Cultural Mandate section of this report) The recommendation is:

All Institutional, Denominational, Christian Churches should rally to this vital ministry saving mission by providing funds to the New Christian Liberties Task Force for Reclaiming America, sponsored by Coral Ridge Ministries – previously described.

A more exhaustive discussion of Stewardship of Christ's Kingdom is included in Appendix B.

Making "Fruit Bearing" Disciples of Jesus Christ:

In keeping with God's assurances to His people, disciples *are* predestined while they are in the womb. But *by-and-large,* disciples achieve their discipleship assignments as they become *"one who will come to believe in Me through their* (other disciples') *word"—and* as they actively accept God's call. This is the means by which the Creator of this Nation/Church has chosen to sustain the structure of His Church. The earlier in a disciple's life that he (or she) begins to hear "their" word, the earlier that disciple will begin to bear the fruit of the Gospel of which he or she has accepted stewardship. And the more accurate and the more truthful and the more "big-picture" the word that they hear, the more fruit will he/she bear.

In order to counter the debilitating effects of *politically correct* and anti-God reaching being force-fed to future disciples today, the Institutional Church must assume financial *and operating* responsibilities for enacting and sustaining *two* programs of education for our "hope for the continuance of our ministry – today's disciples to be. The following, the first of two described, has become critical for Church intervention, because of the *preponderance of half-truths* and the resulting stress on the "less than contributory" (to the achievement of the "ends and aims" of this church building) characteristics of selected "founders" by Public School "educators" in their hiding of the *"total picture" historical truths* from the young students upon whom rests the hope of Christ and of the Nation/Church. Which they do in a deliberate and blatant attempt to destroy that hope! (The second of the two programs will be discussed under *The Cultural Mandate,* following) *These programs must take the form of Sunday Church School classes, Youth Forums* (such as planned gatherings and/or Web Site Chat Rooms or retreats), *many more Non-Denominational "K thru 12" Parochial Schools, Seminars, News Letters, and/or other avenues of communications not mentioned here.* Courses of action must include:

- The true history of the founding and of the founders of this Nation/Church; its ends and aims. This history should emphasize the *overbalance* of the positive accomplishments of the individuals involved against what is now stressed, I.e. The "negative" aspects of their lives and personalities. (Perhaps it could make comparisons similar with what the Bible does with *every human called and used by God,* from Abraham to Paul.) What is taught now implies that "good" history has no value because he who wrought it was not "obedient to law" perfect and we would be better off living the life of pre-event conditions.

- The responsibilities *inherent* with the exercise of God-given and constitutionally guaranteed freedom or liberty, with particular emphasis on rights versus duties; emphasizing *Word of God* teachings relative to rights and duties concerning *free speech"* by applying James' discourse on *tongues* as a guideline. The Church must recognize, teach and practice that the Constitution of this Nation guarantees that speech is to be protected from *government* penalty or intervention, *not from any adverse (albeit peaceful) responses (including economic reactions) by fellow citizens.*
- Accurate explanations of definitions and of acts of *tolerance* under the Constitution are in accordance with Christ's teachings.
- Leadership courses designed to identify and encourage candidates for ordination, theological, specific church education (Public and Christian) *and governmental (including elective office) careers.*
- Across-the-board – ways and means of evangelizing without not excepting family members and "next-door neighbors. The Church must reach out from its traditional "safe-haven" and/or "block home" ministries for *seekers f God,* and become the *grace of God,* like Jesus did when Peter declared his understanding that Jesus was the Messiah, *to those who probably don't even know they need Jesus to come into their lives.*

Utilization of "Already on-Board" Disciples:

A theology of discipleship: The Gospel according to John (3:16) assures us that, in His mercy and at His election and *if* we believe that His sacrificial death was acceptable to God and to us, we belong to Him and will live with Him – *forever.* We are accepted as His disciples *and it was free to us for the asking* – He even (its called Grace) prompts us to ask.

God (s)elected us to be His disciple while we were still in the our mother's womb, and (He) comes to us and accepts us into His "fold" of disciples *as we are Baptized with water and the Spirit.* God accepts us as we are – sinfully short of His glory. We were not "elected" on *our* merit, we have no, *we cannot ever of our- selves attain merit;* **not even by serving as His disciples. We thus become heirs of the Kingdom of God, by His gift of grace alone.**

It is therefore not to *attain* salvation that we become His disciple. We become fruit (or the Gospel) bearers out of the *joy* of our certainty that we have already *and irrevocably* received the salvation we seek. We therefore (are expected to) zealously *participate* in His ministry by *actively* filling *by thought, word and deed,* whatever void there might be in the congregation with which we are "voluntarily" affiliated.

One of the greatest potentials for this Nation/Church's self-destruction is the current organizational tendency of institutional Protestant Christian Churches to *overburden but under-utilize* "professional" disciples who are already in the field.

E.g. *Ordained Pastors:* There is present, wide-spread and constant concern about vacant pulpits in up to 40 or 50% of existing congregations. Many, but by no means all of these congregations are small (less than 100 members) and rural, where *yoking* two or more of them in order to "afford" a full-time Ordained Pastor has *not been* successful in satisfying congregational needs, nor in ministering to the "host" community – nor in advancing the Gospel of Jesus Christ *within that host community.* There is also demonstrable evidence that within Denomination Church "regions" as well as local hierarchies there are purposeful, disguised efforts to "protect" the *Office of Word and Sacrament* by unnecessarily restricting use of *specially trained Ordained Elders* to provide the missing Pastoral leadership. The effort, historically, takes the form of :"burdening" Ordained Pastors with ministering to several groups of Christians (congregations) who have diverse interests, ministerial programming or "host" cultures, which creates a real danger of subjecting the Pastor with a "Jack-of-all-trades, master-of-none" syndrome. The chosen "disguise" seeks to make Denominational Identification more important to *advancing the Gospel of Jesus Christ,* than is the (Christ) intended purpose of *baptizing them and teaching them.* The disguise is made more impenetrable by enforcement (by the "professional" authorities who recommend the approving criteria) of training which is unnecessary and otherwise generally useless (to small congregations with limited resources) elements of congregational ministry.

Small congregations just cannot come up with enough of the disciples required to formally organize and conduct the variety of elements which are collectively called for by the mission of the Church, on a scale for them each to merit recognition as an effective ministry. *Most of those same elements are informally achieved, however, by the small congregation acting as a "committee of the whole" – ministerially speaking.*

One approach for short-handed (in terms of Ordained Pastors) Denominations to solving the vacant pulpit dilemma is:

1) Where a specific congregation is large (or wealthy) enough to support a full time Ordained Pastor, provide one.

2) Fill vacant small-church Pastoral needs with specially trained Elders willing to take on that ministry, even in addition to their "Tent Making" activities. Back them up with full-time mentors who are Ordained Pastors, who will also be charged with evaluation of both the ministering elder and the ministry of the congregation, and with providing "continuing" education in those elements of ministry that will rarely be called for in that specific congregation (weddings, baptism, etc). The Ordained Pastor will thus be able to effectively apply his/her "superior" education by "mentoring" a group of elder/pastors while answering his/her call to Proclaim the Gospel by either rotating preaching opportunities within the group, or by "supplying" within the region.

3) Provide training in *mentor* skills to those Pastoral Candidates in Seminary, who would be interested in that kind of ministry; e.g. Leadership, Problem Solving, Group Stress Management and/or other useful to that type of ministry.

4) Emphasize, from pulpits, the points that Paul makes throughout his letters, that it is incumbent upon *all believers* to search out (with the help of their church elders) and to identify the skills, talents and abilities with which *they* are endowed by their Creator, hone them to their most effective possibility, and apply them to the congregations ministry, *and do it to the glory of God.*

The Denominational Church must also admit within its membership, and educate the man/woman in the pew, that *Christians* who elect to serve in government at local, state or national level, whatever may be their role, *are also fruit-bearing disciples of Jesus Christ —as they do whatever they do, to the glory of God.* In truth, these "Servants of the People" could be recipients of an exceptional call to discipleship which is involved in the 'nation" half of this Nation/Church.

The lessons that need to be learned by *the Church* and ingrained into all citizens of this Nation/Church are revealed to all in the Old Testament Books of Kings 1 % 2 - *how evil rulers brought destruction to the nation of Israel and its people.* The guiding principle for whether to (or how to) make the effort to motivate (in the name of and to the glory of God) believers to *become involved,* is found in James' teaching (4:17): *"...... Therefore, to him who knows to do good and does not do it, to him it is sin."*

God himself says, in that context (2 Chronicles 7:14): *"...... If My People* (extend this to the Nation/Church He created) *who are called by My Name will humble themselves and pray, and seek My face,* **and turn from their wicked ways,** *then I will hear from heaven, and forgive their sin and heal their land.*

And it is also important for the Church to include in their preparation of disciples to assume public office, all that will help or enable them to *overcome the historic tendencies of humans to* **abuse the power they are given to govern.**

"Political" Involvement in Personal Values Issues:

It is incumbent (within Christ's design for His People) for the Denominational Church to rally His People to *actively safeguard* adherence to Biblical instructions concerning values issues being presented for legislation, or which require remedial action because the "slipped through" the Biblical filter. Again, one of the most likely to be successful safe-guard is put Christians in the offices of all three branches of government. And once more, *there is no recommendation herein that "the Church" by any organizational identification, should become a part of the governmental process.* In fact, the opposite has been stressed throughout this dissertation. *There is an admonition that the united church (including non-Christian supporters) must become major input to the processes.*

Legislative Issues Necessary for Safe-Guarding Include:

*Capital Punishment	*Evolution taught in Public Schools
*Economics	*Education (Especially American History)
*God and Government	*Homosexuality
*Marriage and Family	*National Defense
*Parental Rights and Duties	*Pornography
*Religious Liberty	*Sanctity of Life
*School Prayer	*Secular Humanism

The Church must begin *now* to take their positions "Officially" and publicly: *There should be an office in every Denomination of the Institutional Christian Church responsible for coordinating with the others, scriptural "instruction" in God's "input" to the issue or value under consideration, and a translation of those scriptural instructions into "pragmatic" definitions of harm or benefit where warranted.* Some of the actions they should under- take include: Media Releases (Bought if necessary), "Special" epistles to the Churches and local governing boards, Focus Group gatherings of Pastors and Elders – if the case has reached the necessity for "critical intervention," organization of peaceful public protest and/or fundraising.

Individual and national Morality:

It is widely said, mainly by would-be Church leaders who mistakenly advocate separation of God from government decision making, that it is possible to have morality *without* religion. Already presented in this treatise is *evidence* that the founders of this nation and the crafters of the Constitution *neither believed nor advocated* that premise. America's first president, the one who is credited by everyone except current publishers of history books along with public school teachers, as being the *(founding) Father of our Country,* said this in his farewell address about that foolishness:

"...... *of all the dispositions and habits which lead to political prosperity,* **religion and morality are indispensable supports.** *In vain would that man* **claim the tribute of patriotism** *who should labor to subvert these great pillars of human happiness* ...... *and let us* **with caution** *indulge the supposition that morality can be maintained without religion"*

There are now existing, tragic results of prolonged "*labor to subvert*" that basic premise. For more than twenty-five years, the children attending our schools and colleges have been taught that there are no moral absolutes; that *no one can tell them what to do.* They (the children and those in training to teach them) are told simply to choose their own ethics. In the last book of Judges, we read: "...... *every man did what was right in his own eyes.*" (Judges 21:25) This was the culmination of the Israelites' history of immoral living, living according to the "aliens" they allowed within their society. – And the warnings of Joshua to the people, that God, in His anger vowed to no longer drive out from before them, any of the nations which Joshua had left when he died. Joshua 23: 13 came to pass.

James Driscoll says, in talking about our young people who have experienced this fallacy in education in recent decades:

"At their core, there is nothing. At the moral center of many young Americans aged 18 – 30, there is a vacuum, and it is a nearly perfect. It contains *none* of the bedrock ethical values long considered essential to living a decent life. Honesty, personal responsibility, respect for others, civic duty. Instead, this self-indulgent generation passionately only in this: *It (the generation) is entitled.*

It must be said: The Institutional Church *does* describe moral and ethical attributes to those who happen to come in their door searching for *inspirational* answers. The Church does woefully little though, in using the teaching techniques used and advocated by Christ and His Apostles to "truly" make the point; i.e. living examples, *gentle* rebukes, pertinent admonition, and description of the *peace* which comes to those who live within those attributes.

The results these deficits in education of the young are overwhelming (or should be to those who hear the call of Jesus in the Great Commission). Committees of the U.S. Senate and the House of Representatives who are studying the moral situation in America have come up with these appalling results:

- Suicide is now the second leading cause of deaths among adolescents, increasing 300% since 1950.
- Teen pregnancy has risen 621% since 1940. More than a *million* teenage girls get pregnant each year. Eighty-five percent of teenage boys who impregnate teenage girls eventually abandon them.

(This is undoubtedly one of the major causes of "murdering" our unborn babies)

- Every year, substance abuse claims younger victims with harder drugs. The average for first-time drug use has now lowered to 13 years of age.

Non-believing humanist have, in contention that *you don't need religion to live morally,* have drawn up a set of ethics in the *Humanist Manifesto.* But what people who accept that manifesto fail to realize is that *they have turned Christian ethics* upside down, and have taken everything that has been considered immoral for centuries *and declared them to be moral.* Their set of ethics condones gambling, divorce, suicide, free love, fornication, adultery, incest and a number of other things – all of which *for centuries* have been considered immoral acts.

The *tolerant* response is (unfortunately even by many "devout" Church leaders) that *"our morality cannot be imposed on others."* Believe it or not, that is a true statement. But it is not *"our"* that the Church should be championing. The command of the Great Commission said: *"...... and teach them to observe all that I have commanded you."* In insisting on its policy of *"we can best carry out the Great Commission by not involving ourselves in government,* or by putting our involvement on the back burner, once more, the Church is guilty of not practicing James' lesson: *"Therefore, to him who knows to do good and does not do it, to him – it is sin."*

One measure of the perfidy of Church leaders in their response to the call of Christ to be involved in every-day life of His People, is that not only do they discourage the disciples to the Denomination they "shepherd" when it means becoming a participant in the governing of the people, they actually teach them and help them to *disobey* the legitimate laws of the land that hosts and protects them, in which they *refused to assure God's Holy input.* It is almost as if the Denominational Church *disavows* those portions of Peter's and Paul's letters to the churches which they set up. I.e. 1 Peter 13-17; Hebrews 13: 1-6, 17.

The Institutional, Denominational Christian Churches (some Evangelical churches already do it) should organize a nationwide and international boycott of products from those companies who sponsor TV shows featuring "off-color" lifestyles or events; and should begin immediately, with "reality" shows. This would include most present-day "prime time" shows – called "family comedies."

All Churches should immediately instruct the Seminaries and Bible Colleges with whom they are affiliated, to, in a crisis mode, add to their courses of study, reasons *for* and means *to* remedy current, debilitating (to the People of God and to His glory) recalcitrance of Church leaders to emphasize the carrying out *of the teaching portion* of Christ's Great Commission.

Paul, in his epistle to Roman Christians who were having this same battle with *secularist neighbors* and the government, *exhorts them* to proclaim the Gospel and defend its teachings by living righteous lives – individually *and* corporately. In the opening chapter he writes:

"...... professing to be wise, they became fools. Therefore, God gave them up to uncleanness, in the lusts of their hearts, to dishonor their bodies among themselves, who exchanged the truth of God for a lie, and worshiped and served the creature rather than the Creator, who is blessed forever. Amen"

Paul to the Romans continues: *"... and even as they did not like to continue God in their knowledge, God gave them over to a debased mind, to do those things which were not fitting, being filled with all unrighteousness, sexual immorality, wickedness, covetousness, maliciousness, full of envy, strife, deceit, evil mindedness, they are whisperers, backbiters, haters of God, violent, proud boasters, inventors of evil things, disobedient to parents, undiscerning, untrustworthy, unloving, unforgiving, unmerciful, who knowing the righteous judgment of God, that those who practice such things are worthy of death, not only do the same,* **but also approve those who practice them.**

There is one final point concerning the Evangelical Mandate that this writer would make to the "laity" of the Institutional, Denominational, Protestant Christian Church. It is made here with no intention whatsoever of discarding, dissolving or otherwise causing harm to the Church, to the work of which we devote our human life. The point is this:

The first Church that God organized, the Church to which He called Abraham to be the human head, eventually became a "favored Nation" and remained so as long as the people dedicated their loyalty to God, no matter how badly they were from time to time in living His precepts. As long as they tried, they remained in the "blessings" of His Favored People. They ran into "real" trouble when their "professional" leaders, the Pharisees, the Sadducees, the Scribes and the "ruling" junta, the Sanhedrin, became corrupted and began to "interpret" the Word of God to their private material and social benefit. The Church which Jesus Christ organized as He concluded His earthly ministry, the Church on which (as He told Peter) He built on the rock called "faith" rested on a newly defined understanding of the Word, Will and Way of God which He channeled to the People of God, through the then existing laity. You see, Peter, James, John, and the others, were laity when Jesus called them. It was not until after they were called, served an apprenticeship and accepted their assignment, even within its threat of mortal death, that they were empowered and commanded to complete His earthly ministry. And this they did with historical success, at least they set it up so that their successors could complete the task.

They were laity? The existing hierarchy of the Church which they were risking life and limb to "update," thought so. Remember when Peter and John were before the Sanhedrin on charges of preaching false doctrine? Were they not released from "trial" because they were uneducated and untrained in the Scriptures, in the minds of their judges, and so considered to be harmless to the life and welfare of "the Church"? (Acts 4:13) Peter and John were "left go" from trial with instruction from the Church that was, to never again proclaim Jesus Christ.

Peter and John (and later, Paul) along with all the then congregated followers of Christ, denied the Church superiors' jurisdiction over their proclamation of the Gospel, and went forth and changed the world by speaking boldly of the Lordship of the Christ who lived within them and of the salvation to all that He would deliver. (Acts 4: 31)

Category Two – The Cultural Mandate:

As we have already discussed, many – if not most – of the social concerns of importance to the *"daily life"* (the Nation) half of this Nation/Church are equally important to the first, the Evangelistic half. Remedies for the issues that have already done major (and threaten to do more, perhaps fatal) harm to America, are *taught* in God's Word, and are reinforced in the Constitution with which the Church half is so reluctant to *commit its resources to actively defend.* The Great Commission of Jesus Christ clearly *mandates the involvement of Christ's believers* in the affairs of state. From the time God selected Abraham to spawn His People, God set-up the precepts which would make of them a society to become known as His People ... and the Great Commission says "and teach them all I have commanded you." The Commission *does not mandate the involvement of any given Denomination of the church – it does mandate involvement of CHRISTIANS* in governing the (His) people. Thus, as we have seen, said the Founding Fathers in the "start-up" – and thus has said the highest legal authority from the beginning and from this end of the historical spectrum:

But what is seen from the contemporary Church is – succinctly stated: The Church steadfastly refuses Christ's injunction to establish a society which models His precepts, preferring instead to become the cause of societal conflict by leading their disciples of peace to *"civil" disobedience. The Church thus intentionally brings about not peace, but anarchy.*

George Washington, speaking as perhaps the "most involved" of the Founding Fathers, said as he was bidding farewell to the governance of the nation of which he contribute so much to the building: *"Without religion and without morality, **no government will long endure.**"*

William Rehnquist, who served for many years as the Chief Justice of the Supreme Court of these United States, said: *"There is simply no historical foundation for the proposition that the framers intended to build a wall of separation ...... the "wall of separation" between church and state is a **metaphor based upon bad history,** a metaphor which **has proved useless** as a guide to judging. **It should be frankly and explicitly abandoned.**"*

The truth is, however, that if Justice Rehnquist's opinion is to become legally valid, since the Supreme Court is not likely to take its own action to overturn the previous (1947) decision which established the "wall" *– the Church must take the initiative in causing its abandonment, by bringing action to the court.*

The need for the Church to "come out of the closet" and rally its believers to the saving of this Nation/Church is summarized within a historical perspective in the final "thoughts" presented in Appendix B.

The historical frame of reference for this United States of America to be a Nation/Church is solid and irrefutable. But the only frame of reference *with meaning* is described in Isaiah's Prophesy to Israel, as he warns them of their impending destruction as a nation.

In chapter 56, God tells Israel through Isaiah, that all foreigners and sons of foreigners, even as they come from another country or another culture, *every one who accepts ... and holds fast to MY covenant, even them I will bring to My Holy Mountain and make them joyful in My house of Prayer.* In chapters 57 and 58, Isaiah is constrained to warn Israel of the consequences of failure, even as he re-informs them of the blessings of true worship:

Extracted from Isaiah 58: *"...... Cry aloud, spare not, lift up your voice like a trumpet. Tell My People their transgressions. ...... Is this not the fast I chosen to loose the bonds of wickedness. To undo the heavy burden, to let the oppressed go free; and that you break every yoke? Is it not to share your bread with the hungry; and that you bring to your house the poor who have been cast out; when you see the naked that you cover him and not hide yourself from your own flesh? Then your light shall break forth like the morning ...... then you shall call and the Lord will answer; You shall cry, and He will say, "here I am."*

"If you take away the yoke from your midst; The pointing of the finger and the speaking of wickedness; If you extend your soul to the hungry and satisfy the afflicted soul – then your light will dawn in the darkness; and your darkness shall be as the noonday. ...... If you turn away your foot from the Sabbath; from doing your pleasure on My Holy Day; and call the Sabbath a delight; the Holy Day of the Lord honorable; and shall honor Him, not doing your own ways nor finding your own pleasures, nor speaking your own words – then you shall delight yourself in the Lord; and I will cause you to ride on the high hills of the earth and feed you with the heritage of Jacob your father. The mouth of the Lord has spoken."

In chapter 59, Isaiah lists the sins of Israel (which ultimately led to their 70 year exile from the Promised Land). Isaiah warned Israel to no avail. Isaiah now warns us in our "new promised land."

God, through Isaiah, is telling His People (then *and* present day) that the continued "success" of their nation, which only He (God) can bring about, *hinges on the people's return to His Word, His Will, His Way – to righteousness;* and He alone will define their success. And overriding all else, Church "leaders" must make the determination for themselves, and inspire their "followers" when they teach and lead their flowers in the *Lord's Prayer* – are they leading a class in memory development, or do they mean it when they pray: "*Thy Will be done, ON EARTH as it is in heaven.*"

God's People Go To War:

There is a frame of reference within which the discussion contained in this topic must take place. That frame is the only frame in which God has historically blessed and protected His People Israel. God pledged security for the nation and the people, many times in their history, and the record shows that what God pledged, God did, including the many, many times He brought them victory against those who would invade and destroy them, and the times He withheld, finally withdrawing from them as they abandoned Him in their perfidy and sinful ways. His promise is perhaps most clear as it was delivered, personally, to Solomon: "*... if My people who are called by My name, humble themselves and pray, and seek My face and turn from their wicked ways, then will I hear from heaven and will forgive their sin and will heal their land ...... but if you turn away and worship other gods ...... I will uproot Israel from My land* (2 Chronicles 7)

Israel suffered the consequences of turning away from God after Jesus had completed His earthly advent, and their land was no more.

The United States came into being as a Christian Nation, populated 98+ percent by Christians. This is history. Many times in their 200+ year history, God called upon the US to "rescue" oppressed peoples elsewhere in the world. This was done twice globally, many times in selected locales, once within its own boundaries. That gives us the benefits of "favored nation" status. Up to this point in the history of this Christian Nation, the people have maintained, albeit sometimes inordinately well disguised, their identity as people of God. Most of the nations of the world who now belittle, deride, even hate the US, make the point that they "can't stand" the Christianity of our society. In accordance with God's Word and His record of keeping His Word, if the all-out war we are now waging to maintain our identity as People of God, which can only be by living His precepts, if we lose the "secular war" we lose "favored" nation blessing, and we are then "on-our-own" –a historically "losing situation."

177

The Church, as the Body of Christ, has long sanctioned this Nation/ Church's participation in a "just" war. It is so authorized by the Office of the Keys endowed to the Church via Christ's declaration to Peter as He brought the Church into being. At risk of over simplifying to a "lay" mind, a *just war* would be one which is undertaken *not* for the purpose of acquiring by force, another nation's land, wealth or material resources, nor for forcing another people to adopt a particular religion – but *is under- taken* for the purpose of protecting the originating nation's people from a debilitating harm or to free oppressed people from extreme, unjust, suffering, and making visible God's care and concern for those doing the suffering, and is resorted to *only* after the failure of diplomacy. Diplomacy is failed when a self-serving and belligerent nation or people (or their leaders) agrees to stop taking threatening or harmful action against "innocent" people, or supporting proxies in doing such harm while they *secretly* continue to pursue those actions for the purpose of future aggression.

In the Iraqi conflict "possible" consequences from resorting to preemption is widely expressed as a fear by those who oppose war at any cost to the people. But the Church *should* recognize and point out that a preemption decision is not without precedence *within God's chosen People*. It was through "preemption" that the Promised Land was delivered to His People. Several of the battles fought by King David were preemptive against enemies planning to "come up against" the nation Israel; even King Ahab was "advised" by his prophet to begin the battle against thirty-two kings who had allied themselves with Benhedad against Israel.

The people who oppose the Iraqi war fail to give credence to Peter's strong admonition (1 Peter 2:13) to *"submit yourselves to those who govern"* – when the one who "governs" was legally inaugurated in accordance with the covenant (the Constitution) which does the governing. Their claim is: "we are not directly endangered because "he" has not directly attacked us." Apparently they believe that it is not 'just' to take away the ability of a proven and practicing despot, his ability to cause death and havoc *a multiple of times greater than that which the people of this Nat- ion/Church already suffered from terrorists allied to him*, **before he can bring his announced threats to pass.** To "resisters" who refuse to admit that *their* free "pursuit of happiness" *is not limited to self*, in the form of "peacefully" pursuing material gain, *it is not possible to prove to their satisfaction, that **their** jeopardy is a direct extension of the jeopardy to those "others" to whom they would abandon "They brought it upon themselves, let them deal with it."* I guess it never occurs to them, Jesus' hope that they should emulate His willingness to "*lay down His life for His friends.*"

Of course there is a danger that those charged with the decision to preempt an enemy who is willfully building (and has used) his capacity to eradicate "infidel" People of God who have attained material wealth and political influence – by proxy, or from a distance, can decide to abuse the power they have been given. In fact, history records that it is a real and present danger (Kings David and Josiah stand out as two, who in the long history of Israel's kings *did not* revert to such "human" temptation). Many other "kings" of Israel brought all sorts of evil on their people through their immediate or eventual use of their personal power.

But this Nation/Church was created (by Christ through his "founding" servants) with a safety valve. The Constitution blesses its people with inbred remedies to such abuse of power. Three of them are:

- The need for all office holders to stand for reelection.
- For the "Chief Governor" – a two term limit in office.
- If the situation becomes critical, Impeachment. (Impeachment may also be applied to Federal Judges)

This combination of remedial actions is one more reason for the previous discussions about electing Christians to governmental offices.

The current war against world-wide terror is an example of the very necessary, albeit troublesome and unwanted, even hated element of ministry brought to this Christian Nation by our national call to "*… if you love Me, feed (take care of) My sheep*" – the sheep pen being God's world, of which this nation is a special, privileged (but only an) integral part.

The Continuing Need for War

The purpose of God's exile of Adam and Eve from the Garden of Eden was to demonstrate to them and to all successors, the consequences of their sinful decision that they "would take" responsibility for determining right from wrong, good from evil. The peace which He promises man can *only* come from *believing* that God alone can and does (through His Holy Spirit) "shepherd" man (individual and flock) through the valley of the shadow of death which *man's decision opened up to him* ...... and in man's living in trust of God's love, power and mercy during his (man's) earthly sojourn. God never promised to *excuse* man from experiencing trial and tribulation as he journeys. God's promise is that His peace is *awaiting* any (again, individual or nation) who lives that trust in God's "lesson" to all. The lesson is that the created will never be able "think as highly as I think." God himself will set any "call" to war that He feels is necessary to the maturing of man's (or nation's) trust and obedience to Him.

And so the real, great and urgent "need" for the Church to be in its present state of war is that the living Body of Christ is pitted against an organized and powerful array of enemies who are determined to *persecute those born of the Spirit* (Galatians 5:21-28); many of them descendents of Hagar, many more of them simply unbelieving skeptics who, like the marchers of the Exodus from slavery in Egypt, refuse to accept the "end" justifies the means of God's trials of their faith. The enemies are set on preventing this Nation/Church and its people from achieving their assigned "end and aim" – which is to advance the Kingdom of God.

These enemies have become very skilled in using the very Christian precepts under which this Nation/Church was established to first gain wealth and power, and then use their gain to destroy those same precepts for others. *They will succeed in their war against us unless the Christian Church (all its denominations) unites in major battle – NOW – against them.*

The need is for a major battle – but as the history of Christianity bringing down the Roman Empire teaches us, this internal battle against these "civil" enemies *does not always call for, in fact is often better* fought *without* weapons of mass destruction or personal arms; no guns were required, no spears, arrows or clubs.

What *is* needed, is for believing citizens (presently in the majority) to be *constantly* living the Word of God; led, equipped and arrayed as the Apostle Paul advocates in his letter to the Ephesians (6: 10-18). *The Christian, Institutional, Denominational Church must NOW open* *the door of opportunity at which stands the Holy Spirit of God looking for men/women who truly believe: "**I can do all things through Christ which strengtheneth me**" to sign up for this battle.*

There are many, many examples of "I can do all things" faith already in action which are available for the "Christian Army's" reassurance some of them were cited earlier in this critique. But a more recent example will be inspirational, *if the Church gives it the publicity within its own membership, which it deserves:*

It involves a high school senior who, chosen to address a graduating class in Pennsylvania, wanted to, in her address, give Jesus Christ credit for her scholastic and "life" success. The school, in the person of the Principal, presumably backed by the Board of Education, ordered her to take all references to Christ out of her speech, "suggesting" some substitute (politically correct) phrases for her to use.

This young lady, however, felt so strongly that her success should be credited to Jesus, that she took the issue to her Christian Parents, who were strong enough in *their* faith that they all sat down and held a council of war to devise a battle strategy. Apparently, they were able to get "the Church" - in the form of legal assistance - involved. They took the issue to court.

The end result was, by her persistence in faith and with the assistance of the Church, the attempted censorship was adjudged to be a violation of the Free Speech Amendment to the Constitution of the United States, and her speech was restored – *and given to a very receptive audience.*

One lasting result of her determination to proclaim the Gospel of Jesus Christ is that, using legally established guidelines, **students in any Public School may now, publicly and visibly pray in school and at school events.**

BUT THIS IS TRUE ONLY TO THE EXTENT THAT THE CHURCH ACTIVELY POINTS OUT, DEFENDS AND ENCOURAGES EACH SUCH STUDENT OPPORTUNITY!

No bloodshed, no violence, only the weapon of faith in her God, with assistance of her parents and the Body of Christ on earth – this young lady took her faith into the lion's den of ungodliness and slew the lions.

"Passing the Buck" back to the "Professionals"

As was said at the outset of this endeavor, there is no intent on the part of the writer of this dissertation (which does include input from more than one "lay" member of the Body of Christ) to presume all the answers or any wisdom to "reinvent the wheel" called the Body of Christ. It is therefore necessary to pass this call for a "bigger picture" approach to completing the mission of The Body, to wiser and more experienced Christians. Maybe before we make such a pass, we ought to identify our intended receivers (Professional Christians):

A *professional Christian* is one who is elected by God himself even before his (her) conception takes place, who is Baptized within a congregation and by the Holy Spirit of God, matures within a denomination, even if it is an "independent" Church and/or a political party and who, guided by the Holy Spirit accepts his/her "call" (through the Church which He created for that purpose) to a designated ministry, or a combination of several.

A ministry venue may be: Mother; Father; Church Elder; Pastor; Preacher/Teacher; Church Administrator; Business Person; Laborer; Lawyer; Social Scientist; Medical Practitioner; Physician; Township Supervisor; School Board Member; Sheriff; County Commissioner; Elected Representative; Senator; President; "stranger in our midst." *The Christian Professional is one who subordinates denomination and/or political party to making Jesus Christ – one with the Lord God Almighty – visible and the sole recipient of ALL honor, glory and praise.*

Those believers who have accepted God's "call" to assume responsibility for leading the Church into more complete compliance with the Great Commission, whether they are in the "ivory Tower of Academia or are leading disciples in actual ministries, can surely come up with more and better ingredients for mixing into the mortar for cementing the blocks called People of God to the Cornerstone of His Church. What is necessary to their success is, as Paul demonstrated in the forming of the human component of the Church (Ephesians 4):

Extracted: "...... *This I say therefore, and testify in the Lord, that you should no longer walk as the rest of the Gentiles walk, in the futility of **their** mind ...... but you have not so learned Christ, if indeed you have heard Him and have been taught by Him, as the truth is in Jesus ......"*

All assurance for the success of Sackcloth and Ashes is in Paul's assertion (Philippians 4:13): ***"I can do all things through Christ who stregntheneth me."***

Finally:

We began all this prayerfully; we urged that even the planning for *Sackcloth and Ashes* begin with prayer and that two-way communications between God and man be involved, be held constantly open. We therefore conclude the presentation of our findings and recommendations, with prayer:

Holy Lord God, in the hope that we are not too late in undertaking this effort to restore to You what we have stolen from You by sinful inattention to, even by rebellion against what You created to enable us to complete your earthly mission, this Nation/Church – We pray that You will accept our endeavors to repent our failures to make your glory known to all people, to preserve this Nation/Church You founded through those who came first, and we pray that You will prompt your people to answer this call. And we pray for your merciful guidance, your participation, your loving leadership, as we pursue our realignment with the "end and aim" for which You established this Nation/Church; In the name of Jesus our Savior, Mentor and Lord. Amen

Appendix A

Index of Discussion Issues

Appendix B

COMPENDIUM OF IN-DEPTH DISCUSSIONS OF
ISSUES IDENTIFIED IN THE BODY OF THIS
CRITIQUE

Note: Issues are listed in the order they appear in the report and are presented as if written for sermons:

Christians And Prayer

One of the qualities (genes), that made Jesus what He was when He lived in this physical world -- was His self-declared need to pray; and the word He left with us (the Gospel of John) as He was being transformed into His spiritual (eternal) being, was that if we are to have *any hope* of *"if you love Me, keep My commandments,"* we have to pray too.

Prayer is the communicating channels between us and our Heavenly Father, who is the *source* of our new life, the teacher (through the Holy Spirit) the Designer of the Utopia we long for. He it is, the *Architect* of the Nation/Church we are. He, *alone,* can approve any recovery or refurbishing of its tattered being.

The Word of God which we cling to as our hand-book of gestation cites *many* examples of the situations of mortal life which prompted Jesus to pray. The scripture cited earlier, The Gospel According to Mark, in its *first chapter* stresses the need Jesus felt for the sustenance of prayer.

According to Mark, it had been a very busy day for Jesus. He had unveiled a *revelation* (the power and glory of His Father - God) to a hopeless and despondent people; He was visiting the seaside town of Capernaum, but it was not a vacation - *not* a day on the beach. He went into the Synagogue and taught; while there, He cast an unclean spirit out of a man. He, *with authority,* spoke of God's plan of *salvation for an oppressed people* who were overburdened with the necessities of their present day strife and conflict, with their *constant struggle* to maintain *even an unsatisfactory status-quo.*

His tasks at the Synagogue finished, it was a relatively short walk to the home of one of His disciples (Peter), where He healed Peter's mother-in- law, who then got out of "sick bed" and prepared them dinner. Later that day a huge crowd gathered at the door of the house, and Jesus spent a goodly portion of the evening healing the sick and driving out demons. This *man, this very **human** Jesus*, went to bed exhausted, *after* the last man walked away, healed.

The man Jesus *deserved* a day off, at least a chance to *sleep in.* But according to Mark, we are told: *"now in the morning, having risen a long time before daylight, He went out and departed to a solitary place, and there, He prayed.*

Jesus knew that His ministry would take Him to other towns and to thousands of more people who needed His healing intercession. To fortify himself, *His top priority - was to pray!* With a tough day behind Him *and more draining experiences before Him* (not unlike the project *Sackcloth and Ashes* we must take on) Jesus got away from it all, and prayed.

Jesus did, of course sleep in order to restore His physical body strength (other passages of scripture tell us of times when He did need physical rest - see Mark 6:31), but in *this* instance, rather than to take a day off, a vacation, or some other interlude to "re-charge His batteries," *the* **man** *Jesus understood* that if He was to *truly* renew His ministerial stamina, His battery charger *could only be - God, His Father,* through prayer. There were also many other times recorded in Scripture when Jesus felt the need to pray. The most meaningful perhaps, for His people, is recorded in John 17, where He prays for His disciples, whom He assures us, mean us.

Jesus also taught *us* when and how to pray. In fact the over-riding theme of the Word of God teaches us that we can *only* succeed in *our* being transformed into *being God's Son (or daughter)* if we understand *and put into practice,* His way of life. And we can do either, understand *or* change our way of life, *through prayer.* And we learn *what* to pray for *from His teachings.* Our sinful nature makes it impossible for us to transform ourselves, *or our way of life,* on our own.

In Matthew (7: 7-8), Jesus teaches us: *ask and you will receive."* Hence Paul's teaching: *I can do anything through Christ, which strengtheneth me."* What better guarantee can there be that if we undertake the project *Sackcloth and Ashes;* we will succeed in "saving Ninevah." To put it in contemporary language: ***To stand up to the challenges of this world, spend time on your knees.***

And as for *how* to pray: He taught *us* as He taught and discussed with His disciples what we identify as The Lord's Prayer. And please note: The Lord's Prayer ***is not*** to be recited by rote; it is a prayer *acceptable to God* **only** when we have *in our hearts,* the *substance* of the words. He also taught in that same discussion, God *is not* impressed with how many words are in a prayer. He ***is*** impressed with what is in the heart, what the *true* needs are, we bring to Him; and what *we* perceive (He already knows what we need) our needs to be, brought to Him in a righteous, trusting, relationship between us, *and our Benevolent Father, our God.*

By the way, going back to "Ask and ye shall receive" -- the Word of God also teaches what can happen if we are not *very thoughtful and careful **what we ask for.*** We are several times reminded that God *may* decide to give us what we ask for. God is a very doting and benevolent God. He *may* give us what we very deeply want, *even if it makes our journey to where He wants us to go **unnecessarily** troublesome.* An example is when God allowed Samuel to anoint Saul to be King of Israel. God *allowed* Israel to become a monarchy, even when His infinite wisdom knew that was not the best path for them to travel. This was another example of His commitment to their freedom to choose for themselves, His way, or theirs. And ***recorded history*** clearly reveals that things went downhill for Israel from that time. It took the intervention of God himself in *the form of Jesus,* to satisfy the standard of justice He had declared for man - when He exiled Adam from Eden.

But we can defeat *our* doubt and confusion; we can overcome our very own nature, when we remind ourselves that if *we obey His Word, His Will, His Way,* the path to where He wants *us* to go will be smooth and free of pitfalls. He *cares* about us and *longs to give us the wisdom* to handle anything that comes our way (check out 1 Peter 5:7 or James 1:5). In our praying, we *can* trust that God will honor our requests, when ***they are in keeping with His Word, His Will, His Way.*** By the way, are we *studying His Word so that we can know His Will?*

A reminder: Christ teaches that as we pray, God does **not** necessarily promise to **excuse** us from the "trials" of our mortal life; But He *does* promise *to go through with us,* whatever tribulation is going on. God has delegated to His people responsibility for *doing the hard, hard work of sustaining His Church,* but He has assigned to Christ the task of interceding for us when the "burden" of our "cross" becomes too heavy -- Christ's role of Melchizedek (Hebrews 7: 11).

Prayer is where *we* come to an understanding that it is *God* who is supreme. *We **must** be,* our only hope for a successful project, ***is*** to be totally dependent upon Him. In turn, God will let us *know* if we are heading toward the right "Objective," as we like to call it, and if the path we are traveling will take us there . . . and if we listen, He will even *draw us a map* to the path.

Our faith, our transformation to obedient, active, disciple of Jesus *will* grow stronger and stronger, as we realize that He is truly full of grace, that He *delights* in giving good gifts to His children (Matthew 7:11). Humbly, *but confidently,* we can come to Him with our requests. And *if* we *assure* ourselves, *as well as our Benevolent Father,* that we will *gratefully accept* **His substitute, His Will,** in place of what we request; *we become the ones whom He blesses.*

Mark (4:9 and 24-25) addresses our *need* to *hear God's counsel,* as we pray. Communication, *even with God,* is a two-way street. *We need to hear God,* just as we hope He will hear us. It is a provable fact: If there is "noise" on a telephone or a fax line, the message being transmitted may not be understood by the "hearer." It is easy to *transmit* requests to God, but if the *noise of the world* is interfering, the return message *can be garbled* and never understood. *It is "human" that our focus concentrates on what we want to "tell" Him while "blocking out" what He says to us.* If we allow the "noise" of sin or of the cares of life (the Ninevah syndrome) to build up; they will deflect our attention as we study His Word, or "hear" a Sermon, or remain silent in prayer. Again, in the vernacular: **worldly static disrupts communications with God.**

In the Scripture quoted earlier (Mark 4), Jesus says: "*He who has ears to hear, let him hear.* We even have an example of Jesus' willingness to hear, to *accept His Father's will.* On the night in which He was betrayed, He prayed to *be excused from - but He* **accepted** *- new strength, as He anticipated His arrest and crucifixion.*

Does praying for someone else, e.g. those to whom we address our Sackcloth and Ashes messages, *really* make a difference? Remember way back in the Old Testament (Exodus 32: 1-6) when Moses was on the mountain receiving the Ten Commandments? You will surely recall how Aaron, who had been left in charge of the people of God in Moses' absence, left some of them argue him into making a golden calf for them to worship - because Moses "delayed" in returning to them, causing them to fear that he had left them to perish? The people decided to worship a god they could see, and who allowed them to do whatever they could think to do. They *chose* wild parties filled with strong drink, immoral actions and obscene revelry. God threatened to annihilate *all* the people of Israel and select another people for His purpose. With *impassioned pleading (prayer)* Moses persuaded God to apply mercy and to give His people another chance. *Does that Biblical lesson apply to today's* chosen people? Here are two of *innumerable*, contemporary examples, reported by Pastor Jim Cymbala, of the Brooklyn Tabernacle:

1) many years ago, Pastor Cymbala was "appointed" to the pastorate in Brooklyn, at a time when the membership was about 35, and he was required to also pastor a second congregation - - the combined two of them could not really afford a pastor. After a few years, and several disheartening experiences, Pastor Cymbala in a "fit of frustration" went off to Florida, fishing (paid for by his father-in-law) but really to reassess his "call." As he fished and meditated, he "heard" God tell him, "if you go back and pray with your people," the congregation will grow. He returned to the Tabernacle and instituted regular mid-week prayer meetings. More and more Inner-city people heard about the meetings, and came to pray. The Tabernacle now hosts up to 35,000 members (in new and expanded buildings). It now conducts three Sunday worship services of up to two and a half hours duration, and hosts a world famous choir directed by Mrs. Cymbala (who never had formal music training). Pastor Cymbala's book, *Fresh Wind, Fresh Fire,* tells in exquisite detail, what is simplistically related here, the truth of the answers to organized, corporate, and prayer.

2) And Pastor Cymbala freely relates a personal experience with the effects of prayer. His teen-age daughter, in rebellion against the discipline of Christian living ran away from home. She lived with different men for short time periods, in an alcohol and drug culture, in New York City. Neither Pastor Cymbala nor his wife was able to keep track of her, or to reach out to her, even with material help or with forgiving love. She became a constant subject of public (i.e. prayer meeting) and private prayer . . . for more than a year and a half. The burden (for the Cymbalas) became more and more apparent to his parishioners, until one Tuesday night, one of the woman parishioners attending prayer meeting that night, proposed to Those assembled: "let us for this night, forget our own prayer needs and all *of us devote*

tonight to praying for Jim's daughter. That Prayer meeting lasted for several hours.

Nothing happened until the following week. Pastor Cymbala was upstairs in their home shaving, when his wife burst into the bathroom shouting: "Mary is downstairs in the kitchen crying for you!" He wiped the shaving cream from his face and went downstairs to his daughter, who, on her knees, wrapped her arms around his legs, crying to be taken back, and to be forgiven.

To make a long story short, Mary has renounced her *worldly self,* and is now a very vital part of the continuing ministry of the Brooklyn Tabernacle.

In the course of their re-acquaintance conversations, Mary asked: "Who was praying for me Tuesday night" last week? In the midst of my alcoholic despair, I suddenly *knew* that God was *right then* reaching out to take me by the hand and restore me to His grace. An aside: God tells Job *directly*, in the account of *his* many trials, because you (Job) have trusted in Me (God) I will hear your prayers for your well meaning, but O so mistaken friends.

The point of Pastor Cymbala's witness is: If you would influence people for God; *Pray to God for people!* And perhaps it will also clarify *your very own* relationship; and renew it; and strengthen it - *with your Heavenly Father.*

The *original sin* was Adam's decision, *and his action*, to undertake to improve what God had provided. It would be just as foolish, to say nothing about being evil, to begin a project like *Sackcloth and Ashes*, before obtaining the *Architect's* input and approval. And make no mistake, *The Architect is Jesus Christ.* The Holy Spirit is by the original design, **His** voice relaying to us **His** response to our prayers.

Reclaiming America For Christ

Most of the previous discussion *in this critique,* in reference to the *fact* that this nation was founded to be a Christian Nation, reflects (not very well, perhaps) Dr. Kennedy's and Coral Ridge Ministry's pronouncements on the issue, over many years. The following is extracted from a speech which Dr. Kennedy delivered to the annual *Reclaiming America Conference,* in the year 2000. The title *Nation/Church,* is a by-product of what has been learned from his ministry

". . . . How are we going to bring this nation back to God, back to decency, back to morality, back to those things we wish America was like again? I remember reading a statement by a well-known man when he was asked what *he* wanted as a Christian -- what he wanted for America? I think all of us would like his answer. He would like:

- an America where it is safe to walk the streets at night.
- an America where you don't have to triple lock your doors.
- an America where you can let your children go to a motion picture without believing that they are probably going to be shocked at what the contents are; an America where men and women love their neighbors and help them, where people want to be good citizens and godly citizens.

Hardly a radical view of the America *the radicals* of our time would like to *have people believe* we want to see. But we *would* like to see a decent America, a God-fearing country, a country that loves the flag and what it stands for, and doesn't seek to burn it and destroy it.

Two Biblical Mandates

How are we going to do that? I believe *the Bible* gives us *two* mandates that are the basic tracks upon which the train of the Church *and the train of every Christian life* are supposed to run. Interestingly enough, they are the first and the last *commandments* God gave to mankind. The first one is found in Genesis 1:28, where God tells us we are to be fruitful and multiply, and to replenish the earth and subdue it, and have dominion over everything on the earth. This is sometimes called the "dominion covenant," or the *Cultural Mandate. God has given us this world.* He expects us to run it *according to the principles and rules and laws* He has given to us. He expects that *He* will have the glory from it. **We have abandoned much of that mandate to unbelievers.** Ungodly people have taken these things and used them to bring glory to *Satan* and not to God. **And that is a great tragedy.**

We need to get people *(actively) engaged* in our culture. We just gave *"Salt and Light"* awards. The light is the light of the Gospel. Salt is that which preserves meat from utter decay. In fact, it was so valuable before refrigeration that sometimes people were paid in salt. You remember the old phrase - He's worth his salt? And so, salt is necessary to *keep the body politic* from utter corruption and decay.

The problem with America is the difficulty of getting the salt out of the shaker! *We don't want to get involved* with the meat. We don't want to get involved in things that are controversial or where people are not going to be nice to us. Why, somebody might just say nasty things about us. Well. I've had homosexuals marching up and down in front of our church saying: "Kennedy is a Khomeni," "Kennedy is a Nazi." and all of those things. And then they complain that *we call them names*, that *we're intolerant.* I don't call them names. Some people do, but I don't. But it is difficult to get Christians out of the salt shaker; it is so comfortable in there because everybody else is just exactly like we are. In the salt shaker but when you get out there where people are offended by us, what *are virtues and vices to them?* The Bible says, *"Woe unto them that call good evil, and evil good" -- and we live in a time just like that.* Abraham Lincoln said, "Without the Bible, we would not *know* good from evil. When I first read that many years ago, I said, that's a pretty broad statement; I think maybe he would have wanted to rethink that. But as the years have gone by I've realized that Lincoln was wiser than I was on that, because look at our time today. We live in a time when America absolutely cannot decide whether scouting *or sodomy* is evil. And without the Bible, you really can't. So that is why the Bible is so important in the establishment of America. *The Bible was the most read and the most quoted book* in America's establishment period, more so than Locke or Rousseau, or any other of the writers of the time.

In the *Year of the Bible* celebration a quarter century or so ago, *Time Magazine* said that historians are discovering that it was the *Bible,* even more perhaps than the constitution, *which was the founding document of this country.* And that is true.

I think we need to bring the Word of God to bear on every sphere of life. What does the Bible say about how we should live our own lives? How should we treat our wives, or husbands? How should we rear our children? How should they be educated? How should government be formed and operated? What do our freedoms mean, and how do we maintain them? What about our entertainment? What about our media? *The Bible has something to say about all these things*

The amazing thing is that for the most part, Christians haven't been *driven back* into the salt cellar, *they have withdrawn! They have retreated. They have left the playing field to others* **voluntarily,** hoping that all that unpleasantness might just go away. *But folks, it is not going away. It's getting worse!* And I think unless Christians decide that *they're going to get active,* we don't even begin to know how bad it could be.

So *one of the tracks* the train of the Church and the Christian life runs on is the *Cultural Mandate --* **to bring the Word of God to EVERY sphere of life,** to get out **and be salt** in a corrupting society to prevent it from total corruption. Salt is that which stands with feet spread apart across that door that leads to all goodness and righteousness and purity, and says to all wickedness: Thus far, and no farther shalt thou go.

We need **to get involved in everything.**

What are you involved in, in **your community?** Are you involved in your libraries? Libraries *used to be a safe place to go. That is* NO longer true. *Children* can go into our libraries all over the nation and see all kinds of pornography. And the *Library Association* will adamantly *defend* their right to let children watch *any of that.* The children can't go into a motion picture theater and see it, but an eight year old can see it in any library.

Are you involved? What about the school board? *School Boards are the approving authority for what is taught, and the books that are taught from, in the schools they supervise.* What about running for office? About five years ago a young man was sitting right where your are now (at a meeting of the convention). He was so moved by the various things he heard and saw that he went back home and ran for Congress. "When I was in Washington giving an award at the *Center for Christian Statesmanship,* he was there. He is a member of the United

States Congress. He decided to get involved. *He's making a very real difference.*

Someone once said that in this Christian nation *which God has given us,* it behooves Christians, and it is **their responsibility**, **to** prefer and elect Christians to rule over them. Now I guarantee you that in this culture today, a lot of people would find that a foreign concept, an alien concept, an un-American concept, and a concept that is not tolerant -certainly foreign - from all that America stands for in its pluralism.

That statement was made by John Jay -- one of the principle founders of America. *He was the first Chief Justice* of the first Supreme Court, appointed by the father of our country, *George Washington.* He also, with Madison and Hamilton, wrote the *Federalist Papers,* which explained and sold the *Constitution* to all of the states. Without John Jay, we may never have ratified our Constitution. *Our first Chief Justice* said that we should *prefer and elect Christians* to rule over a Christian nation By the way, you will notice what kind of nation *he believed* this was. The first Chief Justice said it was a *Christian Nation.*

May I point out to you that it is not possible to elect Christians to rule over you if Christians are not running for office? Some of you ought to get out in your community and put yourself on the line.

It's not easy, but *some* people are going to make the sacrifice, and some people are going to do it. And some people *who are very ungodly* are going to do it. "I have been amazed, right here in Ft. Lauderdale, to see some of the ungodly attitudes, the hostility to Christianity kinds of attitudes that have come out in this recent fray about the Boy Scouts. Now who are these people? They are people who *are* willing to make the sacrifice to run for office, and we are *stuck with them* for at least another two and a half years. Some of *you* should be out there doing that.

*The Christian Church withdrew from the Cultural Mandate for most of the last century. The result has been this post-Christian, ungodly era that we are living through, and **which is only going to get worse if WE don't turn it around.***

The Great Commission

The second rail, upon which the Christian Church *and every Christian life* must run, is the *last commandment* God gave to us. It is the great commission, or the *evangelistic mandate,* which is to go preach the Gospel to every creature -- and that is the responsibility of *every single one of us.* It is *not* something that was given just to pastors. A lot of lay people say, "Well, that's clerical George's job. We'll let *him* do it. That's why we pay him so much money."

The Scripture says: *"Therefore they were scattered abroad and went everywhere preaching the word"* (Acts 8:4). The phrase *preaching the word* is a translation of the Greek, which means *evangelizing.* They that were scattered abroad went everywhere evangelizing. This was after the persecution that arose from the preaching of the deacon *Stephen.* We read in the first verse of that chapter, the context. Now a text *without* a context is a *pretext,* and that has been a pretext for a lot of lay people *not doing anything* in the area of evangelism, "because it's the pastor's job." But *this* is what the verse says: *"They were all scattered abroad . . . except the apostles."* (8:1)

It wasn't the apostles he was talking about; it was everybody else. Now the Apostles *got* in *their* licks, but Luke did not have that in his purview when he wrote the book of Acts. *Everyone* went *everywhere* evangelizing and *that is how the early Church conquered the Roman Empire.* But, alas, so many Christians have *voluntarily* withdrawn from the *evangelistic mandate* as well

". . . . Do you lead people to Christ? I hope that you do. That is the *great hope.* May I say to you that the Cultural Mandate (*Reclaiming America*) **without the Evangelistic Mandate** is, in my opinion, an exercise in futility, You are not going to impose Christian morals and Christian values on a majority of a predominantly non-Christian culture. It will not happen. They will rise up and throw it off. They will not submit themselves to it. *Therefore we need to do both. We need to be winning people to Christ.* "I would say that the *most effective political action you could take would be to go and lead your neighbor to Christ.*"

"I talked to a man I led to Christ thirty-some years ago, and he said: *Our entire lives have been changed. We have been involved in leading people to Christ in our culture.*" In fact, his wife (Barbara Collier) was handing me the *Salt and Light* awards this evening. He said: "We have grown sons. They are all active in the Church; they are active in society. They are all voting and doing the things a good American citizen would do" all because thirty-some years ago, I took an hour or so to share the

Gospel with them. And that will go on generation through generation through generation."

The most effective political action you could take is to lead someone to Jesus Christ. If the person becomes a *real Christian* -- not just a *professing* Christian -- then Christ, who lives in his or her heart, will guide them in what they ought to do *and how they ought to vote.* You won't have to keep going back and writing letters telling them what to do and how to do it. *God will show them.*

Some Good News

About 86% of the American people *profess* to be Christian. Unfortunately, in our day a great many of those who *profess*, do not *possess* what they *profess.* They are merely *nominal Christians -- Christians in name only.* Christ has never come into their heart; they have never been *born of the Spirit of God.* They are not *new creatures* in Christ. They have not been *changed* by an *encounter* with the living, risen Savior. They are simply *Church people."* "I was one, so was my wife, and so were most of you at one time -- merely church people, but not Christians -- *nominal Christians. There are millions like that in this country.*

One man I know who is actively engaged in leading people to Christ, said that when he accepted Christ (and he was a rank unbeliever) his life was so totally changed. *Everything about him* was changed. He said: "Even my entire *political perspective* was changed." For some people, that does not happen overnight. *Sometimes it takes a little while* to get all of their life and their views in accordance with the Word of God. *But it will take place,* even if gradually.

The problem is in getting people to become active. One of the things we have seen in the last election is that many Christians just weren't enthusiastic, so they just stayed home. Folks, we need (and that's where the Cultural Mandate aspect is so very important) to get Christians registered and voting. "I have never voted in an election for *anything* for myself. Never - *I have always voted for what I thought was best for the United States of America,* **and what I thought was best for the Kingdom of God.** For many people, this is startling.

Do you think *George Washington* would have voted to get something out of it? And yet, how many Americans are "voting their pocketbook?" They are voting for "me and mine." Washington *never accepted a penny of salary* for the eight years he was president. He certainly would never have voted for anything for himself.

But we need to vote for what is good for America, for what is good for the Kingdom of God, and for the morality and the virtue and the godliness of this nation. *"When the **righteous** are in authority, the people rejoice; but when the wicked beareth rule, the people mourn:* (Proverbs 29:2). There has been a lot of mourning in our country in recent years, I am *afraid* about what has been going on morally in this land.

We need to get Christians to vote. I think that as these two rules -- this twin effort --to bring people to *know the living God*; to bring people to *understand* righteousness and morality and godliness and *get them involved* in the culture, "bear fruit," that we are going to see some- time *in the next decade,* a tremendous shift in this country. I think it is going to shift *markedly* toward the good and the righteous, the beautiful, the moral, the godly -- things that once made this nation great, *and were the wonder of the worlds.* And that is *my* great hope.

The number of Christians *in the world* is growing fantastically. This is evidence of ministries like Robert Schuller's TV broadcasts being heard by tens of millions in Russia and Africa, who have been *"searching"* for spiritual enlightenment, i.e. God, or have been *officially* kept from Him for decades of their life-time.

Many people don't know it, but according to the Center for World Missions in California, in 1900 there were 943 converts to Christ per day, world- wide, up from about 100 a day in 100AD. By 1950 that number had grown to 4,500. By 1980 it had risen to 20,000. By 1995 it reached 100,000. Extrapolated for the end of the year 2000 to be 200,000 per day, world wide *the harvest is excitingly there, but laborers are few.*

If we were to use scuba diving as a *"parable,"* where when one goes below even dark murky water where the bottom cannot even be seen from the surface, and looks at the bottom from that vantage point, all of a sudden beautiful vistas not even imagined, open up. We could be describing the state of our nation: All around us we see *ungodliness* growing and gaining, but *beneath the surface,* God is at work. And He is changing the hearts of millions of people around the world. We are in the midst of the greatest ingathering to the Church in the history of mankind, and most *nominal Christians* don't even know it. One of these days, when we reach that critical mass and the teeter-totter shifts from *ungodliness to godliness, from immorality to morality,* the secular, god- less world - is going to get the *biggest shock of their lives*

Dear friends, *be a part of it.* **Make it happen.** Become a witness for Christ. Institutional Church, *train your lay people* to witness for Jesus Christ. Be part of the greatest, most marvelous endeavor in the history of mankind -- the greatest enterprise ever, of redeeming the *world* (including our own nation/church) for Jesus Christ.

The Cornerstone Of This Nation/Church

We are taught, erroneously, in a popular song some years ago, that East is east and West is west, and never shall they meet. But midway through the nineteenth century, we came to a rude awakening in World War II. At *Pearl Harbor,* East met West in a very definite, violent way.

We very quickly learned that behind the military and economic might of Japan, there existed the power of the *Shinto* religion; which was the *true motivation* for the attack. The Japanese people believed that their *emperor was god,* or at least, god's descendant. And that they were *his people,* and therefore, they could have the audacity to take on a nation many times larger than theirs. It was not possible they could lose; "god" was their emperor.

Four years later, on a battleship in Tokyo harbor, the *empire* of Japan surrendered, and the emperor, on radio, which the entire world heard, *confessed* that alas, *he was no god. The Shinto religion collapsed, overnight.*

Then, four years later, the *Confucian Religion,* another religion that Americans were really only coming to know something about -- was overwhelmed by the masses of Communist soldiers led by Mao Tse-tung. The last vestiges of Confucianism had been smashed into dirt. That left three of the five great Eastern religions that were meeting the West in the twentieth century. We move east, through Japan and China, to Buddhism and Hinduism and Islam.

Until now, *none of them* have been involved in wars *involving us.* But they do *now* bring a great deal of confusion, if not consternation, to a great many people where *they* are, as well as in our Nation/ Church. *"What about all those other gods"* has been a question which millions of Americans have asked. Are they real? Are they false? What should we think? Some people have said: "Well, you see, there is really *just one religion, with different faces,* and we're all basically, going to the same God, only by different paths. **This in the face of Christ's own and undeniable, impossible to misunderstand statement: "I (alone) am the way, the truth and the life. No one comes to the Father except** *through me."* (John 14:6) To these "one religion" people, this was a way to *"tone down"* any *conflicts* that may arise. But then, other people began to look at these other religions a little bit more carefully, and we have discovered that of those three -- Buddhism, Hinduism and Islam:

- *Islam is a radical **monotheistic** religion,* leaving no room for even the ***Christian Trinity.***
- Right next door (so to speak) where Islam abuts India, is *Hinduism,* which has anywhere from 300,000 to 3 *million* gods. *Nobody knows for sure.*
- Keep going east, and you run into *Buddhism,* **and they have no god at all,** at least most of them. Some Buddhists couldn't quite handle that, so they tried to make a god out of Buddha. But for the most part, *even they* are skeptical about the question of god -- as was Buddha himself.

The denominations of the Institutional Church all state in their charter or governing documents: "We believe that there is *One God in three persons.*" But *some* of the "professors" in their *Institutes of Higher Learning,* "*imaginatively,*" in the throes of determining if *Jesus* really meant what He taught in John 14:6, have published and promulgated "*suppositions*" to the contrary, *that Jesus is **not** the only way to the eternal God.* The combined churches have done *little or nothing* to refute these public *announcement*s, which have carried over into some pulpit *proclamations.* On the contrary, bending to what they, counter to the Word of the God they would serve, call *academic freedom,* the Institutional Churches, in a debilitating and *faith busting, mistaken,* "*tolerance*" of intellectual " *freedom,*" which Jesus died for combating, is threatening to destroy their "institution." This is of course, *their* pursuit of *Reformed, always reforming,* the theology of man's faith and beliefs, in an errant and futile attempt to *make God's Word "relevant"* to today's "way of life," so that they don't have to go through the "trauma" of making ***today's life relevant to God's Eternal Word.***

Just recently, in 1993, at the *World Parliament of World Religions,* 6000 people from all over the world met to try to straighten out the mess, solve the problem, and figure out what was really going on in the arena of competing, sometimes conflicting beliefs. They finally issued a paper which was *intended* to explain to all, God and religion.

But the paper never *mentions* the word *"God" or the word "gods."*

You see, the Buddhist priests wouldn't *allow* it, because they don't believe in one, or in many gods. They said: "when *we* pray, we are just meditating. Prayer is psychology in practice, and the only person who hears our prayers, *is we.* So what was the solution? There was none. All they did was to come up with some *ethical suggestions. Religion* had been dissolved entirely, by the World Parliament of Religion. Irony of ironies, The World Parliament of Religion became the death knell of the *idea* that all religions are basically the same.

If they are *not* all the same, what are they? In Romans we read: *"When they (mankind) knew God, they glorified Him not as God . . . but became vain in their imagination. Professing themselves to be wise, they became fools, and changed the glory of their incorruptible God, into an image made like to corruptible man, and to birds, and four-footed beasts, and creeping things. Wherefore, God also gave them up to uncleanness, and they worshipped the creature more than the Creator, who is blessed forever* (Romans 1:21-25) Irwin Lutzer says: "I believe that the *Scriptures* require us to view other religions, (in order) to view *other religions as flawed attempts of man to reach God through human effort and insight.* Jesus, you may recall, in the Gospel of John, says: *"All that ever came before Me, are thieves and robbers. The thief cometh not, but to steal and to kill. . . . . I am the good shepherd; the good shepherd giveth his life for the sheep.* (John 10:8 & 10-11) *No one else ever laid down his life for the sheep."* So Christ says that these *(other gods)* are not by any means, gods.

The Apostle Paul said (in 1 Corinthians 10:20): *"And I would not that ye should have fellowship with devils."* This admonition is true all the way through the New Testament. There are some today, who say that we should bow down and *reverence all religions,* in the interest of honoring political correctness, which is the process of making *cultural diversity (the acceptance of "other" gods)* our "new and better" way of life.

Question: Was *that* the attitude of *Elijah* on Mt. Carmel, as he "dealt" with the prophets of Baal? Elijah *commanded* they be destroyed. Was that the attitude of the Jewish people toward *Dagon,* the fish god who fell flat on his face in their own temple when the *Ark of the Lord* arrived? How about Molech, that detestable Semitic god, to whom at one time, they made sacrifice *right outside the walls of Jerusalem?* They had a gigantic *metal image* of Molech that was hollow. On certain festival occasions, they would build a huge bon-fire inside the image, until it glowed red hot. *Into its red hot, glowing, outstretched hands, they would place their babies, and then beat louder on their drums so the babies' screams couldn't be heard.*

When the Jews finally destroyed the idol Molech, they made it into the *garbage heap* of Jerusalem. It is in the Valley of Hinnon. *Valley is the word "ge" in Hebrew. ge' hinnin (Valley).* We say it as Gehennah, which is one of their words for *hell.* So this place of worship for one of their pagan gods is a place that ***Jesus chose*** as a description of hell. -- *Hardly a place of reverence. Godet,* a great *Swiss* theologian, put it this way:

> 'The Apostle Paul does not even take the trouble of
> *stating* the negative answer which he gives to these two
> questions; he passes *directly* to the ***affirmation*** which
> concerns him. *Jupiter, Apollo, Venus* certainly ***are not***
> real beings; but ***Satan is*** *something. Behind the*
> *mythological and fading fancy of image, there*
> *lay, concealed**, malignant powers without being*
> ***Divinities nevertheless****, very real and very active.*
> They are demons, or *fallen angels --* ***dominions of Satan.***

Princeton Theological Seminary's Professor Charles Hodge, considered to be America's greatest theologian, said:

Men of the world do not ***intend*** *to serve Satan when they break the laws of God in their pursuit of their desires. Still, in doing so, they are really* ***obeying the will*** *of this great adversary, yielding to his impulses and fulfilling his designs. He is therefore, said to be the* ***god of this world.*** *To him,* ***all*** *sin is an offering and homage. We are shut up to the necessity of worshipping God, - or Satan*

There is *only one option.* There are *thousands* of pagan religions, but *they all* really boil down to one, excluding of course, *Christianity,* which is the *largest religion in the world;* but is ***not really a religion*** in the truest sense of the word. Christianity is a ***relationship between God and the people He has called unto Himself.*** In all *pagan* religions *there is only* ***one underlying reality;*** and that is *essentially,* ***people are worshipping without knowing*** that those whom they worship ***are***

fallen angels, and that all their efforts, therefore, *are to **try** to bring about their own salvation.*

The two great questions that religion asks are: *"Who is God? And how can I be with Him, forever?* God and salvation. And all *pagan* religions, never-the-less, boil down to man's efforts *to save himself.* So worship is given to the creature. And it is the *creature's effort to save himself, that all **his worshiper's hopes** are built upon, **as opposed to Christ,** who **is the Living God**; who has proved Himself as such, **by His resurrection from the dead** and who freely **gives eternal life, by His grace;** a gift, to **all** of those who trust in Him.* So the two religions, **the only two that exist on this planet,** are diametrically opposed to each other.

Therefore, what is our attitude to be towards all this? Well, we live in a very tolerant age. *Netland describes* something about this tolerant age that we *need to understand, i.e.* there are *three* kinds of tolerance.

First, we see *legal tolerance* - Which means that legally, *in this nation,* we **tolerate** ALL religions -- or NONE. In America, *anyone* can hold to any religion he wants, or to none; and *he can proclaim it from the highest rooftop or radio tower.* It is not *illegal* to be of *any* religious persuasion in this country. That is *not true* in *all* the nations of this world. E.g. it is *illegal* in Saudi Arabia, to worship any god but Allah In many countries, *Christians are being burned, crucified, tortured, and peeled,* for refusing to accept *Islam.* The matter of legal toleration is an *incomparably valuable treasure* we have in this country. And further, the *government* has *no **power*** to enforce *anybody's* participation in *any* religion, or in *no* religion, and **that, we would always fight for.**

Secondly, there is *social tolerance,* which is putting up with *ideas* that we don't agree with. *That* has *always* been American, and *Christians* ought to endorse that, *more than the average.* And we should do it *graciously, lovingly, and kindly.* We are to love our enemies, *even if they are hostile.* We are *not* to shout, or scream, or curse, as some do, when they hear something they don't like.

So there is legal tolerance and social tolerance. Thirdly, there is *intellectual tolerance,* and this is a *totally new* idea that is just being developed in America. It is totally foreign in America. Its idea is, that we are *not only* to accept other *persons* (social tolerance), *but that we are to accept every other view.* Whether it is intellectual, *or moral,* the proposition is that we are to accept it as being *equally true -- with every other view.* That is called *moral relativism.* Therefore, we are *not only,* as they are pushing now in some colleges, to accept them as true, *but to encourage them, equally. Nowhere in the Constitution of this nation are we required to, and the Word of God **prohibits**, our acceptance of other gods or religions as equal to our God, or to our "abundant" life. In fact we are promised **terrible consequences** if we do.*

The idea that we Christians would accept *one religion more than another is totally unacceptable **to** the people who insist on **"political correctness"** today.* The idea is *ridiculous and absurd to Christian believers.* But it did not die out after being introduced about 15 years ago. *On the contrary,* in the last decade or more, it has become more entrenched and stronger and stronger. It has been elevated to a new level. To *not* honor it, is called *"hate crimes,"* and it has become a major threat to all of us who are intellectually more honest. *Hate Crime* laws have been passed in a number of states and, within the past year, the *Federal Congress* failed to pass a hate crimes bill *by a very narrow margin. That would be the first time in the history of this Nation/Church that the intents **of the heart** were thought to be subject to the judgment of men - - **in place of God; and the crime would be not merely an act -- but an emotion.***

Shades of George Orwell and his book *1984.* Remember his *"Orwellian Utopia?"* It proposed something called *Thought Police.* Do you think it *couldn't happen?* It has already happened in countries like the Soviet Union (in the past), and China; and Saudi Arabia; and Iran; and Iraq; and North Korea; *and others.* If one were to go into Saudi Arabia and criticize the Koran, their Bible that would be a *hate crime, **punishable by death** -* urged on by the state and executed on the spot. No trial, ***immediate execution.*** Have you ever heard the Bible criticized in America? Of course you have, *many times.* But you couldn't do it in countries with hate crime laws. *There is a **legitimate fear,*** that certain *intellectual elites* are step- by-step passing such laws. They have their long- range agenda clearly worked out in their minds. Christianity, of course, *does not believe in that sort of thing.* In America, we *now* have freedom to practice our religion, *and free speech.* **Hate Crime** *legislation would make preaching Christian beliefs,* **from a pulpit, a crime!**

We have something else being raised in America, *a new "right"* has been proposed. Fortunately, it hasn't reached the Supreme Court yet, to receive the *imprimatur* of our government, but it is claimed as a "right." It is the right *"not to be offended."* "You *offend me*"- "That *offends* me." I *don't like that.*" "That is an *offense* to me." You see, **I have the right NOT to be offended.**

O really? Where did a "right" like that come from? This is still, *as of now at least,* **America.** In some countries, *some* people, at least *the Muslims* who live there, have a legal right not to be offended. **But not in America, at least not yet.**

What about those other gods? What about conflicts? What *are* we to think? In truth, **Christianity** *solves those* **apparent** *conflicts. First, it abolishes t*he one god of Islam, next the million gods of the Hindus, the "none" of skeptical Buddhism. **Christ solves** the one as well as the many and the none. We believe in One God, but in the Godhead there are *three persons* - and the great religious and philosophical quest of the One, and the many, is solved -- *in Jesus Christ and the Trinity.* And we have the command of Jesus himself to **proclaim that Gospel -- to all people, especially those who follow those other gods.**

This is notable to *Christian Churches* in reference to *"reformed"* theology and current "concern" that we (in the United States or in the world) might be trampling on the "rights" of people who worship "other" Gods. We who accept the *Great Commission of Jesus Christ,* are **called** to believe and accept, that the *Creator God* we worship is certainly *capable* of having a means of grace **which He may apply** to those who worship *"those other Gods,"* but we who *by His Grace* are **followers of Jesus Christ,** are not invited to that *"My thoughts are higher than your thoughts"* arena. To involve ourselves where we have not been invited is to attempt to build another *Tower of Babel.* **Followers of Christ are called (and limited) to proclaim the Gospel of Jesus Christ, and to teach what He commanded us** - - *even to those "other God" worshipers.*

By the way, as we go back to being "offended," how many of you have *not heard* the name of *Jesus Christ* taken in vain by blasphemous people? **That offends** *the heart of every person who loves Christ* -- and yet **we believe** that *free speech* is a *God-given right.* We believe in liberty. But for those for whom *the very, mention of Jesus* is an offense, I would say: "in case you haven't noticed, in America more than 200 years ago, *we gave up any **supposed right** to be offended* by *anything anybody* might say; when we voted for *and accepted* the right of *freedom of speech.* You can't have both. You *must choose* one or another, and if everything offends you, I suggest that *you're in the wrong place.*"

A final thought, *Jesus **died*** to give you the benefit of *personal* choice, and He *rose from death, - to prove His deity.* What about those other gods? *There **are no other gods.***

This Nation/Church Views Sin

In any refurbishing project, if any of the *old material,* if any of the original specifications, if any of the "time honored" and traditional allure of the old is to be restored, the material usually has to be *cleaned up and repaired* before it can reclaim its contribution to the whole. In the case of the *building blocks* which are reasonably expected to attach to and *validate the creation of the Cornerstone,* such a clean-up must deal with the natural *"substance"* of the blocks; .e. SIN; -- *personal and corporate sin.*

".... *For when you where slaves to sin, you were
free in regard to righteousness. What fruit did you?
Have then in the things of which you are now ashamed?
For the end of those things is death. But now,
having been set free from sin,* **and having become
slaves of God***, you have your fruit to holiness, and
the end, everlasting life." (Romans 6: 21-22)*

Since Adam, *ALL have sinned and come short of the glory of God."* The logical conclusion then has to be: If everyone in a given group (read that as congregation of the church) is short of His glory, then the group is no more free of the stain of sin than the most "sinful" of its members. The group is more so, because in any group, the *product* is greater than the sum of all the parts. Or in the case of sin, is it? The purpose of any "fellowship" is to *build on available strengths.* We are called into (eternal) fellowship with our Savior. We are called to *be His presence among His people on earth. We are called to complete His earthly ministry, which is to bring salvation to God's fallen people.* **We are slaves to Jesus Christ!**

Can we truly free others from sin if *we live as we did when we were in sin?* If we are to become of value whatsoever to Christ in refurbishing His Nation/Church, we *must remain free of the sin from which His death cleansed us.*

Human tendency, *and as long as we wear this earthly body* we **remain human,** when we accept the freedom He brings to us, we respond with an infantile like attitude to the *discipline or authority* our *New Slave-master* applies to our *reborn life.*

Human infants begin early to test the waters of *individuality* for themselves. They probe and stretch, a very little at first, the self interpreted as very vague guidelines, not only of their parents, (or if they are *Christian Adults,* Ordained Elders) but those of "school," or society or Christian Doctrine or "new life" stricture placed upon their daily lives until they *in their own minds at least,* have a definitive understanding of whom or what they are, and what they want to do with *"their very own lives.* Note: **It is at this point in their disciple maturing programming, that the Institutional Church can best apply its developmental responsibilities.**

Paul teaches us: *"When I become a man* (or woman), *"I give up my childish ways"* as I come to understand that to love God, to love our neighbor, to love our self, is to **live and act and be like Jesus.** And to live, act and be like Jesus, is to *give up* our now, our comfortable routine lives, and to dwell constantly and completely -- *in His Word.* **Be like Jesus:**

Can you picture Jesus testing the IRS, which by-the-way is an honor system for stating tax liability; can you picture Jesus teaching His children, even by His example, to fudge their tax return so they could reduce their financial burden? *Did not Jesus teach: "Render unto Caesar what is Caesar's?* (Matthew 22:21)

Or imagine Jesus saying: "I did that but I can get away with it by blaming George. *"What does God's Word say about bearing false witness?* (Proverbs 19:9); or would Jesus say: "She *must be* sleeping with someone; she couldn't afford a car like that on *her* income. Not just Proverbs, *all* of God's Word cries out against malicious gossip, or jealousy (covetousness) or vindictiveness -- to say nothing about Jesus' admonition to the harlot, *"Go and sin no more."* (John 8:11)

Or would Jesus leave the scene of an accident victim lying on the side of the road, so that He wouldn't have to get involved, or so He wouldn't be sued? How does that equate with the parable of the Good Samaritan. (Luke 10: 29-37); Would Jesus say - I know that the fire burned all their belongings, or, it is *his* bad judgment that he built his house too close the river and could not afford flood insurance, or - they wanted kids (or were careless) so bad, but they can't afford to raise them, they made their own bed, now let them sleep in it; I have my own needs, or Would Jesus *really* have the attitude, "charity begins at home?" Or what did Jesus mean, when He told Peter: *"If you love me, feed my sheep."* (John 21:17)

Do you think Jesus would teach His children, *you and I are His children,* it is all right to cheat in school or at work, or to take credit for someone else's triumph, or to smoke that weed, or to pocket money you saw someone else drop, -- it *must* be all right, *everyone else does it.*

Would Jesus teach that sex is nature in action, so indulge yourself, *but do it safely?* Jesus taught: *But those things which proceed out of the mouth come from the heart,* **and they defile a man.** *For out of the heart proceed evil thoughts, murders, adulteries, fornications, thefts, false witness, blasphemies . . .* "(Matthew 15: 18-19) And Paul wrote to the Romans concerning "unnatural" sex practices of "unbelievers" (2: 26-27): *"For this reason God gave them up to vile passions. For even their women exchanged natural use for what is against nature. Likewise also the men, leaving the natural use of the woman, burned in their lust for one another, men with men committing what is shameful, and receiving in themselves the penalty for their error which was due."*

Do we misunderstand Moses' consternation when he discovered why God had threatened destruction of the Israelites who engaged in sexual orgy as they were waiting for his return from the mountain?

Contrast if you will, these New Testament teachings, buttressed by age old Word of God teachings such as those found in Leviticus 18:22, which declares that homosexual practices are forbidden; or 1 Kings 14:24 (abomination); or Leviticus 20:13 (punishment described) or Romans 1:24, 26, 27 (unclean) -- with "up-to-date" *Reformed Theology, which according to the Dean of an Episcopal Theology School, on national TV in June of 2003, said:* **The Apostle Paul (ignoring Jesus' teaching on the subject) would never have envisioned diversity in sexual practice, WHICH WE NOW CELEBRATE** *as God* **approved - God created sex and He doesn't create anything bad.** I wonder how that Seminary would teach Romans 6:13-23.

Other reformed denominations, in almost every annual national meeting, spend an inordinate amount of time hearing Ordained and Lay Church leaders debating whether to ordain as congregational pastors, those who **refuse to repent homosexual practices (not orientation**

– practices). We have to admit, Jesus and His Apostles (all of whom taught from O.T. Scriptures) would never have envisioned celebrating diverse sexual practices by believers; But as Church Leaders, are we (the laity) to *also forget Paul's warning to Timothy about latter day **false teachings*** designed to *"support" personal indulgence?*

Is not sin simply the deliberate, willful decision to make self-serving misuse of that which God made "good?"

Did His Word ever reveal that "You can't be a Christian, *you weren't born with the right name, or color, or into wealth,"* or *"you're not welcome at my table, you're not "silver spoon" caliber; you can't join this club - or **this church** -- try the one on the other side of the tracks.* Does *not* Scripture teach that *all are equal in the sight of God?* Paul illustrates this point as he speaks to the several parts of Christ's Body (the Church) in his first letter to the Corinthians (13:25) ". . . . *That there should be no schism in the body, but that the members **should have the same care** for one another . . . .)* We are ALL lost, without His mercy.

If we "Christians" become too busy acquiring personal wealth, in doing our own thing, or in looking after "number one," we *won't* get involved, we *won't* offer our time, or money, or energy, or talents, helping someone else solve *their* problem. Is that in keeping with Jesus' teaching about going into the by-ways and *driving them into* His Master's feast ? Or does that square with the lesson about the steward who refused, *out of false fear, to use his* talents to *increase what was entrusted to him?* What Jesus has entrusted to His Church, is the *completion* of His mission to *reconcile God's people to the home of their Father.* **All people!**

And be advised: *There just **is no** small inconsequential sin!* The popular notions that a *little lust, or pride, or sloth, or greed, **in moderation of course,*** are fun, and that's what makes the world go-round, is a notion that *is the breeding ground for what is known to some believers, as **Cardinal Sin.*** Jesus taught, according to Matthew (5:27-30) for example, in the sin of adultery, it is dangerous to let a little sin go. He went further in verses 29 & 30: *"And if your right eye causes you to sin, pluck it out and cast it from you; for it is more profitable for you that one of your members perish, than for your whole body to be cast into hell. And if your right hand causes you to sin, cut it off and cast it from you . . . . "* **Can there really be any doubt of consequences for him (or her) who**

by the way they continue to live on earth, rejects His call to "repent and sin no more."

Sin, even *small* sin, is insidious. The more we deliberately *excuse ourselves* from living according to *God's Will*, the more comfortable we become with it, the bigger and more destructive and more *self deluding* our sins become. The famous, or infamous, murders of Nicole Brown Simpson and Ron Goldman for example, *were not sin.* They *were sinful actions, the **result of sin.*** The **sin** was the killer's deliberate decision that God *erred in allowing them to live* after he (the killer) became jealous, or to hate them. The **sin** was the killer's **decision** to correct God's "error" as the killer perceived it.

For consequences of sin (mentioned above) just look at the history of Adam and Eve. As they faced temptation for the first time, many things were true for them that have never been true for us. They lived in a perfect environment and an uncorrupted society. No family, no social influence could be blamed for *their choice* to do what was wrong in the eyes of their Creator. No sinful heritage, no ravaged surroundings could be blamed for their downfall. There were even many sins that they just *couldn't commit.* They couldn't commit adultery; they couldn't steal from anyone; they couldn't dishonor father or mother; they couldn't bear false witness against their neighbor; they couldn't covet their neighbor's property. They killed no one -- **but they sinned.** And God declared that they *and all their descendants would suffer **death** for sin.* And that first Sin was their *defiance* of the Word of God; of *refusing* to live and to act and to be – like God created them to be -- **in His own image.**

We today, *even when we have "accepted" Jesus' death as punishment for **past sins**, we are called to "persevere" in our re-born state, and realize that sin can **still** destroy our personal relationship with God.* Parents *and/or the fellowship of believers* (the Church) sometimes, suffer all their lives for allowing their children to become what they, *the recalcitrant one, want to be,* and damn *those who believe **they** know* what is best. " *I have to live my own life, do my own thing."* The problem is that *everyone, not just* the *"rebel,"* must live their remaining life with the "earthly" after-effects of their *combined* (hands-off) decision.

The **good news** of *God's eternal involvement and control* in our task, for we who have been the sinful children of God, is brought to us by Him whom we call *Savior:* i.e. That God, our *Heavenly* Father, even though He established the penalty *death* for sin, *and He steadfastly holds to His judgment "for our own good,"* in the form of His only Son *who never sinned,* took onto *Himself* the penalty He decreed for us – *If we admit to Him, to our self, and to all mankind,* that we must depend on the mercy manifested in the *death and resurrection of Jesus to keep us free of the consequences of the sin we tend to continue to become guilty of, as we "mature" as His children.* He will not only forgive our sins, He will remember them no more.

Jesus Christ became man so that He, *as God*, could ransom man from the gates of Hell, *which is the appointed consequence of sin.* He *paid* the ransom by taking upon himself *our penalty, i.e.* **death,** which was pronounced by the Creator of *all* life, in Eden. He paid that penalty *once, for all mankind,* then, now, and for all time to come; His sacrifice, followed by *His resurrection,* demonstrated that God, with a power that only He has, and in indescribable mercy, could and would *recreate into a new person,* **anyone** who accepted His offer, and **gave up** *(repented) his/her old sinful being.* Before making that ransom payment, Christ revealed to man the eternal glory that would come to him/her *if they demonstrated their belief by* **becoming** *that new person;* and He taught and demonstrated how any *new-born* child of God **differed from the old.** That was His three-year ministry on earth. *Redemption is* **free** *for any who trustingly, willingly, change from the old to the new.* The new redemptive forgiveness He brings calls for us to take on that c*ompletely new life,* **by relinquishing to His death** *the old life,* with the help of *His Holy Spirit,* which He bequeathed to us for that purpose. We, this Nation/Church are *"called" to* concentrate our *"new"* lives to what He leads us to do through His Body, *this Nation/Church.--* To satisfactorily *complete His ministry of salvation for all people.*

217

The Relevancy Of The Gospel - Today

In August or September of each year, a new term year begins. We will once more be *tempted* to hand off to *"professional"* educators, responsibility for passing along to our "future," our children, whatever *"professionals"* consider being appropriate knowledge. State-of-the-art is the way *they* describe appropriate or perhaps *more* definitively, *politically* Correct.

BUT- let *us* speak this morning, to the feeling that many, too many people in today's world feel that the *Word of God,* more specifically, the teachings of Jesus Christ and His Apostles, *and His present day Church,* are **irrelevant** to the circumstances of life, as *"we"* have *"advanced"* them.

The real hardship in countering the apparently prevailing feeling of *irrelevancy,* is that first the baby-boom, and then the "X" (now some of the "Y") generations, *today's parents and grandparents,* have gotten so far out of the mainstream of *the followers of Jesus Christ,* that it might be beyond the capability of those of us who *remain in His flock,* to convince them otherwise. or -- so say the hand-wringers and doomsday prophets among the *so-called* faithful, who look more to tradition in *form* of worship services, than they do to *innovation* in developing ways of *communicating* the *good news of the presence of God in today's society,* and of *salvation being* offered *even to today's supposedly lost generations.* I guess they don't believe Paul's assurances of possibilities in Philippians 4:13.

Now in order to prevent anyone from concluding that this statement indicates that I am *contemptuous* of traditional worship practices, let me assure you that I am not. As of this date and time in *my* worship life, I am *more than content* to be labeled a traditionalist. But I have *already accepted Jesus Christ* as the Cornerstone of *my* life. I find *inspiration* in the *traditional* worship service. ***That does not, however, mean that others, who are so caught up in "state-of- the-art" advances in their lifestyles, must be locked out*** on any opportunity to accept the grace of God, just because I am **unwilling** to speak to them in a language not too out of date -- for **them** to understand.

The point for today is, *it is up to us who accept the stewardship of the Gospel, to adapt the* **proclamation** *of it to a form, as well as a language, which* **they** *will stop and hear and be challenged enough by that they will want to explore it themselves, under the auspices of the Holy Spirit,* just as you and I have done for all our lives, *and should still be doing.* When you get a chance, time-wise, review Acts 2: 1-12, the account at Pentecost, and remind your- selves how important *Peter* felt it to be to pro- claim the Good News of Jesus to His people, in a language *which they* understood. Please notice: I said *adapt the proclamation* of the Gospel to them, I **did not say,** adapt the *Gospel* to their lifestyles. The goal is, to *amend life circumstances to fit God's Word,* not the reverse.

If we are to make a successful effort to translate the teachings of Jesus to contemporary language, perhaps our first step would be to achieve an accurate definition of the so-called uniqueness of those "hearers." Here's a way we can do that:

The foremost social analyst of his time says: "Young people today will be the ruination of our great country. We are not talking about *children,* we are not talking only about *teenagers,* we are also talking about *young adults,* some of them parents, who as a class, have succeeded in breaking the bonds of parental, or social, discipline and authority. They are contemptuous of social values; they believe their so-called education, *which in reality is little more than extensive memorization of facts,* makes them *immune* to any need to adhere to natural or man-made law. They waste themselves in strong drink, or drugs, or promiscuity; self-glorification, dishonesty, self gratification; and imposition of their will by violence, seems to be their order of the day. They accept no guilt for their own actions, blaming their actions on previous generations and practices. They *resist* the thesis that the freedom they demand, *only works in direct proportion to the responsibility* **each free person** *applies to its maintenance.* They *worship self* enough to believe that their parents, their society class, their country or their educational "inferiors" *owe them* material support, *regardless of the frivolous nature* of their life-styles.

The *Social Scientist* we are paraphrasing is no longer living among us. His name is *Socrates,* who made comments like these *hundreds of years* before *Jesus of Nazareth* made His appearance as our Messiah.

The people who today refuse to *accept the Word of God* -- **are not unique at all.** They are merely *copycats of history.* It *is* true that much, much more is *available* to them in the arenas of science and technology; they have been able to transform beasts of burden to over-night delivery; ass or donkey into super-sonic plane or space shuttle; or stone tablets into Internet or e-mail; or blood letting and amputations into organ transplant. But their so-called *today technology* continues to be nothing more than *accouterments* of mortal life, *still subject to the same kind of greed, or avarice, or abuse, or exploitation,* as were the aides to living from which they evolved.

Socrates spent his career trying to *teach the axiom* that **knowledge,** in and of itself, *is only the first step to wisdom, and it takes inordinate wisdom to make freedom for all work for all.* Socrates knew what most *politically correct* educators today *fail to demonstrate* to *their proselytes.* That knowledge is acquired by learning facts; *Wisdom* is found in *learning to apply knowledge* to the various conditions (good or bad) of mortal life. This is of course, the *worldly* distinction between the two. God has His own definition of wisdom. *God created wisdom,* just as He created everything else that has ever been, or that is, or that ever will be.

Wisdom which *is* of God (that is spiritual wisdom) has knowledge as its *entry point,* just as does worldly wisdom. But that knowledge is worthless, it cannot ever be profitably applied *without understanding* how that knowledge fits into *God's* plan, *or if faith is the applicator.* e.g. we are forced to believe that *confused knowledge* falsely inspired the 39 members of the "Heavens Gate" cult, (remember them?) all of them college graduates, many of them with advanced "state-of-the art" degrees, to commit suicide, so that they could beat the rush to catch "God's spaceship" to eternity, which *they believed* was following a comet. Their supposedly *superior* knowledge led them to forever *forfeit any chance* of their attaining God's wisdom. We could put it this way: *Knowledge* can come from college, but *Wisdom* comes from God!

Wisdom, *Spiritual Wisdom,* is mentioned more than 130 times in the Old Testament; at least 76 times in the New Testament. The *Books of Proverbs* and Ecclesiastes are dedicated to *very practical wisdom.* It seems to follow then, that our second step in translating the *Word of*

*God would be to **know** the Word of God.* How do we get to know the Word of God?

A text on the *Word of God* has existed for *thousands of years,* which will help us, *teach us,* how to accomplish our personal, our *believer* responsibilities in *communicating* the *Good News* of the *only* means of *salvation, of eternal life* with God, (which is) available to *all people.* Brought to us by God, interpreted by inspired man, passed down over many generations by word of mouth from father to son; canonized almost 500 years *after the death of Christ,* some say the first complete book ever printed; a text containing 4000 years or more *of testimony to the **timeless** might, and power, and steadfastness* of God, who *created man and his (man's) present world, and to His (God's) personal love and mercy for His creation, **forever.***

That text *is* actually, of course, the recorded Word of God, which we call *The Bible.* **And that Word of God is as relevant to today, as it has always been - to man.**

The *problem* remains age-old. Not of *relevancy,* but of man's *rebellion* against the discipline of *living with God, on earth.*

The *Word of God* speaks to this problem today, just as it did to Abraham and Moses, the same as it did, *through Christ,* to the 12 and to the 70, to the 500 and to 5000; to *countless generations.*

Only the accouterments have changed - *not necessities – accouterments* of life have changed. The *Word of God* speaks to the same problems today as it did *before* Abraham, since *Adam and Eve;* it speaks to man's sin, and just as is true today, *each of those* Biblical generations also had their own *language and way of life of their own..* But the *Church* succeeded in translating the Gospel, to *each, to every one of **those** generations,* with the help of *The Holy Spirit; just as it will help us, **if we call upon it to do so.***

As a *test of the relevancy of God's Word,* read the New Testament *letter to the Hebrews.* Hebrews was written during the first century A.D. The writer was *concerned* because of a *very evident drift* of believers from a vital faith, and from *their personal commitment to it.* It is true, *some **were** wilting in the face of persecution,* but ***others** were beginning to doubt* because of secular, ***humanistic*** philosophies *being taught in that time period.* It sounds like when it comes to the 21st century, *only the date has changed.*

We know, of course, that like any other text, *The Bible does not* do its job in a vacuum. The Bible was *never intended* to stand alone. The Bible is only *one part* of the equation for spiritual wisdom.

For us to *understand* the *message* of the Word of God, and to remember that as we read, that understanding how *knowledge* of God is intended *by God* to fit into His plan to *save man* from *eternal damnation*, *and from hell on earth*, -- for us to come to a true understanding of the knowledge of God's Word, we must combine a life-long, *continuous, repeated study of His Word, with faith and prayer and fellowship with other believers, and lifestyle.*

In order to *become* knowledgeable about the perfect Will of God as it applies to our very present state-of-the-art lives, we must meditate (read that as *study and restudy)* His revelations to us throughout the history of man; but *most assuredly,* through His Son, Jesus. (Identified as Messiah, Rabbi, Savior, Teacher, Son of God) And to *understand* the knowledge we gain from that study, we must *depend* upon the *counsel* that *Jesus assures us* is ours by faith; I.e. *His Holy Spirit.*

We are promised faith *and* His Holy Spirit by God's grace. *But,* God *requires* that we (you and I) **use** that faith, in order for it to be relevant in our daily lives. *And how do we use faith, coupled with our knowledge acquired by study of His word?* We *invoke* the counsel of the Holy Spirit, by prayer. We must subject ourselves to prayer. Often, quiet, personal, private and public, *in all our daily circumstances, in any form -- Prayer.* **And that does include hearing what God has to say to us!**

Just as Jesus used His knowledge of Scripture which was ingrained in Him from infancy by His mortal parents, as *He faced temptation,* not only in the wilderness, but *throughout His ministry,* so must present day *believers assimilate the Scriptures into their own beings.* And once more, they best do so by constant, repeated study of His Word, made *understandable* by *prayerful intervention of the Holy Spirit.* We must learn how it is that God would have us change the *focus of our lives* from being *of* this world, to *being God's people* who are presently *in this world.*

There is another element in the formula for translating *knowledge* of God into *Spiritual Wisdom.* **It is the element of Christian Fellowship.** It is in sharing with *other Christians* the act of Public Worship, *as well* *as* sharing experiences of joy and of our own personal difficulties in Christian living, that God *demonstrates* the means by which His Will can triumph; and in mutual support and nurture, that we are able to make the teachings of Jesus *meaningful **and relevant.***

God created *man to live in community,* which we call fellowship. It is really not possible, or at least not as likely, that one can be "as good a Christian," by living as a *spiritual hermit.*

Prayer, Study of His Word, Faith, Fellowship. These are, *all of them,* in concert with each other, the elements of *Spiritual Wisdom, **given to us by our God,** and **our only means** to **combat** un-godlike* lifestyles, which we ***allow to corrupt our participation in building the Kingdom of God.***

And let there be *no mistake,* **successful** *combat* begins with *each single one of us. Combat **is** the correct word.* The arena in which we minister for Jesus Christ is a *battleground, not a playground.*

But believe it or not, there *is* a silver lining to the cloud of difficulty called relevancy. It is recorded that *many thousands* of college students, as they complete their collage careers, are finding *outside the academic curricula,* a way to put *some ultimate meaning* into their lives, which their education and their *"guidelines"* for future success *fails to provide.* By the thousands, they are seeking *religion* as a capstone of their preparation for adulthood. It is a statistical fact that the *greatest percentage of new religious converts, **is on college campuses.***

Vincent Krische, a campus chaplain and Director of Campus Ministry at the University of Kansas, says: "Students are *hungry* for religion, because many of them were raised *without it."* He continues: "I think there has been a *failure in passing to them,* meaning and values; something *internally* inspires people to search for them.

The *silver lining* is that the very people we tend to throw our hands up about, and write *out* of our proclamation of the Gospel would most *likely be receptive* to the message we proclaim ***if we make the effort to speak their language.*** And, they might even "someday" understand the need for *combat discipline.* Not now maybe, *but someday.*

Just a tip: *No spoken word, in **any** generation, is more accurately understood, as is Parental, or older Church Member, **lifestyle examples.***

The need for immediacy, *before college,* is: There are many more "religions" than *Christianity* available for those trying to *fill a void. Try*

Buddhism, Hinduism, Shintoism, Islam, and others. They are also, *and more aggressively than Christianity,* on college campuses. And these others *also* make themselves available to *those who never go to college; i.e.* in High School, or *even more dangerously,* in "social" environments.

If we, *you and I,* solve that part of the problem *that is ours,* i.e. *making the Gospel known to our own children,* **and to those in our congregation/community,** we will make it **possible** for God to replace *worldly "foolishness" with spiritual wisdom.* **We will have applied the <u>only</u> relevant medicine to the ills of mankind,** and as the results of that treatment fans out; spreads:

- There will be no more personal depression
- There will be no more violence (particularly tragic is the tendency of teenagers to inflict violence on *teenagers; too often, as suicide)*
- There will be no more social suffering
- There will be no more racial hatred
- There will be no more injustice

There *will be* peace, and joy, and an abundant life such as *no political party, or academic* effort ever formed by man, can even imagine, let alone bring about. And God, our Heavenly Father, will reap the honor and glory and praise that *are* His just due. What a way to usher in the *Kingdom of God.*

The hope of being "relevant" to youth, rests in using youth, substantively, in planning, and in executing, worship services -- and in "reach out to others" ministry.

Values, Standards And Such

"......*Also I heard the voice of the Lord, saying: "Whom shall I send, and who will go for us?" Then I said, Here am I, send me. And He said, "Go and tell this people: Keep on hearing but do not understand; keep on seeing but do not perceive. Make the heart of this people dull and their ears heavy, and shut their eyes; lest they see with their eyes, and hear with their ears, and understand with their heart -* **and return and be healed.**" (Isaiah 6: 8 - 10)

God, concerned with Israel's rapidly accelerating slide into evil, in His mercy, called to Isaiah in a vision, asking *"Who shall I send?* Isaiah responded: "Here am I, send me."

By responding to God's call, Isaiah took on the very troublesome task of being the Prophet, the Counselor, the Spokesman of God, whose 40 year term of office was directed at the "upper class," and the religious leaders of a mightily prosperous Judea.

Isaiah's prophesy foretold that *if there was not a general repentance across the nation, a change in the lifestyle they were then living,* **God would deliberately withdraw His protective favor, and the absolute destruction of Jerusalem would follow.**

Isaiah was required by God to *warn the rich and powerful* Judeans, at a time when peace and prosperity prevailed and their standard of living had never been so high in their long, long history, that corruption, immorality, injustice to their own poor, and *preoccupation* with frivolous elements of the lifestyle they were then enjoying, *were prompting them to push God out of their lives. Isaiah had to tell his own friends and neighbors,* that God *saw through* the **facade of their worship practices,** i.e. their "faithful" attendance at worship services, their regular celebration of religious festivals and holidays, their practice of tithes and special offerings, their public piety and prayer -- *they were just* **not living** *the way that God, through His historical stream of spokesmen, from the time He had appointed them as His people, had* **taught** *them.*

The people of God were once more *demonstrating* their **illusion** that their wealth and power resulted from *their own* mastery of life. Oh, they did give God *lip service,* but they had relegated Him to *insignificance* in

225

their daily lives. They were *in truth*, worshipping *idols* -- some of the idols were graven images, *most of them were **excesses in their "standard of living."***

In their false worship of God, the rich and powerful of Judea had **learned** the **values and standards** which God *had established* for them to live by, but as they prospered and became more and more affluent, *they became corrupt* -- they *ignored* the precepts that had sustained them *as the people of God;* they went so far as to *assume* that since God lived among them (in the Temple in Jerusalem), they could never be harmed *no matter what they did, no matter how they lived.* By the *way people were living,* they were in fact **redefining** *the values and standards which they had been taught* by their benevolent God, and it was Isaiah's task to *warn them, God was **in no way,** pleased.* And, unless they made a *complete turn-around* in their way of life, *God would punish them as terribly as if they had been returned to slavery in Egypt.* Even more so, they would lose their cohesion, their unity as God's chosen people. (By the way, *history records* that Judea *was* destroyed and the people exiled to far disbursed locations, until *that generation* died off, -- 70 years.

Why should we emphasize Isaiah's *warning* prophesy today, rather than his foretelling of God's ultimate grace, the coming of the Messiah (which *was* the other side of the story)?

Look around you at today's lifestyle in this Nation, in the cities certainly, but also in rural areas, even in our own community. It is *not hard to see the parallels* between Isaiah's Judea and the way life is evolving, out of control, *right now!*

This Nation is the most affluent society in the history *of the world.* Our current standard of living *has never been equaled* -- if you think that *you and I - Joe/Jane working stiff* - are so poor that that affluence *does not include you and I* -- compare our standard of living with those who live in the Far East or other third-world country, where if a child brings home a stray dog, *it does not become a new family pet,* **it becomes their evening meal.** If that does not *implode* on our conscience, we *have no claim to Christian life!* Or just look at the man-in-the-street in present day Russia. Because of poverty, shortages of staples, a *survival of the fittest mentality,* years of government oppression of Christian teaching, a Russian's average life-span has dropped from 62 years in 1962, to 57 years, today. *Almost 20 years less than in the United States.* Or look at the pleas for help for *children, all over the world,* by the Christian Children's Fund. In countries where greed and avarice have not yet overheated their economy, it costs ***$20.00 per month*** to provide for a child. *Certainly,* that is an over-simplification. But you and I seem determined that the measure of success *in* how well we raise *our children* will be *how much we spend on them;* what we are able to buy for their pleasure. We think *we are impoverished* if we can't spend *twenty times* $20.00 per *week (not per month)* on them.

We feel *so strongly* that way, that we *relegate* their day by day *learning, values absorption, needs satisfaction, love quotient, to someone **we hire off the street*** (or a "state approved" program facility manager) so that we can spend *"our"* time earning the where-with-all to *pay for our parental substitute.* We so foolishly define our love for our children thusly, that we pay for material things we *give* them, rather than by *our presence, or by our example,* or by *what we demonstrate as values, to them.* Are you aware that Child Psychologists have determined that *values absorption begins at age three,* and those beliefs *frameworks* begin to take shape *at age five?*

We, *you and I* who *now* study the Word of God, *also* know God's values and standards. We know them *even better* than did Isaiah's Judeans. We have the *Holy Spirit* of our Savior to enhance our study of *their mistakes.* We also know, even though we are reluctant to admit it, that *His Word **cautions of the need for** personal and for corporate (Church) self-evaluation* from time to time *invoking the help of The Holy Spirit,* in order to assure ourselves that we are not yet, nor are we about to, *stray from Him who created and sustains us.* Is there a more appropriate time than immediately? Yom Kippur is an annual day set aside on the Jewish calendar for *re-evaluation.* We Christians *pretend* we do that *personally and constantly,* but maybe we should do it *formally, and together.* The Church, for example, through its assembly of believers, *should* advocate *spiritual* rather than *material* objectives of "human" endeavor. *Too often, the Church's primary effort is in **raising money,*** so that their ***doors can be kept open,*** *rather than "promoting" Church ability to adhere to the teachings of Matthew 25, or to more effectively comply with Evangelistic or Cultural Mandates.*

And let us not *delude ourselves.* Let us not "pass the buck" back to our tempters. The trials, tribulations, hardships, anguish and suffering

227

we endure, can *usually* be traced to *our own* resistance to the *values, the standards* which, if we do not turn our back to them, *God assures us* will attain for us the *peace and spiritual prosperity and the self-fulfillment* we so desperately seek in our lives. But before we go any farther, let us come to an understanding of what we mean by *value.*

According to Webster, a *value* is something of *primary importance to us.* Not really hard to understand at all. If it is *important to us,* it qualifies as a value *to us.* A *standard* is the life factor by which a value is assigned its worth.

God's plan for perpetuating His values, in the construction of His Church.

Now, let us begin our self-evaluation with an examination of the *basic building block* of God's *New Jerusalem,* which He reveals to John, on the island of Patmos (Revelations 21). It is *true* that Christ is the Cornerstone, but the basic building block, according to *any reading* of God's Word, *is the family.* In Genesis (2:24), God says *"Therefore a man leaves his father and mother and clings to his wife, and they become one flesh."* And we profess as we participate in a wedding ceremony, that *we accept God's standard: "Till **death** us do part."* We do this in our *wedding vows, **which are made to God, before** making them to each other.* In Genesis, God also commands us *to be fruitful and to multiply, **to bring forth a family.*** More than 250 additional times in succeeding chapters of God's Word, the *family* is brought to the forefront. The *product of man and wife, **according to God's plan,** is family,* either by natural birth or by adoption, or even if there is no child.

Let us also realistically recognize that there *are* some exceptions to the *"until death do us part"* standard. *Christ* teaches that being *unfaithful* to one's spouse is an *acceptable* cause for separating the *"one flesh." **Adultery,*** according to His teaching, does not *require* a divorce (see the prophet Hosea's marriage woes), but it *is the only acceptable cause* for an annulment of the marriage vow. There are, however, *times* when physical or mental *abuse* (spousal or child) makes divorce a *lesser evil.*

But in our mislead zeal to be *"understanding"* and or compassionate, we have *officially, secularly,* and unfortunately *within the Church,* **changed the standard** implicit in God's Word. We cite *incompatibility, or hardship, or health, or personal ego* (the need to be "our own" person) *or neglect, even "no fault"* as "legal" permission to break up a family.

We have prompted our *societal* legal system to *supersede God's standards;* and *much more* than 50% of the building blocks we *do* build, are *shattered. And that statistic says nothing about the families, or at least the children conceived **without benefit of marriage vows.*** The Fabric of Christianity that we claim as our national banner is getting a whole lot of snags in it.

It is widely said, many times by would-be Church leaders who mistakenly advocate separation of **God** from government decision making, that it is possible to have *morality **without** religion.* There is more than ample historical, available to the public, evidence that the *founders of this nation and the writers of our constitution, **neither believed nor advocated** that premise.* America's first president, the one who is credited by everyone except current publishers of history books and public school teachers as being *The Father of Our Country,* in his Farewell Address said *this a*bout that foolishness:

"*. . of all the dispositions and habits which lead to political prosperity, religion and morality **are indispensable supports.** In vain would that man claim the tribute of patriotism **who should labor to subvert these great pillars of human happiness.** And let us **with caution** indulge **the supposition that morality can be maintained without religion.**"*

And there are tragic results of prolonged "labor to subvert" that basic premise: For more than twenty-five years, the children attending our schools and colleges have been taught that there are no moral absolutes; that "*no one can tell them what to do.* They (the children and those in training to teach them) are told simply to choose their own ethics. In the last book of Judges, we read: "*. . . . . every man did that which was right **in his own eyes.**"* (Judges 21:25) -- and God, in His anger, vowed to no longer drive out from before them, any of the nations Joshua left when he died.

We go even farther, we actively strive to *tolerate,* or to officially recognize marriage between *two males or two females, or "families"* comprised of one parent (usually, but not *always* female) whose child-bearing results from either "*renting" or "borrowing"* someone of the opposite gender, to conceive the child. We "practicing" Christians seem to *be demonstrably* more worried about, and we revere, "*political correctness," much more* than we do God's standards.

*And I am **not** suggesting persecution, or even ostracism, of those misguided mortals;* in fact, they should be singled out for intensive *evangelistic* outreach.   **But if they refuse repentance of their chosen way of life, if they insist it is their "right" to live as they choose, over God's way, they must never be made "officers" of the Church -- nor ordained in the Church.**(1 Timothy 3: 1 - 11)

As a direct result of *"secular" acceptance and corrupted Christian theological "tolerance" of this standards abuse,* in some areas of this *open and diverse society* we so fervently defend, *one out of three children have only one parent -- the National average is one in four.* It has been *proven* that one parent *cannot possibly* fill both roles alone. It is recognized of course, that through death, desertion or other rare cause, single parenting *can be* the only option available; *which is when the fellowship of believers **should** kick in and do what it can to fill the void caused by the missing parent.* And the parenting role of which we speak is also spelled out by Isaiah, as he tells his nation: *"The father shall make known **your** (God's) truth to the children.* We are **not** talking here of arranging for (paying for) so-called *"wholesome"* activities for children, in lieu of *quality time* together.

No matter how much a parent decides to sacrifice, to strive, to scheme, to help, to promote or to "push" children into what is *euphemistically* called *higher education,* or those so-called *wholesome activities,* before children "hit" *any* books (or personal priorities), *they need to know* that the *most important things they will **ever learn,** come from "the" book, the Bible.* It is **the parents' responsibility** to make that fact known to their children. That is something we *must* therefore consider, as we *parents* decide whether *we* should attend Sunday Church School, or should we sleep in, rather than seeing to it that our child *gets* to Sunday School, or to make a Christian youth/fellowship organization a *top priority* on our child's "*belong to" list*

Having thus examined the *values and standards* of a family in God's Kingdom, let us now evaluate His *perspective* of life in this world. Let us do so by asking ourselves some questions: "Am I so wrapped up in the *form* of our worship services, that I dilute its substance and drive others who *would* join us, away? Or do I get so ecstatic over (or do I have an immature need to) *repeatedly hearing* that Jesus makes my salvation possible, that I *overlook the **fact*** that Jesus also **calls** me to *complete His* *ministry* on earth? Is the time I spend generating income (overtime, second job, etc) *overriding my capacity* to serve God, to serve His people? Do I work for the *basic necessities* of earthly life, as Paul did with his tent-making, or do I strive to pile up *personal* wealth, or power, or name recognition, *more than* the "Jones'" -- or more than God? Do the *two* of us parents work *in order to feed our family,* or are we using our God-given skills and spiritual gifts to build up *personal "retirement" treasure* - which Jesus pointed out will rust and mold and be *useless* to our eternal soul? (We *can not buy* a "retirement" as good as we are *given)*

Moses was the first (human) to proclaim that God's Word is a *family* endeavor (Deuteronomy 6: 4-9)

Do we use our "hard earned" material gains for *indulging our selves, and our children* in worldly luxury, or do we really *trust Jesus* when He teaches: *"Do not be afraid of the Father, for it is His good pleasure to **give** you the Kingdom.*

Do we find our fulfillment in the *chase* to become king (or queen) of this earthly heap, *ignoring our knowledge* of God's values, or *regardless* of the *destruction* of the family we have built, *originally to His Glory,* or is our *delight* (fulfillment) truly in bringing joy to His heart by *living* His values and standards.

As can easily be seen, this evaluation cannot be made meaningfully in the vacuum of our individual self; God did not create us to be *hermits.* It is in the context of *our* family, our *congregation,* our *society,* and our *nation,* that we are tasked *by our God* to exist. The unvarnished truth is: *unless the basic building block (the family) is strong and incorruptible,* the whole structure falls.

Perhaps the entire self-evaluation should be in the context of John's vision on the Island of Patmos, when Christ spoke to him of the Church in Laodocia: *"I know your works, you are neither cold nor hot. Because you are lukewarm, and neither cold nor hot, **I am going to spit you out of my mouth.** For your **actions** say "I am rich and need nothing; you do not realize that you are spiritually wretched, pitiful, blind and naked."* Christ says further: *"I reprove and discipline those whom I love."* Isaiah's prophesy *admonishes* us: *Be earnest therefore, and repent your lukewarmness.*

Fortunately for us, *there **is** a saving grace.* Our saving grace *can only be* God's indescribable love and infinite mercy, as *He* evaluates our personal *and our congregational **and our community*** lives, for which we earnestly pray for guidance from *His Holy Spirit.*

The question for those of us now in Isaiah's shoes is: Have I, in truth, stood up and answered a call from my Lord God: **Do I as charged by Peter, through whom the mantel of the ministry of Jesus Christ was passed, address a chosen race, a royal priesthood, a holy nation, God's own People?**

Let *us* (as the Church) see what we can do about keeping a *good momentum* going. We *have to recognize* that keeping it going, takes ***more** than wishing* on our part. It takes ***our involvement*** in public life, and in social volunteerism, ***and in politics***, and in *Christian support and fellowship*. **Let it be so!**

Forgiveness

When we kids in our neighborhood were ten or twelve years old, we would go down to Jack's Creek and play in a miniature park, around the "historical" *Old Arch Bridge*. At that age, not many of us thought about the engineering, but for our purpose today, perhaps by visualizing the arch, we can transform the bridge (at least its arch) into our theological discussion, into the stately entrance, the *narrow and only* doorway into the eternal *fellowship of children of God*, which we can make reference to for our purposes, as the Church.

Picture if you will, how the line of an arch curves from a wide base (the width of the "church structure") upward on an angle, until the Structure is joined, not as a half circle, more like a curved sided triangle. The engineering principle being that an arch such as we describe would provide strength enough to hold up a roof, even when the walls are interrupted to provide a door, the *only* door through which entry could be made. The arch, in fact the "building," is made of stone "quarried" from creation itself (remember Genesis, et al?); each succeeding stone placed closer to the center as it goes into position, until the arch is completed and closed. The secret of the *strength* of the arch is the *three* stones that come together at the top, the center stone we will call the *keystone*. If the keystone or *either* of its companion stones were to be removed from their position in the arch, the whole structure collapses. The roof will no longer shield the occupants from *fiery* elements, and the entry to "the Church" becomes an impassable pile of rubble.

If we can use the arch as a picture of God's plan for our salvation, that makes the keystone *Jesus Christ*. Jesus says: "*I am the way, i.e. the only way to the Father.*" And *if* Jesus *is* the way, the pathway to eternity, the *companion pieces to* the keystone would have to be (if we accept all that we have learned from the Word of God) *would have to be* **Love and Forgiveness.** The two are *intertwined,* and equally support the keystone of the arch.

For now, let's talk about the stone called *forgiveness.* Jesus became the way to the Father by becoming the means by which God would *satisfy His Judgment Decree* that the penalty for mankind, for **sin** would

233

always be - death. ***Sin would require the death of the sinner.   But* . . . .**

Jesus, ***the very Son of God,*** who had no sin of His own, *alone in the history of man and* **alone** *acceptable to God* ***for that purpose***, stepped to the front of Judgment, before God; *lovingly, willingly took upon Himself the consequences* ***of yours and my sin; was crucified until dead.*** And ***if you and I accept His death for our own*** (God does, you know) God will ***forgive yours and my sins.*** He does this out of His *indescribable love* for us. Jesus ***thus became the keystone*** of God's engineered entry for yours and my sojourn in eternity with our creator. The keystone is supported on the side we look into today, by the stone - ***forgiveness. We have our entry to forever, through the forgiveness of our sins.*** *Not by pay-back* ***after we recognized our sins,*** *but by Forgiveness* ***before*** *we recognized our sins, as a result of the sacrifice of God's only* ***begotten*** *Son;* ***And if we accept it.***

Forgiveness is *one of the three* **indispensable stones** at the top of the arch. If this stone is removed, ***the whole structure falls.*** The keystone, *Jesus Christ,* will no longer be able to hold up the structure.

In Matthew 18 (vs 15-35), Jesus teaches the Apostles about forgiveness, but ***not*** just His forgiveness of us. Jesus was teaching His disciples about the necessity of *all believers* to forgive ***any who sins against them!*** Peter, wanting to be sure that he understood, asked: "Lord, how often shall my brother sin against me and I still forgive him? Till seven times?

Many of us, as we read this question of Peter's, *miss* the understanding that in proposing seven times, Peter had *already accepted* Jesus' teaching that it *really is* necessary to forgive someone who insults, cheats or otherwise wrongs us. If fact, Peter was being *more generous* than we give him credit for. You see, Peter was raised and trained in the Judean tradition, and was recalling that he had been taught from birth, by Pharisaic teachers, that a devout Jew was *required* to forgive his brother **three times.** To a Judean, if the matter was not resolved after having been for- given *three* times, ***forgiveness*** was withdrawn.

Within *his* life-long frame of reference, Peter was being very generous with his seven times, but the number *Jesus* responded with was astronomical *from the rabbinical* point of view. The math of *Jesus'* response (70 times 7) aside, Jesus was saying that man had to forgive his brother an **unlimited** number of times. Jesus was setting a *radically new* standard for forgiving, and lest *we do* as most humans are prone to do, which is to grossly *misunderstand Jesus' teaching*, let's realize that Jesus was **not advocating unlimited sinning,** *Jesus was teaching* **unconstrained** *forgiveness.* And as we look farther into His teachings, we will discover that the **forgivee** has equal responsibilities in the process. But now, let us remember: We, who forgive, are **not responsible** for how the forgivee reacts to our forgiveness. It is necessary to discuss this because we humans are *prone to reject out-of-hand,* this **most important part** of the **discipline of living our faith:** (Many "humans" find it too extreme to forgive a brother, especially more than once for the same offense, - **or** we are willing to forgive - on condition). We **might** forgive if the offense does no harm to us or a loved one, - or perhaps after we *get even,* or extract a revenge, . . . but to forgive outright, without condition, and to forever **not** hold that offense against that person again, is something we humans are **not usually prone to do** . . . and we are not talking about **forgetting** the offense.

It *has* been proposed that we must forgive *and forget.* Humans *might* forget, but **not as a means of forgiveness. More likely,** because we forgave. It is just **not** practical to expect the human mind to *forget a major offense.* We teach that God *does* that, **we do** not. We teach that, but when we do, we *misrepresent* what God's Word *actually* says. Hebrews 8 (12) says: *"Their sins and their lawless deeds I will remember no more."* God does not say He will *forget* our sins, He says He will remember them (*against us*) no more. His Word tells me, that *after I confess,* **repent,** *and am forgiven*, He will never again bring *those deliberately, calculated sins* against me - - *not that He will forget them.*

The forgiveness Christ calls for is that we *consciously decide* that the offense done against us **will not prevent us** *from including the* **offender** in our efforts to proclaim the Gospel to *all people,* which is what Christ commands us to do. The lost lamb, the lost coin, the worker hired just before quitting time, the thief on the cross, just *might be* the person *we must forgive* in order for him or her to *truly glorify God,* by accepting the Gospel we proclaim.

As He did so many times in order to make His point, Jesus went directly from His answer (of Peter's question) of 70 times 7, into a story, in this case, a parable - designed to illustrate to the disciples - to you and

I - the *meaning* of what He was teaching. If we translate the parable Jesus uses for His forgiveness lesson, we understand that the king in our Scripture, represents God, and you and I become the servants.

The servant we *concentrate* on, the *ungrateful one* has built up a huge debt. Jesus uses the example of 10,000 talents (translated by *some* as 12,000,000 current dollars), a figure that the servant would not *ever* be able to repay - in his lifetime. What we so often fail to take into account, is that the extreme figure which Jesus uses to describe the debt of this servant to the King, equates to the *sin in yours and my life,* and the penalty for which, *since Adam and Eve,* was adjudicated as **death for the sinner . . .** to the sin in yours and my life, *which we will **never** be able to repay **on our own** . . . to the sin for which God's only begotten Son was **sacrificed** to pay **for us.**

In this parable, the King (God) *forgave* the debt of the wicked servant, **not** *because the servant begged for more time to repay what he owed,* **but because the King, in His own mercy** knowing full well, even better than the servant, that the debt could **never** be repaid **by the servant. The King forgave the debt and set the servant free.** The servant was so grateful (tongue in cheek) that he immediately went out and **refused** the same kind of mercy to a fellow servant who owed *him* a minuscule amount. He threw the minor servant in jail until he could pay his *very minor debt.* Goes to show how intelligent some of us servants are, the wicked servant gave no apparent thought as to how the indebted servant would *become able to pay the debt, if he didn't have any money and was to remain in jail, losing any ability to earn the money to pay him off.*

Several lessons of *Jesus* jump out at us, from this story. One - the King forgives out of His indescribable mercy, **not because He hopes the debt will be repaid; Two** - the King **does** expect that because the forgiven person *accepts* the King's forgiveness, the forgiven person is to likewise forgive *any who owes him a debt;* and last (but not least) the King reserves the right to **revoke the forgiveness,** if the forgiven *person* is too hard-hearted to pass that forgiveness along to anyone who wrongs him/her, thereby demonstrating that he/she in either *unable or* **unwilling to live or act in the spirit of mercy.**

You see, *Jesus saw nothing **inappropriate*** in the actions of a King who can be full of mercy and forgiveness, but who can *also* become frustrated, *and call for punishment. Mercy* has **never been a servant's birthright.** The King offered mercy as He (the King) desired, *and He gave it generously.* The King's mercy **could not be earned; it** was given because the **King** was good, **not** because the *sinner* had done enough to deserve it.

The second, perhaps more important point of the parable: The servant in this story, however, responded to the King's mercy **ungratefully,** by **refusing** *to act mercifully toward his fellow servant,* **in fact,** *by acting* **without any mercy.** He acted legally, mind you, but totally opposite to the mercy *he had received. He had his fellow servant jailed.*

This "wicked" servant was then hauled back in front of his King and was re-dealt with. The King was applying the same "mercy" used by his servant on his fellow.

There are other Biblical references pointing out the **need for followers** *of Christ to be as forgiving toward others,* as we pray for Christ to be *to us.*

Here are several that stand out:

In Matthew 5 (24), *Jesus* teaches those if you come to the altar of worship with something in your heart against your brother -- leave your gift and go find your brother and *settle* the grudge. *It is the only place in God's Word, where we are told to qualify our worship!*

And Mark 11 (25) tells us: *"When ye stand praying,* **forgive,** *if you ought against any,* **that your Father who is in heaven may forgive YOUR trespasses."**

Matthew 6 (14-15): **"If you forgive men their trespasses,** *your heavenly Father will forgive you,* **but if you forgive NOT men their trespasses, neither will your Father forgive your trespasses.**

Let us now realize that forgiveness in **not** some sweet platonic ideal to be dispensed like perfume sprayed from a bottle. It *can be* (for humans, it usually is) achingly difficult! An unfaithful spouse; a rebellious child; an abusive parent; a traitorous friend; a stranger who commits a crime against us . . . *no doubt* any one of these can cause severe personal pain. When these kinds of happenings devastate us, we *wrestle* with deep anger and sorrow that threatens to become bitter. We ask: "how can we **possibly** forgive?"

Jesus gave us a demonstration of (obedient to God) forgiving love which can motivate us to forgive, *even when it hurts.* His demonstration was given while He was on the *sacrificial Cross, for the hurt (sin)* **we did** *to Him.* He prayed to His Father: *"Forgive them for they know not what they do."* It is **only when we focus on how much WE have been forgiven that WE become free to forgive.** We can, **and we must** *forgive, because* **we have been forgiven.** We can *always* be aware that though we (in our own mind) are not as guilty of as big, or as much sin as others we know about, **our sin was enough for God to sacrifice His only begotten Son**

We *are called to* **live** *the adage - that every action we take reflects our faith (or lack of it) in Christ.* If we fail to forgive, *we damage our Christian witness.* Others, *not necessarily involved in our dispute,* may point to **our example** - to justify their own lack of forgiveness -- and children, and young (or new) Christians may develop insecurity in **God's forgiveness for them, since WE are their examples of how God forgives.**

When we pray *as Jesus taught us:* Forgive us our debts as **we forgive our debtors** - do we really mean for God to forgive us only under that condition? That is what God, in *Jesus Christ* teaches. Are we thus *sincere* when we pray that people of our acquaintance will receive God's mercy, *through us?* How could we be sincere, *if we refuse to forgive them for* **any** *affront they have perpetrated against us - or someone we love?*

Love

A sequel to the dissertation on forgiveness immediately preceding:

Two weeks ago, in a discussion on forgiveness, I used a metaphor (the Old Arch Bridge) to help us visualize how *God* made use of *two "stones" (forgiveness and love)* as structural support to the keystone (*Jesus Christ*) in constructing a "door" as *the* entry into His "Church."

The *doorway*, with its "matching" stones, which became the *sole entrance* through which God would allow any who would spend eternity with *the Heavenly Father*, to come into His Holy Presence, the *only possible* entry, *acceptable to God,* and which is our *transformation* from worldly, human, physical, form, into the *spiritual* form which *Jesus Christ* (the keystone of the arch) makes possible for us through His revelation of *God the Father, His (Christ's) life without sin, His willing, love-driven sacrificial death on the Cross of Calvary and His resurrection from the dead.*

The metaphor was that the arch could accomplish its purpose of holding the structure (the Church) together, *only as it was **intertwined** with* its two companion stones, one on the right side, and one on the left.

The stone on the right hand of Christ, was identified as *forgiveness;* the gist of which was (it is worth repeating here) if we have *any hope of being cleansed of **our** sin by His sacrificial death, **we must also forgive any who transgresses against us, making forgiveness a way of life under God, for all mankind. The key phrase** in the forgiveness lesson for us being: If you forgive men their trespasses (against you or yours) your Heavenly Father will forgive you . . . **but if you forgive men NOT their trespasses, neither - will you be forgiven.** (That statement straight from the mouth of Jesus . . . recorded in Matthew 6:14-15 and also found in Mark and Luke.)*

The stone on the other side of the keystone is **love.** Love is what we talk about today: God's l**ove** for you and me, our **love** for God, our **love** for each other. I guess if we want to have any *meaningful* discussion of love, we need to come to common agreement of a definition of love:

Webster says: 1) Love, a noun, is an emotion of affection, a state of being. God's Word says (as does Webster's 2nd definition): *love is a verb.* Love is a **self-sacrificial action.** In God's Word, to **love is to give.**

How much easier it is to *abuse* love, when it is held as an emotion. *as* an emotion, love is - too often - *used as an excuse to do something, Usually,* to do something to satisfy self, an inward indulgence, or even a self-gratification whim; e.g. How often do we hear, admittedly in the extreme, but how often do we hear of a love *killing,* where someone's *life* is taken because he/she does not have the same depth of feeling for the killer, as the killer has for the victim? -- The "If I can't have her, *no one can have her* syndrome." Or how often do we sympathize with, or even *excuse* someone for doing something demeaning, or infantile, or downright *physically* harmful to someone they *claim* to love, in an (usually vain) attempt to change that someone into *their own version* of an object of their love.

Or, as an emotion, love becomes a reason *not to do something which should be done.* E.g. the discipline of a child, or a *friend,* out of fear that love will be destroyed. *What a contravention of* **Biblical Instruction!** The entire 12th chapter of the letter to the Hebrews deals with how important *discipline* is to God, be it administered by a *parent,* an *Elder of the Church;* **or God himself.** (Proverbs 3:12 tells us: *"The Lord disciplines* **those that He loves)** And in Revelations 3:19, *Jesus* reminds John *". . . those whom I love, I rebuke and discipline."*

Which brings us to how we, as humans, are prone to *mis*understand what God's Word tells us about His loving intervention in our lives? From God, love is **always an action. The very basis for our faith** is our belief that God (Jesus) *willingly, lovingly died for our sins;* and the **basis for our hope** is that God, as He created Man out of His love, *pre-destined each one of us* **to be His,** while we were still in the womb. Our *mis*understanding is that *pre-destination* means that everything that *does* happen to us *is God's Will.* **That erroneous belief** is, unfortunately, **double pre-destination,** which **is not** what *God,* or *Jesus,* or the *Holy Spirit of God* teaches, or what the *Holy Word of God* implies.

What His Word *does* tell us is that *whatever God commands* to happen in, or with, or through our lives - **will happen.** Our confusion comes from our *self-indulgent* exercise of the freedom His Love *permits us* as we travel the path He lays before us. Even some Ordained Pastors regularly confuse pre-destination with *double* pre-destination. We need to understand that God's Will has at least *two* dimensions: What God *commands* to happen, and what God *allows* to happen.

It is true! We *are* pre-destined to be God's child, or man, or woman. (that *is* what *God's Word* tells us in many places); but *only* as we *come to believe* that *Jesus*, in obedience to God the Father, died for *our* sins; AND if we evidence that love by spending our life on earth *trying* to become like God's only begotten Son . . . *"in His image."* Remember Jesus' words to Peter (John 21:15-17) *" . . . if you love me, take care of my sheep."* That conversation with Peter was part of Jesus' final instructions to Peter, *after the resurrection, and after Peter had repented his denials.* It was Jesus' way of **re-instating a beloved, forgiven** Peter - as a full-fledged Evangelist, after Peter had three times denied Him *at His trial before the Sanhedrin.* (The culmination of Jesus' final discourse *before* the crucifixion is described in John 15, in which Jesus assured them *"If you obey My commands, you will remain in my love . . . just as I have obeyed my Father's commands and remain in His love. My command is this: Love each other as I have loved you, then the Father will give you whatever you ask in My name. This is My Command: Love each other."*

And also, in the whole of His teaching, *Jesus* cast a *vision* of what His disciples (you and I) were to do to reflect His (Jesus') love -- and then He trained them to transform *that vision into fact.* (That is the value of Bible study for *us,* in reference to the ministry Jesus *entrusted to us* as He ascended to His Father). And *that vision always prompted any believer* to see to the welfare of *others . . . before even considering self.* But even more than that, He *gave* them (us) *the power* to bring His *vision* into *reality.* **His Spirit** works through each of our unique personalities and skills, to touch the World with the *Good News:* ". . . *That God so loves the world that He gave His only begotten Son to die for their sins."* Jesus' teaching on how far *love* is to go, was (again, John 15) *"No greater love has man than this that he lay down his life for his friends."* *"If you obey My commands,"* Jesus told them, *"you are my friends."* **Jesus laid down His life for His friends.**

The paradox is that too often in our continued preoccupation with *self,* we confuse, that is (remember *double* predestination?) - we *blame* God for the consequences of something (un-Godlike) *we choose to do.* The fallacy of our reasoning is that *God loves us so much that He **allows***

241

us to make our own choices about how we live our life, *even **after** we make the key choice, **to "believe."*** Yes, He *will* guide, guard and protect us as we open our personal door to *His Holy Spirit* (remember Revelations 3: 20, where *Jesus,* speaking to the *Church at Laodocea,* describes His *involvement* with man-kind, thusly -- *"here I am, I stand at the door and knock; if **anyone hears my voice and opens the door, I will come in**"*). **The Choice** is ours. Jesus *knocks (that's called grace) and His light is there to shine on us, **but we must open the door.*** Jesus is *not* a gate-crasher! *God loves us so much, that He **allows** us to **choose** Him, or **refuse** Him.* **The choice is ours.**

With His ministry, His sacrifice of His own life, *Jesus* makes eternity with Him, *one with the Father, **possible** for us.* **But not by force!** He *makes it possible, but **we make it happen,** with our free choice.*

I heard a speaker chairing a clinic, once say: "You must love your child enough to allow him/her make their own mistakes, at least enough to help your child recognize that his/her chestnuts (put there by their own mistakes) are in the fire, and to ask for help, *before* extracting the "burnt" chestnuts for them. *That is Biblical.* Using free choice, that is the way *Our Heavenly Father,* loves us.

Jesus *allows* our free choice. He *will* guide us in making that choice, **but only if we open the door to His knock.** *Either way, our opening the door, or not, Jesus **gives us the choice.*** And *even when we **fail** to call upon the Holy Spirit to guide our choice and **we spill our chestnuts into the fire.** If we recognize that our chestnuts are getting burned, **Jesus will still help us pull them out of the fire,** as we confess our sins to Him* (as did King David, remember the Bathsheba affair?).

God will not *necessarily remove* the undesirable, worldly, consequences of our poor choice. The history of David's continuing reign as King was played out within the consequences of his *choice* to *take* Bathsheba. Consequences included their (illicit) first born son being still-born, - and continued through the rebellion of his subjects (who tried to replace David as King), and so on . . . David's entire forty-year reign, was experienced with sword in hand (for which David was told *not* to build God's personal house) after he had Bathsheba's first husband killed by sending him into battle with the enemy, while *withholding* supporting troops.

But even though God *may not remove* the worldly consequences, He *will*, *if we, again, choose to obey, He will make a silk purse out of the sow's ear* (as the saying goes). Again, in history, even *within the consequences, thanks to full and complete, recorded confession and repentance, and trust in God's mercy, His promises, we have come to know David as the model king of Israel, the forefather of Messiah.*

God can, and *His love will,* make something *good* come out of our poor choice. To repeat, His promise is: As we *confess and repent, and return to our absolute dependence upon Him* (that's called righteousness) God will not *revisit* our sin and withdraw, *for that same reason,* His love, His mercy, His presence, *our destiny,* from us. He will help us; even *drag us through,* the consequences of our poor choices.

But choices *do* have consequences! And the consequences *are usually* the result of something we *choose to do, in contravention* of the better (spiritual) judgment *He gives us.* Our trials, tribulations, heartaches are *not* something *God brings to us* (His decision to "test" our commitment, not withstanding). e.g.

When we, who consider ourselves to be *good, obedient* people, drive at too fast a speed, and our car fails to make a turn, and we are life-flighted to a hospital (or a morgue) how can we (or our survivors) *blame God?* God *did create* the principle of centrifugal force, but *God did not drive the car. We* drove the car too fast, *God didn't.* God's love and power and healing, is applied *after* the result of the choice He gave us. I know, God *could have prevented the accident if we asked Him to, and if we slowed down.* He could even have given us a "special" warning - *if we had opened our door to His knock; but* in His love, *God gave us the choice, even knowing that He would have to apply His mercy, grace and healing power after we learned from our mistake,* after the accident.

Or we become crippled as a result of our causing a DUI accident, *or worse,* if that same accident *resulted in injury, loss of property or death to an innocent victim,* and we are no longer allowed by civil authorities to drive, and we had heretofore *made our living* driving truck, our *human response could be:* If *God loves me like He says, How could He, after I say I'm sorry and will quit drinking, how could He let this happen to me?* The answer is, of course, God had nothing to do with our drinking, God did not pour a drop of alcohol down our throat and raise our alcohol blood level, or damage our motor skills, it was *our choice* to ignore *all the warnings and to continue drinking,* and God had given those "civil authorities" the freedom to establish the penalty for this "sin." And as for those *innocently involved,* God has *always promised and will deliver - to those who open their door to His knock,* healing, comfort *and salvation.*

Or for the fifty percent, or more, of marriages ending in divorce, contributing to *as many as one out of four* children in the United States living with only one parent; *Can we blame God? Or is divorce a result of a series of poor but correctable choices, none of which now puts the spouse and his/her needs first in our "love."*

Or, (and here we listened to a Pastor) in counseling a teenager coming, pregnant, to the Pastor for "advice," to the *agony* of the teenager lamenting: "how could God do this to me," the Pastor *proper response* (prior to "guiding" the teenager to God's open arms) the Pastor's response *could be:* Young lady, I don't know how you did in Biology, but *Jesus did not do that to you - - it is a consequence of choice.* God's creation, called nature, is designed so that certain consequences *can occur, if and when certain acts take place* (God only needed one Mary in His plan to redeem mankind from sin), but God gives *us the choice of whether, or not,* those acts will take place.

Or, referring to the Aids epidemic in the "Christian" *United States: No matter what anyone's belief or opinion is about homosexuality, or "free" sex, it* is pretty hard to get Aids *without exercising the choice of having sex of one kind or the other -- promiscuous sexual activity, is a matter of choice. The love of God comes into play after the fact, and is expressed by God (through "Christian" believers) treating, healing or taking the "victim" through the experience, even up to losing mortal life.,*

One could go on and on with examples of *people making choices and challenging God* over the consequences, but it isn't really hard, *with a little thought, meditation and openness to the Holy Spirit's counsel,* to *understand what has been discussed.* The key to it all is that in accordance to God's "lessons" to us concerning Adam and Eve, *man's choices bring on the consequences GOOD AND BAD.* And before we lay all the blame on Adam and Eve for *our* earthly trials, remember God's Word teaching *us: "we have ALL sinned and come short of the glory of God.*

From Genesis to Revelations, the whole of Scripture tells us, and *faith,* driven by the Holy Spirit, *assure us* of God's love, *active love,* for us. He *sacrificed the life* of His *only begotten Son to "pay" for the remission* of **our** sins; and He keeps the *Holy Spirit of God* on 24 hour duty, ready to lead, guide, guard and protect us as we *persevere in our belief* in His (the *only*) means of salvation. And the *Word of God . . .* in Paul's letter to the Romans (today's Epistle Lesson) describes for us how God expects *us* to apply *our love to His glory . . . .* And his (Paul) letter to the Corinthians (1 Corinthians 13) describes in minute detail, *what the characteristics of love are. Jesus* himself *demonstrated the efficacy* of love *as a component of forgiveness,* **and as a stand-alone active force,** *in reconciling mankind to his God. Jesus himself commands,* **in no   uncertain terms** (in John 15): **we are to love one another, as He has loved us.**

Earlier, allusions were made to some *good* consequences (in describing not so well) in *choosing to obey* Christ's command to love one another. And *choosing* to love is an *intellectual act,* not an *emotion.*

But now, let's make a quick summary of the *good consequences, of* **choosing to love.**   Paul summarizes for us, in his letter to the Romans (13: 8-10): *"Let no debt remain outstanding, except* **the continuing debt to love one another,** *for he who loves his fellow man has* **fulfilled the law.** *The commandments Do not commit adultery; Do not murder; Do no steal; Do not covet; and whatever other commandments there may be,* **are summed up in this one rule: Love your neighbor as yourself.** *Love does* **no harm** *to its neighbor; therefore, love is the* **fulfillment of the law.**"

Jesus did not *do away* with the Ten Commandments, He merely made *asserting compliance with them no longer necessary, for those who* **love God, and neighbor.**   And Jesus awards the *ultimate good* of the *choice to* obey His commandment to love one another. *Jesus* says: *"My peace I give you. I do not give to you as the world gives. Do not let your hearts be troubled, and do not be afraid."* The *tangible good of choosing to love,* includes the **elimination** of anxiety; unrest; fear; nervous breakdown brought on by self-driven *desire to climb to the top of the worldly heap, or to provide more "material comfort"* to our progeny than does our neighbor; or any "need" to embellish our own name or reputation.   We are *all equal* **in God's sight,** *and share equally in His benevolence.* Jesus *knew whereof He spoke,* when He commands us to love one another. And Paul, in his letter to the Romans, makes it even *more understandable.* Paul advises us: "You shall love your neighbor as yourself." RBC Ministries, in their publication *Our Daily Bread,* interprets the command to love neighbors this way: "The statement by our Lord, and by Paul, is **not** *a command to love* **ourselves** *more. It is a recognition* that most of us *already* look after *our own welfare,* in reasonable ways. That is, we love ourselves enough to feed and clothe ourselves, to keep a roof over our head, and to avoid being cheated or injured. In practice, we should love our neighbor *at least* that much."

But the complete love of God is - - for us -- for you and I – is freedom to *love or* **not** *to love Jesus,* is a **choice** His love for us, *gives to us.* Remember the earlier discussion of forgiveness - *how we must forgive others -* **or we forfeit** *our forgiveness from God?* Forgiveness is also a deliberate *act of love,* an intellectual act, and as we confess, repent, *and demonstrate our love for Him,* we possess Jesus' love.

The arch supporting the doorway to eternal life, *the Church,* created **by Christ** to be the agent of the wondrous news of *Salvation* to all people, to you and to me, will remain forever, will not, **can not** collapse . . . *with Jesus as the keystone, supported on the one side by the stone forgiveness, and on the other, by the stone love.* **The Church of Jesus Christ will not survive, without the arch!**

The choice is *ours,* the consequences are *ours.* **Jesus has decided to stand by our choice.**

Stewardship

" …. *After that He poured water into a basin and began to wash His disciples' feet, and to …… He said to them, "Do you know what I have done to you? … If then, your Lord and Teacher have washed your feet, you also ought to wash one another's feet.* **For I have given you an example, that you should do as I have done to you …….."** (John 13: 5+)

The Apostle Paul's first letter to his protégé Timothy, describes how he, as their Pastor, should exhort his parishioners to *Godliness with contentment.* The substance of this exhortation is to revolve around man's preoccupation with material acquisition, with physical possessions - with money. Paul points out to Timothy that when man becomes obsessed with wealth *only to satisfy personal gratification - he will never achieve contentment.* In 1st Timothy 6, Paul tells Timothy about such a man. Paul is reinforcing in the churches he began and passed to successor Pastors, a built-in means of carrying forth, as well as perpetuating The Body of Christ's capabilities to complete the ministry of salvation of all people, entrusted to His "Church" - the raison d'etre for its creation. As this discussion proceeds, it will describe two parallel paths over which the church should concurrently travel if it is to successfully complete that ministry: 1) The "steward- ship" of the management of the where-with-all (material things) of human life, and 2) The enlightenment and the oversight of the people of God appointed to do the works of both carrying out the ministry and of maintaining a "social" environment where-in "recruits" in the Gospel will be able to grow, mature and prosper and become equipped to carry out their specific "call."

Management of Material Resources: As far back in the history of God's chosen people as Moses, the people were being taught *by their ordained leaders,* the sinfulness of total preoccupation with acquiring "excessive" personal wealth *for the purpose of their own comfort and well-being.* Moses, just before they took over the land that God had promised them, warned them against relying on their own handiwork to provide for their own security. Even the original sin of Adam and Eve was that their *actions* evidenced doubt of God's veracity in His promise of abundance - *to be provided by God.* Solomon taught (in Ecclesiastes)

247

"there can be nothing but grief and sorrow in man's striving after pleasure, or great pride in accomplishments, or in hard labor (for selfish gain) even in man's struggle for wisdom. Solomon called it all *vanity*.

A focus of **Jesus'** teaching, perhaps high-lighted more than any other was His teachings on pride of *self accomplishment* re: personal wealth and security. Recall His parable of the *Rich Man and Lazarus* (Luke 16:19+) and of the *Rich Young Ruler* (Matthew 19:16+). Notice - in this lesson, Jesus *did not* say to the young man - that he should stand for elective government office on a hypocritically *contrived* platform of compassion for the poor, so that he could overburden the "not so rich" by taking from them in the form of taxes what they could, if they retained their earnings, do for themselves, and give *that* to the poor. Jesus taught the young man - "sell what *you* have and give it to the poor. The sum of Jesus' teaching was that His followers would, *out of love,* freely, willingly, even sacrificially, take care of the poor and give to God - not to the government - the glory. And in Luke (14:33) Jesus said: *"......whoever of you does not forsake all that he has cannot be My disciple."* **Neither a Socialist nor a Theocratic government is in the plan of Jesus!**

It is most common (in this writer's 79 years experience) for congregational pastors to practice extreme reluctance to emphasize God's command for believers to **tithe**. It is *mentioned* by most - almost as a "behind the hand" whisper; *but there is no call for discipleship more strongly taught nor argued by the Apostles, than is the need for using material gain with which one is blessed by God - for the well-being of others not so blessed.* Instead, the Denominational Church appears to be determined to spiritually support *non*-tithing by "forgiving" members who *will not* spare the time, talent or wealth for participating in the ministry of Jesus Christ. The Church gives "sympathetic" support to families "enduring" two wage-earner lifestyles so that they can afford luxuries equal to or better than their social peers, or to pay taxes commensurate with the income necessary to achieve that "equality" in their lives. These Pastors would "never dream" of admonishing Christians that if they would live more austere lives, *and tithe* a single person income, they would be able to live the kind of fulfilled, *at peace with themselves* fellowship demonstrated by the first Christian conger- gation (described by Luke);

and the God they acclaim, not their government, would receive the glory.

Oversight of Disciples and the Social Environment: There is no longer a viable argument that can be made against the very public and well documented, on-going war by secularists/humanists being con- ducted with the goal of *eliminating God* and His teachings, not only from all Government decision processes, but from the "hearts and minds" of our daily lives. The battle is being waged in the courts, in front of carefully (pre)-selected judges who are "trained" to be sympathetic to pleadings by "professional" educators and self-acclaimed "intellectual" theologians, who use false witnesses and fabricated scenarios and trumped up privacy and/or cultural issues - sustained by contributions from "patrons" with illicitly gained wealth. And the war is being fought with very real and unbelievably effective campaigns in the schools, in the courts and in the public mind; and because of the cocoon like practices of the Denominational Christian Churches - *the humanists are winning the hearts and minds battle.* What to do?

The Denominational Christian Churches must reconsider their 40 to 60 years of concentrating the teachings of Scripture on "announcing" salvation through belief in Jesus the Christ (the milk of the Gospel - 1 Corinthians 3:2) on the assumption that believers remain unable to digest the *meat* of the Word of God. The history of the Scriptures reveals that when leaders who have the spiritual courage to teach the whole Gospel do so, the people will respond and the Kingdom of God will advance. Matthew 28:19, 20 calls for the churches to do just that. But it truly teaches not just to "talk" without leading in the living by doing of the teaching (the text which opens this discourse). Scripture has many examples of *"I can do anything through Christ who strengthens me." (Phil 4:13):*

Some Scriptural examples: 1) Joseph, son of Jacob, by living His precepts and relying on guidance from God, established himself (effectively) as ruler of Egypt, and in "ruling" a nation, furthered God's plan for gathering, redeeming and "training" His people (Genesis 39-50). 2) Joshua, in assuming "rule" over Israel and obeying his charge from God, conquered Canaan and assigned lands to the twelve tribes, their allotted "homes." (Joshua) 3) the judges appointed by God to salvage His people each time they required their "chestnuts" to be pulled from the fires of the people's disobedience of God. (Judges) 4) David/Solomon led the people of God into great prominence on earth by their wise and God fearing rule (2 Samuel and Kings 1-3) 5) Mordecai/Esther by "getting involved in the politics of the king, saved the People of God (Esther). Leaders, not in scripture, who in obedience to their beliefs/faith led People of God in advancing the Kingdom of God: 1) George Washington led a fight for freedom from tyranny and thereby established the peoples' opportunity to govern their selves. 2) Thomas Jefferson, using his tenure as Education Commissioner, concurrent with his presidency, required that the Bible be the primary textbook of students in public schools. 3) Abraham Lincoln led the nation in a war to free a major segment of believing people who could not free themselves. 4) The 100+ members of congress affiliated with the Center For Christian Statesmanship, Washington, D.C.

We are called to tithe our "first fruits" - we are entrusted to GIVE our TOTAL, time, talents, and abilities to the completion of Christ's Ministry of Salvation for all people.

Rallying The People Of God

Why do the nations rage and the people plot a vain thing? The "kings" of the earth set themselves and the rulers take counsel together against the Lord and against His anointed, saying: "Now therefore be wise, O kings; be instructed, you judges of the earth. Serve the Lord with fear and rejoice with trembling. Kiss the Son, lest He be angry and you perish in the way when His wrath is kindled but a little. Blessed are those who put their trust in Him." (Psalm 2 - a warning given by God through Solomon, to all earthly kings and governments who choose to ignore God's right to judge kings and governments.)

Let us begin with recognizing how unusual it is throughout history that cataclysmic events ever occur without warning. In nature, rarely has there ever been a catastrophic hurricane or cyclone, a blizzard or ice storm, volcanic eruptions, even a tsunami, that was not predicted far in advance. Most man-made catastrophes, such as the World Trade Center bombing, the "insurgencies" of Iraq, the holocaust of WW II, major forest fires, major flooding of New Orleans (a combination of man deficiencies and of nature) are also able to be seen far enough in advance to be prevented, or their effects minimized with foresight and "wise" plus "heroic" action.

Historically, the destruction of cultures is likewise forewarned. Spiritual, moral and economic crises do not happen overnight! They begin as "minor" conflicts, which the truly wise can see coming long before they become crises.

The population of America, this Christian Nation - brought into being by its founders who were following the Holy Spirit of God, and for the stated purpose of advancing the Kingdom of Jesus Christ (the Mayflower Compact and the New England Confederation Agreement) has been resisting for more than forty years, signs of a pending crisis in its probability of survival as founded. Moral relativism pervades the nation and shouts aloud to anyone willing to listen. Abortion, failure of its public education system, sexual perversity, **loss of religious freedoms,** deteriorating marriages/families, the successful encroachment of secular humanism, are all very visible signs that America stands today on the brink of its likelihood of continuance as a Christian nation.

And the radical decline of this Christian Nation, accompanied by its predicted probability of failure to achieve its founding "end and aim", are in major part due to the phenomenon of "the church" in all its major denominations, passively subverting its responsibilities under the great commission (Matthew 28: 19-20) in order to "obey" deliberate misinterpretations by secularist non-believers, of the constitution which is the covenant of daily life, established by its Spirit led writers as the means of perpetuity of the freedoms fought and died for, which gave opportunity to its founding purpose.

It (the USA) began like this: The Reverends Jonas Clark, William Emerson, John Witherspoon (President of the college that became Princeton University), et al, ordained Presbyterian Ministers, having prepared and trained their congregations through the pulpit and through daily interaction, became actively involved leaders of the "first responders" (the minute men) when the perpetrators of the tyranny which their ancestors had fled to a new land to escape, followed them, bringing violent oppression. Their enemies came to call them *The Black Regiment*, their uniforms being the black garb of their religious calling. For nearly 200 years, Christians led by the Church guided this nation in its pursuit of its end and aim, and the US became renowned in the world for its Christian influences on all societies, saving many of them from debilitating tyranny.

But in the 1960s, the church, choosing a different path, began to move into the closets from which rebels against the Word of God had emerged *demanding, and sometimes receiving,* leadership roles in the hierarchy of the church, even to ordination as pilots of the "Mayflower" to advance the Kingdom of Jesus Christ. In effect, leaders of the various protestant main line denominations began to second their responsibilities as stewards of the Gospel to a misguided interpretation of the First Amendment of the US Constitution, triggered by a 1954 amendment to the IRS code sponsored by (then Senator) Lyndon Johnson as a means of defeating a political opponent, to which church leaders made no objection. In turn, causing many successor disciples to begin to seek other "home bases." and/or renewal points; and the Political Correctness to which some churches have been so self-defeatingly successful, is their persuasion of peer Christians that the US Constitution prohibits government office holders from expressing or practicing their spiritual beliefs; or that "good" Christians will not enter the political arena in the first place. Equally damaging to the mission of the church - the advancing of the Kingdom of Jesus Christ, has been the churches sympathy/support/excusing/forgiving the tendency of individual members to give first priority in their daily lives to advancing their own earthly, material well-being - over their "call" to participate in Christ's sacrificial ministry.

The consequences of the churches decision to hide in the closet is that the nation *is* on the brink of self-destruction as described above, that unless the door is opened, *humanism* will become the house that contains the closet. Compare this situation with the success of those believers who brought down the Roman Empire without ever taking up arms, even at the cost of the historical "hungry lions" and the conversion, by Nero of those caught evangelizing - into human torches. *Be assured, the Church of Jesus Christ* **WILL** *prevail on earth. But as Mordecai prophesied to Esther; "If you remain completely silent at this time, relief and deliverance will arise for the (People of God) from another place, but you and your father's house (US main line denominational churches) will perish. Yet who knows whether you have come to the kingdom for such a cause as this?"* (Esther 4:14) The Church has created a secular nation. What must we do?

John Adams, founding father, born again Christian and 2nd President of the US says it to us as to his compatriots: "It is the duty of the clergy to accommodate their discourses to the times, to preach against such sins as are most prevalent, and recommend such virtues as are most wanted. For example, if exorbitant ambition and venality are predominant, ought they not to warn their hearers against those vices? *If public spirit is much wanted, should they not inculcate this great virtue?* If the rights *and duties* of Christian magistrates and subjects are disputed, should they not explain them, show their nature, ends, limitations and restrictions, how much soever it may move the gall of Massachusetts (people who are offended)?" (Emphasis mine)

The Church in America must understand this truth: *Though Federal Law currently (it CAN be modified) prohibits churches from direct involvement in influencing the outcome of elections,* **no law** *should keep* *pastors from speaking out boldly on the great moral, political, spiritual issues of our day!* The church must re-invoke the conviction of the first-century Apostles who declared they *could not keep silent* about what they knew to be true (Acts 4:9, 5:29).

Though the Church is silent, we study the same Word of God that those colonial Church leaders studied. What was true in 1775 is true today. God has not changed His declarations about the very human and moral issues that face every generation anew. The question is - on what kind of ears will His Word fall today? Crises do not start out as such. They begin as "challenges" to the status quo which often grows into schismatic conflicts which if not taken up can spell ruin for a nation. What are minor today become a crisis - and then a full-blown calamity. Only the disciples of the Christian Church led by the Holy Spirit can open the door to the closet into which they have been wrongly, if not inadvertently hidden.

Appendix C

There is a popular axiom that "a picture is worth a thousand words." The action suggested (with all its supporting justification) in this dissertation contains some 95,000 words. To reduce the whole message to picture form would require 85 pictures. That's too many. But it might be worth it to summarize the key thematic suggestion by converting it into three diagrams, which attempt to put it into a bare-bones perspective

The diagrams are known as *functional analysis tools*. They are read by stating the Goal of the effort on the left margin (of the first diagram); reading to the right reveals the actions chosen to achieve the objective; the HOW. The chosen HOW actions are validated by reading from right to left; explaining WHY those particular actions where chosen.

As described above, the diagrams put into bare-bones perspective, a *suggested plan* for achieving the goal, leaving out the flesh of detail. *Functional Analysis* can also be used to "brainstorm" any level of detail desired to put flesh on to the bones. Each block of text on a diagram, if designated as an "objective" for a detail plan, will become an achievable "target" for in-depth brainstorming. *A caution: There is an opportunity in any diagramming session, - to go into too much detail.*

SACKCLOTH OPERATIONS PLAN

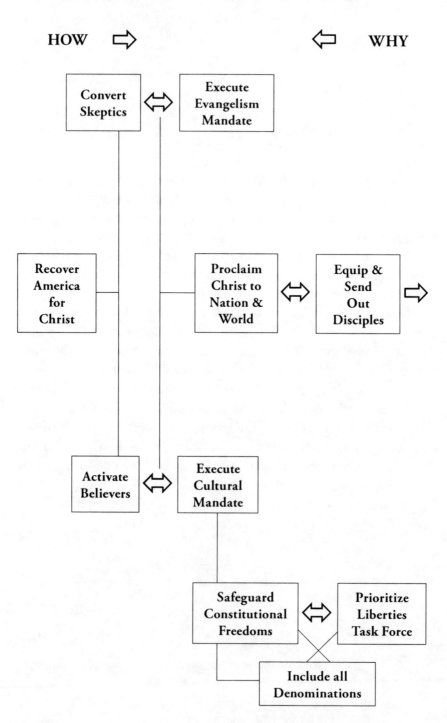

HOW ⇨ ⇦ WHY

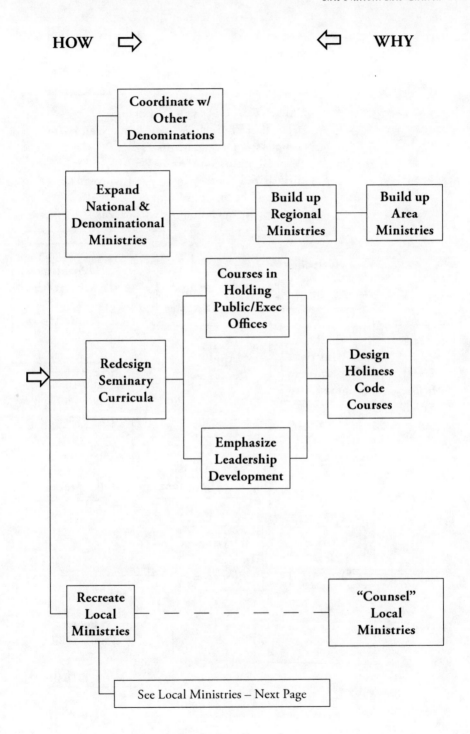

HOW ⇨   ⇦ WHY

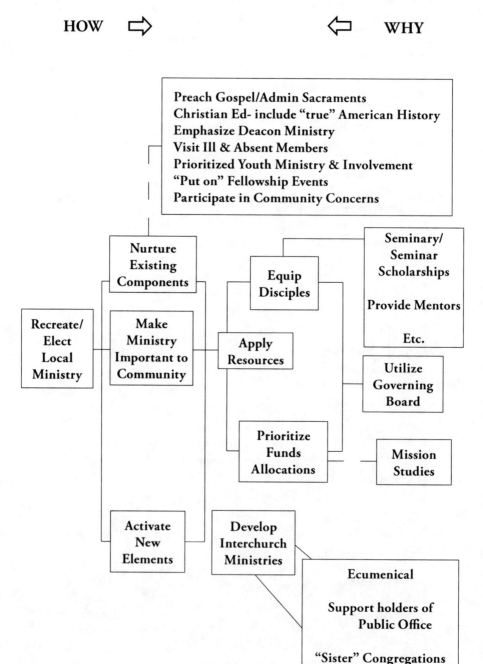

Preach Gospel/Admin Sacraments
Christian Ed- include "true" American History
Emphasize Deacon Ministry
Visit Ill & Absent Members
Prioritized Youth Ministry & Involvement
"Put on" Fellowship Events
Participate in Community Concerns

Nurture Existing Components

Seminary/ Seminar Scholarships

Provide Mentors

Etc.

Equip Disciples

Recreate/ Elect Local Ministry

Make Ministry Important to Community

Apply Resources

Utilize Governing Board

Prioritize Funds Allocations

Mission Studies

Activate New Elements

Develop Interchurch Ministries

Ecumenical

Support holders of Public Office

"Sister" Congregations

About the Author

Don Goss, has been filling pulpits of four denominations since the 1960s, conducting worship services and discussing with worshipers their thoughts on the influence on society of their denomination. He also participated in two studies of the efficacy of smaller churches as components of nation-wide ministry. Don also served for many years at "district" levels of two denominations. Don, with his wife, devoted 40 years as "officials" of Youth Ministry, counseling and helping youth and parents relate "unique" experiences to the Gospel of Jesus Christ. Don's "tent-making" career during those same years was in serving as Internal Consultant to agencies of state government, serving five Governors covering both political parties. Don's professional "nature" is to apply issues and concerns to the "Big Picture."

Printed in the United States
71284LV00003B/79-87